In Gypsy Tents

Francis Hindes Groome

IN GIPSY TENTS.

BY

FRANCIS HINDES GROOME,

AUTHOR OF ARTICLE 'GIPSIES' IN THE 'ENCYCLOPÆDIA BRITANNICA.'

Second Edition.

EDINBURGH:
WILLIAM P. NIMMO & CO.
1881.

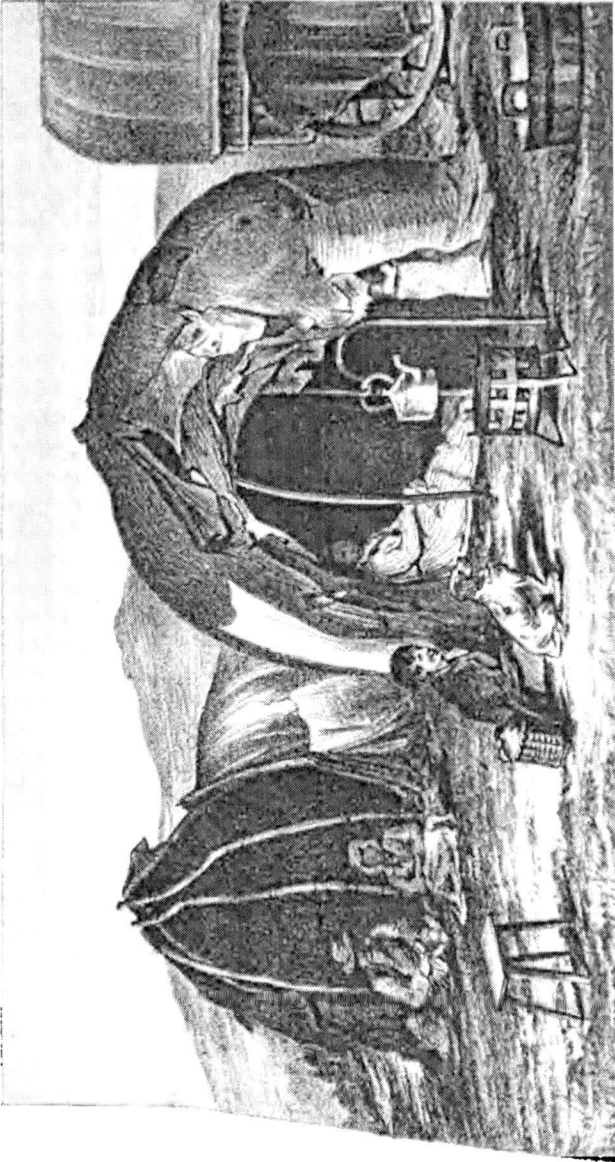

List of Illustrations.

"PAZORRHUS."

OR INTRODUCTION I was writing a cartel of defiance, when my adversary kindly cut his throat, and by an odd coincidence I was summoned to sit upon his remains. *Requiescat in pace*—henceforth he may lie in peace, inasmuch as it boots not to measure weapons with a suicide. Speaking though of boots, there was once a Parisian shoeblack who trained his dog to dirty the clean boots of passers-by. He wanted a job, poor lad ; and, had he had no dog, would doubtless have somehow filled its place himself ;[1]

---

[1] *Note to Printer.*—These lines to be spaced out widely, as there is much to be read between them.

but, be this as it may, I must get on to make my acknowledgments to dead and living.

Dead—for, alas! the "Nine Men's morris is filled up with mud;" the author of *Gipsy Experiences* died whilst its reprint was passing through the press. But Silvanus Lovell is flourishing, so are John Roberts and Sylvester Boswell, and them I most heartily thank for their "exercitations" on behalf of their race. John starts to-morrow for the Caernarvon Eisteddfod; and, when last I heard of them, Sylvester was at Blackpool, Silvanus "creeping slowly up for the Black Mountains."

Next on my list of creditors stand Dr Bath C. Smart and Mr H. T. Crofton, authors of *The Dialect of the English Gipsies;* M. Paul Bataillard, author of *L'apparition des Bohémiens en Europe* (1844), and of many later works; the Rev. S. B. James, author of "English Gipsies" in *The Church of England Magazine* (August–December, 1875); and many contributors to *Notes and Queries*. Next, Lieut.-Colonel Fergusson; Sir Walter Elliot; Messrs Hyde Clark, Fitzedward Hall, H. Sydney Grazebrook, W. T. Marchant, F. A. Blayde, J. H. Turner, C. E. Mathews, H. S. Brickhill, H. Kilgour, and E. Cockburn; and the Revs. R. W. Munby, T. Walton, George Eller, G. F. Blakiston, C. P. Greene, H. W. Plumtre, E. H. Everett, J. Collier, W. D. Underwood, W. D. Parish,

J. W. Murray, J. H. Morton, H. Mitchell, A. D. Taylor, J. Smith, and J. R. Jefferson.

To these clergymen, last but not least, I am mainly indebted for what séems to me the most curious portion óf my volume—viz., Chapter Fifth, which deals with Gipsy burial. Some day I hope to expand this chapter into a separate pamphlet, to be distributed among my Romani friends in England and the Colonies. Therefore I beg of any one who may light upon registers or other documents relating to the subject, to forward them either to *Notes and Queries*, or to myself direct.

And so my book "goes," in John Roberts' phrase, "before the world." Save where my hobby breaks away here and there, and carries me maybe into unfamiliar country, I have tried in it simply to represent the Gipsies as I have found them, taking neither the best nor the worst of their tribe, but just those Gipsies whom I have longest known. Three-fourths of my readers will never have exchanged a word with Gipsies, and may be disposed to pin their faith on bad names given centuries ago. I will only remind such readers that harmless blindworms are looked on by the peasantry all over England as venomous beasts, to be hewn in pieces whenever occasion offers. Not that Gipsies are by any means faultless. As William Pétuléngro said to me only

three days since, "We're just middlin' kind o' people
not perfect like górgios, but"—only multiplied dashes
could complete the sentence.   His cousin's wife, Mr
Alfred Reynolds, had been reading to the family a
book called *Gipsy Life* (London, 1880), in which
Gipsies are represented as firing ricks, farming
górgios' babies, and kicking their own to death ; in
which "gutter-scum Gipsies," "ditchbank sculks,"
and "agents of hell," are among their more kindly
epithets.

PORTOBELLO, *July 23, 1880.*

IN GIPSY TENTS.

Chapter First.

NDER the shadow of Cader Idris a byway
leads from Dolgelly to the Cross Foxes
Inn. Halfway along that road I sat on a
summer evening in front of a Gipsy tent,
which was pitched, with six others, in a long narrow
meadow, fenced by a low stone wall. I had noticed
the Gipsies three hours ago passing above me as I
stood fishing in the stream below, had marked them
down to the accustomed camping ground, and presently, with seven small trout for contribution to their
tea, had joined them at that favourite Gipsy meal.

Old acquaintances most of them, they numbered
some thirty souls, of various ages, from a baby scarce
two months old to the grandfather of threescore years.
The latter, Silvanus Lovell, is worth describing. A
hale old man, he stands over six feet two ; his merry
nutbrown face is lighted up by dazzling teeth and a
pair of glittering hazel eyes ; his grizzling hair curls

A

round the brim of a high-crowned ribbon-decked hat. A yellow silk neckerchief, brown velveteen coat with crown-piece buttons, red waistcoat with spade-guinea dittos, cord breeches, and leathern leggings, make up his holiday attire ; his left hand wields a silver-headed whalebone whip ; and from a deep skirt-pocket peeps forth the unfailing violin.

Seven sons has Silvanus, sons worthy of their sire, all strapping fellows, and black but comely all, with one exception—the first-born, Pyramus. His ruddy, "gorgiofied" aspect betrays some far-away strain of Gentile blood ; but at heart he is truest Gipsy of the lot, the deepest speaker of the old Romani tongue, the most widely conversant with men and manners. London is Pyramus' headquarters ; but Jersey, the Highlands, and Ireland—he knows them all ; he has met Mr Julius and Lavengro, " leastwise a portly, white-haired gentleman, as told me more than ever I knowed myself ;" and lovingly he speaks of Eversley's knickerbockered parson, " who went to heaven upon us Gipsies' prayers." In Eversley church he wedded Lucretia Pinfold, a Gipsy beauty of the Eastern Counties, by whom he has only two children, against the six of his oldest brother Plato, whose wife Richénda comes of the swarthy Hernes. Wisdom and Nathan have married two sisters, Rodi and Alabīna Wood, members of the chief Gipsy tribe of Wales; but Lóverin, the fifth and best-loved of the boys, is both a widower and an "innocent," his wits lying buried in the grave of a girlish bride, away in Clavering churchyard. Lancelot and Anselo—one twenty, one sixteen years of age—are still unmarried, as also are their two youngest sisters, Ruth and Starlína, though these have broken the hearts of half the lads in Wales and in the Border shires. Patience and Shúri, the eldest daughters, are absent both of them, the first with her husband Goliath Stanley in America, the other in Blankshire, where she is married to a substantial yeoman. But Sinfi, the middle girl, has brought gudeman and bairns from Scotland to join the old people in their summer ramble; and they have made her welcome as the flowers in May, albeit her marriage with a low Tinkler like Willy Faa was looked on as a terrible come-down.

Grandchildren, horses, ponies, donkeys, and dogs would almost outnumber Homer's catalogue of ships; but Mistress Lementina Lovell demands a formal introduction, if only for her sometimes royal rank. Not much like a grandmother, this Gipsy queen; but then she is only fifty-seven years old, straight, lithe, and able to walk three miles an hour, handsome withal, if somewhat weatherworn. In girlhood she is said to have strongly resembled her beautiful kinswoman, Charlotta Stanley, and still she retains her girlhood's ornaments. A gorgeous handkerchief covers her coal-black curiously-plaited hair; her ears are pierced by old-fashioned hoops of heavy gold; a necklace of amber, coral, and coins runs thrice about her neck; and her hands are bedizened with massy rings, one of them wrought by Plato from a guinea welded upon

three wedding rings. A parti-coloured apron over a
short blue woollen dress, and naily boots, complete,
with a cutty pipe, Dame Lementina's "landscape," for
she has doffed the *mónging-gúno*, or alms-cloth, in
which, as in some mendicant friar's hood, are stowed
the bread-winnings of her daily rounds.

These Gipsies, I said, were old acquaintances, seen
first at Chester Races thirteen years ago, and last in a
Gloucestershire lane a twelvemonth back, and our
present meeting was as pleasant as unlooked for.
"How art thou, brother? sit down and eat," was all
that Silvanus said; but the children were noisier in
their greeting, so noisy, indeed, that grandmother
threatened that "hellhound's breed" should pack off
supperless to bed. The threat was emptier than its
recipients by the end of tea, where my poor trout
were lost in the creelful caught by Plato from a
brooklet skirting the Dinas Mowddy road. Not that
fish formed our only fare, for there were eggs and
bacon, oatcakes and mighty loaves of Welsh brown
bread, cheese and fresh butter, tea such as only Gipsies
brew, and milk bought warm and foaming at a penny
the pail from milkmaids in the meadow opposite. So
"frightfully satiated," in German phrase, we sat around
the fire, as Gipsies sit even on summer nights, and
spoke of the year gone by, of absent friends, of matters
of Egypt generally, but first of the weather, as was
but natural in rainy Wales.

Pyramus told how, having left his waggon at Chester,
he joined his father up in Anglesey. "It was well

enough in the Island, but soon as ever we got among the poverty mountains it came to rain,—rained as if it was never going to hold. First night we stopped the other side of Bettws, on the slope of a tump that was like a waterfall by morning, and everything got drownded there. I wanted to stay next day at Bettws; but no, my daddy would have us keep racing on like dogs; so race we did, through mist and rain, to just this side of Herod's Castle "—

"Herod's?"

"Ay, him as killed the babies, brother; and there we got the tents up, though the ground was that sopping wet that Nathan said the brook was the driest place; and hardly a bit of straw to lie on neither. Well, bor, we had just got made, when, blest if the wind didn't turn slap round right into the tents. It was too late then to shift, so by-and-bye half the places were blown clean inside out, and the rest all scampered off to a great big barn close by, where they got up a roaring fire, and managed pretty comfortable. That wouldn't do for me, though, for I'd no mind to see all my bits of things drownded again; and, if you'll believe me, I was up over half the night digging trenches, and sticking in pinthorns, and piling stones to keep the blankets down. You'd hear the wind come roaring down the valley, then it would go dead still a minute, and then rush it would come, and the rods would be bending and blankets flapping just like a great gig-umbrella. Ay, and I was the umbrella stick, for I had to hang on to the ridge-pole to keep

things standing. Dórdi! dórdi! I smoked a whole
rickful of tobacco, and said my prayers twice over ;
and how I kept looking at the time every five
minutes, against the light should come. Before then
the wind dropped a bit, and I dropped too, glad
enough, with all my wet rags on, into bed. By-and-
bye I fell a dreaming as I'd been up fiddling to Squire
Patersall's, and the butler had filled me out with cider
till I was three parts drunk, and Plato was pumping
on me to get me sober. I woke up, half like, and, sure
enough, there was drip, drip, drip coming right on the
tip of my big nose. And where do you think it came
from ? why, off old Tinker's tail ; for three of the
neddies, poor animals, had backed into the tent, and
there they stood, all three of a row, just like a valentine
what a young lady (not you, Lucretia) sent me from
Beckbury once. I couldn't for the life of me help
laughing, though I was angry too ; but there ! you
might shout to those blessed donkeys. They'd just
budge an inch, and then keep back, backing again,
and looking round at me as much as to say, ' I'm very
sorry to disannul you, sir ; but outside there is more
than a man can stand.' I was better off than Wisdom,
though, for one of the creatures got into his place, and
ate up three whole loaves of bread."

"As bad a nightmare, Pyramus, as Zacky Lee's
white donkey."

"Zacky Lee," said Silvanus, pausing in act to poke
the fire ; "I mind him well, reía, but nought particular
about his donkey. How was that ? "

" Only that he was stopping one night in a meadow at Pewsey, and thought he saw his donkey loose outside the tent, so went to hobble it. But the nearer he tried to come at it the farther off it always was from him, till at last he knew it was the Devil, and a pretty dance it led him half the night."

" Comical that was ; but, bless you, I've often known the same myself. Lots of places we never could get one wink of sleep at, and then in the morning folks have told us as some one had been murdered there. But the curiousest thing that ever happened to we was at Friar's Ditton, off by the Clee Hills yonder. It must have been nigh about twelve o'clock at night, and we were stopping in a bit of a wood, with a little brook running down below. It was Lemmy here, she heard some very curious tunes right atween the tents, but nigher the boys' than ours. Just like a lot of fiddles it was, a long way off, but wonderful clear and sweetsome; and Lemmy kicked me—but there! I never took no hearkenings, only grunted ; leastwise so she said next morning. And the boys, they hadn't heard nought neither, but the bailiff of the fine doctor said, ' Oh! I've often heard that myself; that's the fairies.' "

" Fairies! The last occasion, I take it, that fairies were heard in England. How long ago may that have been ? "

" Three years come Nathan's birthday. But these Welsh farmers, some of 'em leastwise, set bowls of milk out every evening, and they're sure to be empty by morning."

"A cat, or snake, maybe. I know of a dairy down
in Dorsetshire where they found the milk going, and
set a snare, and caught a snake a night for ten days
running."

"Ay, ay," said Lementina; "Dorsetshire's terrible
overrun with reptiles. I mind me well, when I was a
girl nigh Lina's age, Perun (God rest his soul!) and
Emperor Buckland were cutting corn at Gillingham,
and we went on and left them at it. My daddy had
a lot of ponies then, and me and my cousin Savoury
stayed behind with a little bay and a brown one,
letting 'em eat along the road. And at the cross-
roads we stopped to put down pátrins[1] for the boys.
And as I pulled a bit of moss from the bank, I got
rolling it and rolling it about in my hand, speaking to
her the while, about our sweethearts belike, rubbish as
all young Romani girls gets chattering. Well, I felt
something tickle the middle of my hand, and when I
opened it to look, dórdi! there was a young snake
sticking its head up out of the moss in my hand.
Down I pitched it 'mediately, and it scrawled out at
its full ugly length, and Savoury and me picks up a
stone apiece, and killed it between us. Lord! and
there was a lot of snakes thereabouts in the walls—
adders. I'd rather walk on a mile any day than sit
down aside the road.

"Then I remember Perun, when he was only four-

---

[1] *Pátrins*, heaps of grass or leaves laid at cross-roads to indicate to
loiterers the route that they must follow. Gipsies of England, Germany, Norway, &c., are all familiar with the "pátrin-chase," as also
were the Thugs of India.

teen, but that was in Devonshire. I had been washing
the day before down by a little stream, and close to
where I had made the fire there was a big flat stone,
and underneath that stone there was a great grey
snake. Perun had seen it, but I never did; it was a
mercy it hadn't stung me. Ay, bor, so my poor
brother he got up early next morning in his shirt, no
shoes nor nothing on, went to the place where he had
seen this snake, and lifted up the stone. There it lay,
curled up and frightful to look at; but it would take
something to fright him. He killed it, and brought it
on a stick to the place—a long one it was, and awfully
thick—and he hung it up on a fir-tree close by my
mammy's tent."

"Now, our old people had a curious way with
snakes," said Nathan's Welsh Gipsy wife. "When one
of us children killed an adder, my daddy would cut it
in half with a whip or a stick, and the head he would
put on the right side of the road, and the tail on the
left. Then my mother would walk between them
first, my daddy next to her, and all we children after
them in a row, from the eldest down to the littlest.
And my poor mother used to say some funny words
to herself, what none of us never knew or ever did;
but for certain when we used to go through that performance, my mother would not be long before she
had a pocketful of gold."

A pitying smile played on Silvanus' face, as he
gravely observed, "That was a superstition, Alabīna,
and superstitions are things I never vindicates. If

you want superstitions, you must go to your Uncle
Gilderoy."

"Gilderoy! I was near forgetting him. How has
the world been using him, Silvanus?"

"Oh! right enough, for anything I can tell. He's
balder a bit than when you saw him, and—but, I say,
refa, have you seen that nice gentleman by Cheltenham lately?"

Silvanus spoke with reserve about his brother, who
I knew was suspected of dabbling in godless arts, and
his question was plainly meant to change the subject
of our conversation. But Anselo, free from his father's
scruples, burst forth impetuously :—

"Balder! no wonder, too, when it's his master fetch-
ing every scrap of hair off his wicked old head. He'll
tell you himself plump out that he has sold his blood,
and now he has found out some new wise man down
Aberystwith way. One day you'll see him without a
penny to bless himself, and the children'll say, 'By
Job, my daddy han'na got much money now;' but wait
a week, and he'll be boasting about with thirty pound
in his pocket. He took Lucas with him—that's my
second cousin—last time he went, and Lucas was
telling us all about it. It is some great gentleman
seemingly, a kind of farmer, and he knowed they
were coming, knowed their names, brother, for says he,
'I thought I should see you, Mr Lovell, before very
long.' There was ever so many other gentlemen
feasting and drinking in the parlour, and Lucas too
he feasted and drank, and then the wise man took 'em

into a back room, and then he fell to beating the sods "—

" Beating the sods! And what may that be, Anselo?"

" Oh! I don't quite know rightly, but that was what my cousin said. He sat on the sods, and beat 'em; and then they comed away. But a few days after Lucas and Dosia met him out in the road, and he made them so as they could'nt stir."

" And what do you say to all this, Silvanus?"

" I don't quite know, refa; anyhow, I don't hold with such doings noways. To go running in the face of the blessed Lord like that is heresy; and heresy is a thing as *I* should be disdainful of. It does'nt do no good neither. I'm better off than Gilderoy any day, for all his cunning men; still, I know some of they gentry can do things as would make you open your eyes a bit. Maybe you never heard of the waggoner's boy at Chapel Bottom."

" No. What of him ? "

" That's near Knighton in Radnorshire, and this boy's master set him to mind the crows, while he went off to Knighton fair. He was'nt gone five minutes when the boy was after him, and by-and-bye they came against one another in the crowd. ' Be you tenting the crows?' asks the master, main angry; and the boy he answered, bold as brass, ' Oh! yes, sir; I've got 'em all in the barn.' Sure enough, when his master got back and came to look, there was the crows, all in the barn together, and nought but a rake to stop 'em.

He had put the rake like at the pitch-hole, and there was one white crow among the lot. That boy growed up to be an old, old man, and was a regular sort of a conjuror. Why, the farmers have told us that scores and scores of times, when we went up to the farms a fiddling."

The tale was told with that unquestioning faith in the incredible, which, deeply rooted in the Gipsy mind, scorns only unknown "heresies" and "superstitions." It set me pondering. In the rake I recognised the "holy mawle," the hammer of Thor, or, in Radnorshire, rather of some Celtic deity. Thor's hammer was, of course, the thunderbolt, the *Molnija* of Slavonic tribes, a word that as *malúna* has passed into the Gipsy tongue. "When you see the *malúna*, you will hear the *gúriben*" (thunder, *lit.*, lowing of oxen), said Wester Lee to me at Notting Hill; but most English Gipsies can express "thunder" and "lightning" only by such periphrases as "the voice of God," "God's light." Then, what strange beliefs have Gipsies about the Cross, beliefs that carry one back to old pre-Christian days. *Trisula*, the Sanskrit name of Siva's blood-stained trident, has been by them transferred to the emblem of man's redemption, and again has been debased by German Gipsies to signify a club or *kreuz* at cards. And any little English Gipsy child will tell you how, if you see a rainbow and cross two sticks, its colours will fade away. As indeed they will, if only you wait long enough. Some Gipsies set their boots crosswise before they go to bed, fancying thereby to keep away the cramp ; but the Lovells knew nothing of any such practice, and treated it as an old wife's tale. Lementina, however, with grimly conscious triumph, dived into the deep leathern pouch that is worn between the skirt and petticoat, and after much rummaging drew forth a "fairy foot," asking me if I knew what that might be. It was the skeleton foot of some small animal, but of what I could not say ; so, after vainly guessing, I gave it up. "A mole's," she answered ; "and it's good for rheumatism." This led to a discourse on Romani charms, and I learnt, what I knew before, that babies in teething should wear a necklace made of myrtle stems, which for a boy must be cut by a woman, by a man for a girl.

Alabīna declared that an adder's slough, or a bit of mountain ash, was certain to bring good luck ; while Sinfi's children, it appeared, wore round their necks black bags containing fragments of a bat, which one of the boys had killed. In turn, I told them how a wise man near Aldershot, a Gipsy house-dweller, had given me a charm for hurting an enemy, viz., to stick pins in a red cloth rag and burn the same, and how I had imparted this charm to an Essex labourer. He heard me eagerly, and then exclaimed, " I'll try that ; 'strue's alive, I'll try that on my brother, I 'ool," moved solely it would seem by the spirit of scientific research, and lacking a viler subject for the experiment. Oddly enough none of my Gipsy friends had heard of this incantation, which, under varying forms, is as ancient

as it is widely spread. Virgil knew of it, and it was
employed against the Nizam of the Deccan by the
ladies of his harem sixty years ago, much as against
King Henry VI. of England by Margery Jourdain,[1]
the cunning witch of Eye. But Wisdom capped me
with the story of his wife's cousin, Bob.

"When my Aunt Silvína ran off with another man,
Will Solomon, Bob was keeping an inn at Barmouth,
and soon as he heard the news, he left his father, put
his harp on his back, and went off to a cunning man.
He told Bob to buy a pennyworth of new pins, then
to find a toad, and stick all the pins in its back
and belly, till it looked like a hedgehog. Next he was
to go and dig a hole at the foot of a grave where one
of Will Solomon's kinsfolk was buried, and there at
midnight he was to bury the cup with the toad
covered up in it by a piece of slate. The wise man
told him, too, to go in five weeks' time, and dig up
toad and cup, and if he did'nt do that he was safe to
go mad himself; but if it was all done right, Will
Solomon would go off his head. So poor silly Bob
did everything the wise man bade him, except that
he made a mistake in not finding the right grave,
neither did he go there to raise the cup at twelve
o'clock, as the man had told him. Which was the

---

[1] It may be noted that Jourdain was a Gipsy name in the reign of
Elizabeth. At least, in *State Papers*, Domestic Series, Vol. li. No. 11,
is a list of "sturdey vacabownds" taken and whipped at Higham
Ferrers, in Northamptonshire, on 26th March 1569, where we find that
"Elizabeth *Jurdayne* had a pasport delyveryd her to go to Lowek in ye
countie of North' within two dayse."

cause of my cousin going off his head, and died so at Caernarvon. He was an excellent harper."

"That's true, of course, Nathan?"

"True! brother; it's as true as the coaches runs up London streets. Why"—

"For goodness sake don't chatter, boys, no more about such things, if you don't wish to have the devil by you all night long. The wizards are always on."

The interruption came from Lementina, weary of talk of ghosts and witches; the more so in the eerie darkness. For night had fallen and the stars shone down on us through driving clouds. The firelight cast strange, uncertain shadows, and glittered in the children's big dark eyes, while from the hillside came the whirr of the "knifegrinder," a bird whose Gentile name I do not know. So, wishing to shift the current of our discourse, my hostess asked where I had been since I said farewell to them by Chipping-Sodbury.

"Rolling about, mother; rolling about, rubbing off what little moss I had gathered. Across the water, in Germany, and farther still."

"Ay, that's the way; but Garmany! I would'nt go there. That's where the war was, isn't it, as scared us so? Reconcile, my brother's lad, was with us then, and he and the boys got and dressed themselves up in their sisters' clothes, for fear of being took for soldiers. And Reconcile did more, for he got lime and put it on the tops of his fingers, and burnt 'em down, so as he could'nt hold nothing."

"Rather silly in Reconcile; the war had nothing at all to do with us. But that's an old Romani trick. It is curious, too, for Romané fight well enough when angry, or when they see there is anything to be gained by fighting. There were some famous Gipsy prize-fighters, Cooper, Winter, Oliver, Jim Mace"—

"What," put in Pyramus, "is he a Romano?"

"So I believe; but your wife should know best about the Maces, for they, like her, belong to Norfolk. I never set eyes on Jim, though I'm told he has returned from America, and is keeping a fish-shop in London; but Poley, one of his cousins, and I are old acquaintances. He is a thorough Gipsy, if you like; has been in America, too, but travels Scotland now. I expect you must have met him," I added, addressing myself to Willy Faa, who hitherto had modestly kept silence.

Will is a sandy-haired, grey-eyed, raw-boned man, presenting inwardly, as outwardly, a striking contrast to his brothers-in-law. Their tongues are seldom still, and Romanes is their speech among themselves, while from their English you would hardly tell what part of England they are natives of. Will, on the other hand, is taciturn, the more so here, where his brethren laugh at his broad Lowland Scotch; and what little Romanes he has, was learnt from Sinfi, his English Gipsy wife. However, if once he can shake off a seeming deep mistrust, common to Tinklers and ill-used mongrel curs, he has a fund of Border tale and song; and now he answers, with an accent which Anselo mimics, and which I do but faintly reproduce, that Poley and he are very good friends, and were last together at Edinburgh Hallowe'en Fair.

"Eh! mon, there was a perfect ceremony wi' thae Maces and Reynolds when Queen Victoria cam' doun to Dumbar a twalmonth syne. The papers was jeest full o' the Gipsy queen (that's Poley's wife, ye ken), and his gude-mither and her ither dochter. They were a' of them dressed in purple and velvets, and the men in their scarlet coats. Puir bodies, they've had sair trouble sin' then. First the auld gentleman, Master Reynolds, died. He was always wearying to win back hame; and Tammy was clean broken-heartit, and followed his faither before six months was ower. He died at Dalkeith, but they carried him a' the way to Dumbar, and laid him by the auld man's side. Troth! but it's a terrible break-up. They were the only real Rōmanies travelled Scotland, barrin' me" (here Anselo whistled) "and Sinfi; and I mind weel when they first came up frae England, eleven year syne, wi' thae ither Rōmanies wha went aboot gie'in the Gipsy balls. Eh! but they're mighty fine folk the Reynolds, wi' their braw camps, and caravans, and brakes. Free-masons, too, the young men were, and awfu' golf-players. And horses! why, I ken last Hallowe'en Fair, Alfred himsel' had sixteen horses, and that wad be ower twa hundred pound and mair. The *gárgies*'ll jeest mak 'em pay, though, where'er they're campit; a guinea a week I think it was at Musselburgh, and hardly a bite o' grass for the puir beasties. And the scavengers wad come to the camps to clean awa the

B

ashes and siclike, jeest the same as if it was some
grand gentleman's house; and I've seen the highfliers and puir poverty Tinklers come beggin' up to
them; ay! and get mair than they'd get fra the haill
o' Musselburgh. Hoot awa! I'm tellin' a lee, sayin'
I had'na seen them sin' last November. We were
campit jeest oot o' Edinburgh, Sinfi and I, a fortnight afore we cam doun here, at a place they ca'
Craiglockart, in a field belongs to a verra honest man,
wi' a lot o' kye; and on Sabbath I said to Sinfi, I'd
jeest gang ower to Musselburgh to see an auld aunt
of mine. She lives in Fisherrow, and you can see the
camps fra there, gin ony one's stoppin' on the Links.
So I saw thae great big tents, and jeest steppit ower.
Alfred and Poley were sittin' outbye smokin'; so, after
we'd had a bit crack, 'Where's Tam?' says I; and
then I heard that he was gone a fortnight syne, and
I was sair vexed, for he was a pleasant canny body
was Tam; nae sae muckle as Alfred, but keen as a
razor's edge."

Willy was coming out with a vengeance, and Wisdom, ascribing his eloquence to the Cross Foxes Inn,
murmured the Romani byeword, "A hedgehog will
open when he is wet." But it was joy, not eloquence,
that loosened this Earl of Little Egypt's tongue. A
Tinkler is as much more patriotic than an English
Gipsy as he is far more mixed with native blood; and
Willy was overjoyed to meet with one who understood
"braid Scots," knew every hole and corner of Auld
Reekie, and had even conversed with Her Majesty

Esther Faa Blyth, in her cottage palace on the English Border. She is his kinswoman, and he now inquired after the venerable Tinkler queen.

I told him that, when I was at Kirk Yetholm last New Year's Day, she was hale and merry enough— "Blyth by name and blithe by nature," to quote her royal pun. I had found her all by herself, for one of her sons was at Berwick ; another, Prince Robert, had "got into trouble through a dirty póliceman ;" and the daughter was out at service at some great gentleman's hard by. "'Tis a sin and a shame," said Esther, "that she, a princess born, should wait on others, be they ever such highborn gentry. I have said, and I'll stick to it, that they ought to rise up and let her sit down ; but there's chance in life, and the Chancery Court in London." She had chatted away, shown me a sword that belonged to one of her "auncestors," but really, I fancy, was taken in a smuggling fray ; had related how, when she came to Edinburgh, the guards before Holyrood presented arms ; and had told me that Mary Queen of Scots was so passing fair that the wine could be seen as it ran down her throat.[1] Every place that she goes to she "studies its antiquities ;" but as to her powers of *rókering Romanes*, I had to confess, in answer to a question from Silvanus, that

---

[1] I have met with this singular standard of fairness in a recent three-volume novel, and also in the story of Fair Rosamond, as told me by Cinderella Smith, a Gipsy house-dweller at Headington, near Oxford ; one detail in which story is worth preserving,—that close to the Bower still stands a holy briar, which, being enchanted, bleeds if a twig be plucked.

Her Majesty calls "sugar" *sweetnams*, "fire" *glimmer*, "tea" *slàp*, and "a sixpence" *tanner*, while half of her few genuine Romani words are basely clipped or otherwise corrupted. She cannot follow the simplest sentence addressed to her in Anglo-Romanes, as neither can any of her Tinkler subjects, unless, like Willy, they have dwelt with their deeper English Gipsy brethren. The fact is strange, since the Faas and Baillies, the Browns and Youngs of the sixteenth, seventeenth, and eighteenth centuries would seem to have fully equalled the Boswells, Lovells, Stanleys, and Hernes in Egypt's wisdom and Egyptian wiles; but through frequent intermarriages with Gentiles, the stream of Scotp-Romani blood has lost in depth what it has gained in width, and many, besides, of the chief Gipsy families have migrated to England, the Colonies, or the States.

Silvanus grunted. He seemed to have scant sympathy for Gipsies who had all but forgotten their ancient mother-tongue, who called "tents" *camps*, and who could not stomach *hótchiwítchi* (hedgehog), which Willy knew only by the name of "urchin."

"*Urchins*, quotha! and *chitties!*" and the old man jerked a contemptuous thumb at his son-in-law's tripod pot-hook, dear to all would-be painters of Gipsy life, but utterly "mumply" in a Lovell's eyes. "*Chitties!* more like a gallows than a kettle-prop; the very Gloucestershire trampers would scorn to be seen with it."

A storm was imminent; but Lementina artfully

proclaimed that it was time for all good folks to be abed, whither the children had long betaken themselves. So "Good-night, all," and "Same to you, brother;" and, nightcap-pipe in mouth, I made for the farm, a half mile distant, where I was lodging all that wet July.

Chapter Second.

IT was a delicate clear morning, when at seven o'clock I started for the river, to bathe and fish. At the tents I found the elders still abed, all but Piscator Plato, who had taken his angle two hours and more ago; but the children were up, and the boys of course must come and see me swim. Whooping and hooting, the "Jacobīnes" (their grandmother's pet scolding epithet) set off, and I was nothing loth to have their company.

No one is fond of Gipsies, but is fonder of Gipsy children,—odd compounds of pluck and shyness, of cheek and courtesy, of thoughtlessness and meditation, of quicksilver gaiety and quaint old-fashionedness.

> " Who taught this pleading to unpractised eyes?
> Who hid such import in an infant's gloom?
> Who lent thee, child, this meditative gaze?
> Who massed, round that slight brow, the clouds of doom?"

So Matthew Arnold asked of the Gipsy child whom he met by the seashore in the Isle of Man; and that child, I have fancied, was possibly Lavinia Lee,

22

my dear little Gipsy friend of bygone years, whose brightness hid unfathomable gloom indeed. One hour romping with Oliver and baby Omi, the next she would be moved to passionate weeping by the sound of the Painswick bells; and, did you ask her why she wept, would answer, "Because of the poor dead people lying beneath, who cannot hear them." Lavi herself can hear no more the bells; but I, as I stood in the dewy turf-edged lane, could hear the keck-keck of the red-billed blackbird as he flew from a missile shot by Christopher, could hear the shouts with which his miss was hailed by Dimiti, Mantis, Adam, and all the rest.

One carried my towel, another my rod; the rest would have carried me, and, failing that, offered a mount upon Richenda's Jenny. I declined the offer, for who was I to ride upon white asses?—asses, moreover, that were ghost-seers, as was White Jenny, according to Mantis' tale :—

"That was in Pooler's Lane, again the other side of Newport, bor; and it was about ten o'clock in the morning, just when we were going to have our breaks-fast. My daddy was out at the back of the tent washing himself, and the neddy got galloping up the lane, and looking through the hedge, and trembling all of a dither. Nigher to the tent she came; and then, when my daddy called us out to look at the neddy, we was going down the lane to catch her. Short round she turned, and jumped right over the hedge. A high bank it was, very high, and then quickset on the top, and some wooden pales put

abackside of that. I'll swear any horse couldn't do
it ; and such a short distance as she had of it. Then
Anselo runned arter her across the field, and catched
her, and then brought her down the lane and tied her
legs. She keeped looking across that same road, and
next thing we heard was that my old granny was
dead. She always used to ride on a white neddy too,
and you may be sure our old Jenny saw her coming.
And if we children hadn't made a row, you may depend
my daddy or some on us would have seen something
too. But I never saw another neddy jump so in my
life. Lord bless us ! it did jump some height. A real
hunting horse couldn't have done it."

"That was Richenda's mother, Mantis ? "

"Ay, bor; and it was miles away in Yorkshire that
she died. She was a very old woman indeed. 'Old
Abigail Hearne,' the Gentiles called her ; but Sanspray
was her properer name. The people came for miles
to see the funeral, and they buried her close by my
grandfather in Rossington churchyard. Last time we
seen her was at Peterborough Fair, in the fields where
the railways run, and she didn't hardly know us then,
but was going to tell us all our fortunes. And my
Aunt Starlína made herself like some young lady
wanting to have her's told, and she gave the poor old
body a halfpenny for a shilling. My mother did just
welt it on to Lina for that ; and sarve her right."

"And she'd carry clothes-pegs round her neck,"
said Dimiti, "right up to the very day she died. The
moment she got up she'd tie 'em up in a blue silk

handkerchief, and put the mónging-gúno on. Sundays and week-days was just the same to her. And she carried in her pocket a little china dog dressed like a doll. I mind she lost it once, and she was in an awful state till it was found ; and she used to fancy it would talk to her when she was all alone smoking her pipe up in the waggon. You should have seen a pack she had of very old fortune-telling cards, which was painted different colours. She used to select the different ones for each day ; sometimes she would have those with the devil and sarpents on 'em, then other days she would carry those with birds and palaces."

Now, as we walked, there lighted on the road before us a " Romani magpie," or water-wagtail, and Christopher, son of Pyramus, chanted the Gipsy formula,—

> " Is it any kin to me, it will fly, it will fly ;
> Is it any kin to me, it will fly, it will fly."

No, it scarce hopped aside to let us pass, so Christopher proclaimed that we should see strange Gipsies ;[1] and lo ! a turn in the lane brought us in sight of what

---

[1] To Gipsies all over England the water-wagtail is known as the "*Rómano chíriklo*," or "Gipsy magpie," and they believe that its appearance foretells a meeting with other Gipsies, kinsfolk or strangers, according as it flies or does not fly away ; also that the Gipsy lad who kills one of these birds is sure to have a lady for his sweetheart (*suvéla raúni*). According to Dr Richard Liebich's *Zigeuner in ihrem Wesen und in ihrer Sprache* (Leipzig, 1863), German Gipsies also designate the water-wagtail as " *Romano tschirkulo.*" Why, Dr Leibich omitted to inquire. It is a noteworthy fact that the Greeks had a saying, as old at least as the 5th century B.C., " Poorer than a *kinklos* " (κίγκλος = water-wagtail), and that peasants in the 3rd century A.D. called homeless vagabonds *kinkloi*. I do not seek to derive, with Erasmus and Pierius,

seemed to verify his words—two tattered, low, smoked
tents, pitched in a hollow by the wayside. But "tink,
tink, tink," came the sound of a whitesmith's hammer,
announcing that these were no gentle Romané, but
Irish Crinks,—"Some of Lacky Fury's breed," said
scornful Dimiti. At least the wielder of the hammer
was black enough, though whether from innate swar-
thiness or ingrained grime it were hard to determine.
I could but hazard a remark in Romanes, "Sor shan,
pála? rínkeno saúlo si" (How d'ye do, brother? a
beautiful morning). He paused a moment with uplifted hammer, shot a mistrusting glance at us, and
curtly answering, "I dunna jŏn your cant," went on
with the milkpail he was fashioning. We went on
with our walk, and, when we were out of earshot,
Christopher observed that the Crinks knew just as
much Romanes as Sinfi's man.

"Why, Willy knows a fairish bit, and the old fellow
yonder seems to know something too. His 'jŏn'

Cingarus (Zingaro, Tchinghiané, Zigeuner, &c.) from *kinklos*, "a water-
wagtail," believing these words to have been as distinct originally as
Gipsies (Egyptians) and *vipseys* or *gipseys* (eruptions of water in the East
Riding of Yorkshire; *cf.* William of Newburgh's 12th century *Chronicle*,
and Camden, *sub* East Riding). But may not Gipsies have been led, by
the resemblance of its name to theirs, to adopt the water-wagtail as *the*
Gipsy bird? and why did Theognis and Menander apply to the water-
wagtail the epithets "much-wandering" and "poor," unless the bird
was associated in their minds with some poor wandering race? Possibly
we have here a slight confirmation of the theories of MM. Bataillard,
Mortillet, Chantre, E. Burnouf, and others, according to which there
were Gipsies in Europe in pre-historic times. In passing, I would
suggest to a gifted poetess, that water-wagtails do not as a rule "sit
on oak-branches high."

meant '*jin*,' and that is good Romanes for 'know' the whole world 'over. I have often heard tell of the Crinks, but never set eyes on any of them before, and I should like to have a good long talk with these. I expect, like the Muggers and Nailers, they are 'half-and-halfs,' or rather a thimble-full of Romani to a bucket of Gorgio blood."

"Maybe, brother; *I* wouldn't be seen with them. But they makes a sight of money hereabouts with their tins and cans, because they can all of them talk Welsh, and their women tell fortunes for sixpence or bread and cheese. There was one lot we saw at Aberystwith as had been backwards and forwards to America half-a-dozen times. But here's the bridge."

Below the bridge the rocky brawling stream widens and deepens into a yeasty pool, that Nature must have meant for dainty bathing. A hundred yards long, and from ten to twenty feet deep, it is fringed by a sheep-cropped lawn, where one big boulder lies ready to receive the bather's clothes. A minute's loitering on the steep-backed bridge, and we were down in the meadow; another minute, and I was bare as Adam, —not the old Adam, but his brown young namesake, Nathan and Alabīna's son and heir. Swimming is a rare accomplishment with Gipsy boys, and Adam alone of all the lot could swim. He had learnt the art from his Uncle Valentine, and learnt it well. At least he beat me easily in the race we had up and down the pool; and he could dive like any kingfisher. How the cool water bubbled like four-year-old cider, and how the rest did shout at Adam's triumph, while Spot, the terrier, barked incessantly! So we came out, and dried and dressed ourselves, while the others dispersed to dabble in the shallows, or grope under rocks for trout and eels ; and Adam, as we dressed, discoursed about Valentine Wood, with the new-grown import-ance of a Romani Captain Webb.

"Just the same as a fish my uncle is, always in the water, bathing or fishing ; and he'll catch trout out of dear little tiny brooks, where you might try a fortnight and never rise a pilk. They never hardly eat 'em themselves the Woodses doesn't, but he takes them to the farms or into the towns, and gets a fairish penny that way, besides playing the harp of evenings at farms they stop at. A funny way for Romané, always going in barns."

"What, haven't they any tents?"

"No, bor. The Lees, and Drapers, and the Coopers has tents (often more like dog-cubs), but very few of the real Welsh Gipsies has. Winter-time they all take houses over in the Island, and when they do get out in the summer, they're all for stopping in barns. I don't believe Valentine or the old woman ever slept in a tent in their lives."

"Something like your Uncle Willy's people, eh?"

"Oh, bless you! they aren't as bad as the Tinklers— 'stinkers,' I call 'em—not by a long way, reía. They're proper black ; for all the world like copper warming-pans, and they are just deep. They've got the Romani craft and the Welsh craft too, and it takes a long-headed man to get over the Crockans. That's what my daddy says when he's on with my mammy. But horses or donkeys! why a child might cheat 'em when it comes to dealing."

"You don't seem, Adam, to love the poor Tinklers much?"

"Nasty Scotch Faws![1] not I. I have'nt got no

[1] This phrase was in the mouth of Adam's kinsfolk years before they knew who the Scotch Faas really were. A mention of Scotland evokes it from West Country Gipsies, who know nothing of Scotland, and less of its Tinkler tribes; but it is seemingly a survival of the closer intercourse that once existed between English and Scottish Gipsies. The few English Gipsies who visit Scotland now, visit it as they would some foreign land; and Sinfi's marriage with Willy Faa could not, I think, be matched in the last half-century. But formerly there was a constant passage from one to the other country; and even now there are old Gipsies in the London Potteries who as children were familiar with the streets of Aberdeen. In 1549, Baptist, Amy, and George Fawe were committed to Durham gaol for counterfeiting the king's great seal (Lodge's *Illustrations of British History*, 1791, vol i. p. 135); and at Dorchester, in 1559, eight Egyptians (James and George Kyncowe, Andrew Christo, Thomas Gabriells, Robert Johanny, John Lallowe, Christopher Lawrence, and Richarde Concow) escaped hanging, under the Act of 1554, only because they had come "out of Skotland into England by Carlysle, wch ys all by land," and were not transported or conveyed by sea (State Papers, Domestic, Eliz. vol. vi. Nos. 39 and 50, vol. vii. No. 20). The Hernes are now only known as a great Anglo-Gipsy tribe; but in the register of Jarrow, Durham, we find—"Francis Heron, king of ye Faws, buried 13 Jan. 1756;" and the Allans belonged as much to England as to Scotland, Jamie, the famous piper, dying at Durham 28th August 1806, just a twelvemonth after his reprieve from the gallows for horse-stealing. He was buried *in* the parish church of St Nicholas, whose register also contains the entry—"1592, Aug. 8. Simson, Arrington, Fetherstone, Fenwicke, and Lanckaster were hanged for being Egyptians." It is noteworthy, too, that Gilderoy (Gael. "red lad") is a common name with English Gipsies, occurring even as far south as Folkestone.

patience with such mumply poverty people. Look
at my Uncle Will's white-headed children—"barns,"
he calls 'em. Regular Dane's breed, and can't understand plain English, let alone Romanes. Why, the
other evening Mantis told little Maggie their neddy
was down the lane ; and she had'nt no notions what
he meant, till Aunt Sinfi said, 'It's the cuddie he's
meaning.' Lord! Sinfi was a fool."

"Gently, Adam. How did she come, though, to
take up with Willy?"

"It was all my granny's fault. She was always on
with the poor wench, saying as she'd never be worth a
man, till long and by last she took and went off with
my Uncle Pyramus and Aunt Lucretia, when they was
going up to Scotland after ponies. They were going
along the road somewheres up in those parts, and left
Sinfi behind ; and my uncle was just sticking up the
place, when, on looking round, Anselo (he was gone
with 'em too, and he was littler than me then) he cries
out, ' Here's a highflier coming with a bit of a budget
under his arm.' He come walking right up to the
place, and said to Pyramus, 'Good day.' 'Good day,
man,' says my uncle ; and they never took no more
notice of him. So presently he said, 'Mr Lovell' (he
had got the name very quick), 'Mr Lovell,' says he,
'will you give me your sister?' 'Ay, man,' he said,
'you can have my sister, and welcome,' never thinking
Sinfi was behind. And they all burst out laughing.
But he turns back, the highflier did, and brought her
up to the tent as bold as brass ; and when they saw

that, they were so struck they didn't know what to do or what to say. And my uncle laid it on to her like anything, but she didn't mind it in the least. And there and then this Credit (we always call him Credit, because he said once he was a 'Creedit to the family') went over the hedge, and cut some little tiny bits of nut-stick, more like twigs than tent-rods; and green briars they cut to lie upon. My uncle wouldn't give them nothing to sleep in, and she made a tent of her frock. And next morning they heard a kind of half-smothered screaming; and when they got up to look, it was Credit beating her with his naily boot. My Aunt Lucretia said it sarved her right, and they never interfered with her. But they gave him some money to go to the shop for things; and seemingly he sat upon the gate wondering whether he should go to the shop or run away altogether. So that's the end of the man and his ass."

"At any rate, she seems very fond of him."

"Oh, bless you! yes; and if any of US goes atween them when he's beating her, she'll begin on we, say it's her affair, not ours."

Christopher and Dimiti had come up in the middle of Adam's tale; and Dimiti told me that Plato, his father, was fishing close to the Cross Foxes Inn, and wanted to know if I would come and join him in a morning glass of ale. Willingly; but I continued to fish as we went along, having already caught several trout, including one beauty that nearly touched the pound. And as we went we came upon a keeper.

The waters are free to all but salmon-fishers ; and the
man, whom I had often met before, wished me a civil
"*Boren da*" (good morning), though he glanced at my
escort somewhat doubtfully. The boys in turn seemed
equally suspicious ; and Dimiti, a hundred yards lower
down, broke forth,—

"If there's one thing I do mortally hate and despise,
brother, it's keepers.   They're just the same as the
pretty hangmen (policemen), for they've taken the
sacrament[1] to speak the truth ; and precious truth
it is they do speak, nothing in the world but a lot of
lies.   What craftiness they'll use, too, to get our poor
dear people into trouble. Tell him about that lot by
Aberystwith, Christopher."

"What, last summer? Well, bor, it was about eight
mile off Aberystwith, and we had been up the road to
look after the neddies.   My uncle Lancelot had a long
pair of trousers on, and an old long black frock-coat,
and an old box hat, and he had been making himself
like (*i.e.*, pretending to be) a constable.   And the fine
keepers was set in the hedge, squeaking like a rabbit,
just to 'tice us on.   And Lancelot was going over the

---

[1] Whence did English Gipsies get this use of *sacrament* for "oath,"
unknown, I believe, to all our provincial dialects? *Salmon*, according
to *Guy Mannering*, was the inviolate oath of Scottish Gipsies, and, if
pronounced like the name of the fish, would closely resemble *serment*,
the French descendant of Lat. *sacramentum*, "oath."   If, on the other
hand, its *l* were sounded, *salmon* would be identical with the "*Salomon*,
an altar or masse," of Harman's *Caveat* (1567), and might be connected
with the Anglo-Romani *sólohólomus*, "oath," and the Tinkler *sállah*,
"curse."   "*Solomon* David," the Cockney corruption of "*solemn* affidavit," is probably a mere coincidence.

hedge, thinking it was a stoat had got a rabbit; and these fine keepers bolted out, and axed him what brought him there. They wanted to take him; and then my daddy cut off to the tents, and Lancelot came running after, racing right past, and we never seed him till next morning. We all got into bed, with all ours things on; but when we did hear 'em coming, up we jumped, and ran across some boggy ground on to a railway. And up that railway we went two miles, then turned out and came in the road. Then we waited a goodish bit, sat under the bank, till we heard my mammy coming; then we went straight along the road for half a mile, and then turned out along a way that took us out upon some hills. We couldn't find no place in the lane to lie down, so we went over backside of the hedge into a field. There we laid till morning. My daddy got up very early, and went into the road to look for Lancelot. He couldn't see him nohow; so he just put *pátrins* in the cross-road, and we went on. It was an awful funny road, all up rocks; and then when we just got up top of one bank, Lancelot catched us. He had slept in a barn that night, and had never seen the sights of bread. And we went across fields, over hedges and ditches, till it brought us out into the turnpike-road."

"By Job, they make more bother over a poor little rabbit or partridge than ever they would about a Christian," was Dimiti's comment.

"You don't uphold the preservation of game, then, Dimiti?"

"Eh, brother?"

"You think that Romané have as good a right as Gentiles to hares and partridges?"

"Sure! Who do wild things fly and run for, if not for them as is wild themselves?"

"I cannot say, Dimiti; go and ask that keeper. Still I don't think Gipsies get often into trouble for poaching."

"No, bor; they takes good care of that, 'cause then they wouldn't get leave to stop nowheres. My uncle Lancelot, though, he bought a gun last Christmas, a beauty it was, double barrelled; and such a state he made of himself. He and Anselo went up to Squire Morley's a-fiddling; they'd been out shooting, and Lance had the gun in his hand and the shotbelt over his shoulder. The servant girl came out, thought they were some great gentlemen come over shooting, and asked them to walk in and take lunch. Then she saw the violins, and wanted them to play a tune about a man being shot. Talk of state (boast), that was a state for you! But Lancelot was like to have got into trouble about that gun, and my grandfather took it and pitched it right into Chetwynd Pool. Do you know what tune it was the girl meant, reía?"

"Not I."

"Well, I should say it was my grandfather's song;" and Dimiti sang—

> "Three of us went poaching out;
> To kill some game was our intench:
> The laafty pheasant they did fall,
> With powder, shot, and gun.
>   .   .   .

He cried out for help,
And still he was denied.

. . . . .

No more locked up in a maidnight cell,
To hear the turnkay push the bell.

. . . . .

In his breast a mortiäl vound,
While crames of blood did flow."

"A corrupt text," I thought, "with lacunæ deeply
to be deplored;" and the song having brought us out
against the inn, I bade the boys carry my trout as a
present to their grandmother, and departed in quest
of Plato. He was sitting in the porch, talking to the
landlord; and, as I approached, he hailed me Gipsy-
wise:

"Sor shan, pála? av te besh alé. Lián tu váriso?"

The landlord withdrew to fetch a quart of ale, with
a puzzled look upon his countenance. Me he knew,
and Plato he knew, just as he might know a sheep and
a goat; but this lying down of sheep and goat together
was a thing that passed his powers of comprehension.
Plato had noticed his bewilderment; so when the ale
was brought he continued to chatter in fluent Romanes;
then, with a wink to me, addressed himself to Boni-
face,—

"You didn't think, Mr Hughes, I knew this gentleman?"

"I did not, indeed, Mr Lovell; but seemingly you
do. He comes from?"

"Egypt, sir. Yes, he come from Egypt three weeks
last Friday night, through Garmany and France and
Am——."

"America," he would have said, but my "*Ma, dínilto*," stayed him; so with perfect composure he explained that I had landed at the Gloucestershire seaport of Bosbury,—"a wonderful place for shipping, Bosbury."

"In-deed! He'll be a countryman of yours, then, Mr Lovell, and its Egyptian you'll be talking together. But I understood from Mr Price" (my landlady's husband) "that the gentleman was a London scholar."

"Oh yes, sir; you're perfectly correct. London *is* his natival when he's over in England. But you see, Mr Hughes, his father (and he married my wife's own cousin's grandmother) he's king of we 'Gyptians, and sometimes he stops in London, and sometimes in Egypt yonder. A very favourable gentleman he is with all the nobility, never drives out himself with less than a carriage and six, and has got houses all over the country, though he wouldn't live in a house, no, not if you paid him pounds and pounds of gould. But my friend here likes to get away for a bit of pastime now and then; and besides he's got to pay a visit to Sir Watkin. *Ma túti péssa, bor; mandí's got a posh-kúr'na.*"

As we strolled away, "I'd scorn to tell the truth to mumply kennicks," quoth honest Plato; and then in answer to my question, Was it likely the man would swallow such hideous lies?—

"Swallow them, bor! I should just about think he would. Did you see how his eyes twinkled

when I mentioned Sir Watkin? That's the King
of Wales, they call him; and if he was in it, it was
bound to be all right. And all these country gorgios
fancy we come from Egypt. There was Mr Powell
(we were stopping in his field by Bala), and he
come up to the place and got talking with my daddy
very early one morning. I wasn't up, but I could hear
every word from where I was laid. 'You come from
Egypt, you wandering tribes,' says he; and my daddy
answered him, 'Ay, sartain sure, sir; Egypt is our
country. It was one of my uncles built the Pyramids.'
'In-deed,' says the gentleman (you know these Welsh-
men's way); 'and was you born in Egypt yourself,
and did you used to go naked like the blackamoors?'
'Stark mother-naked, every Jack of us,' says my
daddy, very solid like;—but there! I forget the rest.
Lies! They'd swallow any mortal thing, and ask for
more."

"Like Oliver."

"Ay, he always was on the getting line, was Oliver
Lee. But now I want to ask you one question, brother.
Where do you really think we Gipsies origined?"

"Where do you think yourself, Plato?"

"Well, I can't rightly tell, bor; I never took much
notions of it; but for sartain we must be a very ancient
people. I reckon there were Gipsies in England generations before English and Welsh was ever thought on,
'cause, go wherever you will, you're bound to come
on Gipsies. Now no Englishman can't understand
a Welshman, but Romanes is the same all parts; for

look at they Langarians [1] that Pyramus and Belcher
Lee seed up by London.   Belcher was going to buy a
pony off them ; little bits of animals they are, and
goes in pairs with their forelegs coupled.   You'd
never say as they were good for nothing to look at ;
but just you try 'em, they'll fly.   Well, Belcher was
a looking at this here pony, and all the while one of
their women was walking round and round.   She had
got a baby in her arms, and she kept rocking it and
rocking it, and singing away.   What do you think she
sung ?   '*Bángo grai, bángo grai*,' broken like ; but any
fool might know she meant the horse was lame.   Leastwise Belcher did, and all he said was, 'You can keep
your *bóngo grei*, and I wish you a very good morning.'
That shows if it is'nt a very antiquated language."

---

[1] I cannot tell why Plato gave this name to the Hungarian Gipsies
who visited England some few years ago ; I only know that once before
I heard it used by some of the Taylors, who were staying on Rush-
mere Heath :—"They came from the Langári country, and they were
called Langarians."   It can hardly be identical with *Lingurari*,
Roumanian-Gipsy makers of wooden spoons, and I cite as a mere
coincidence the following passage from Marsden's "Observations on the
Gypsies" (*Annual Reg.*, 1784), p. 82 :—"His Grace the Archbishop
of York suggested to me the probability that the Zingari may have
derived their name, and perhaps their origin, from the people called
Langari, or Langarians, who are found in the north-west parts of the
peninsula of Hindostan, and infest the coasts of Guzerat and Sindy
with their piratical depredations.   The maritime turn of this numerous
race of people, with their roving and enterprising disposition, may
warrant the idea of occasional emigrations in their boats, by course of
the Red Sea."   [Thus I had written when I learnt from Marsden's
Memoir (1838), p. 61, that *L*angarians is a misprint for *S*angarians.   I
let my note stand as a warning against theories founded on resemblances
of sound, *e.g.* of *Zotty* and *Djatt*.]

"Oh yes, the language is the same the whole world over. Since last I saw you, Plato, I have been in Hungary, the very land that those Langarians came from. Whole Gipsy villages you find there, and Gipsy blacksmiths, and Gipsy innkeepers; and there is hardly a musician in the country who isn't a Romano. I stayed at a little town called Siklos, close down by Turkey, where they've just done 'fighting with the great big Russian bear,' and a little to the right of the Danube river (you know the Blue Danube Waltz?). I was stopping in a big hotel, where there are hot springs, just as at Bath and Cheltenham, and at this hotel there was a Gipsy band. Eight of them there were, one with a dulcimer, one a base viol, one a violoncello, and violins the rest."

"That was proper, reía."

"Ay, and so black they were, and so well dressed. The dulcimer player was really a beautiful young fellow, with long, black, frizzly hair, parted in the middle; and he was as vain of his good looks as any young girl. He carried a little comb and brush all in one, with a velvet-framed looking-glass let into the back; and every two minutes he would pull it out, spruce himself up, then gaze with delight upon the charming effect. It was late on a Saturday night when I arrived, and first thing next morning I was wakened by their music, for in summer they begin at six o'clock, and Sunday there is the great day for playing and dancing."

"That'd be the country for me, brother. The

gorgios hereabouts all think they're going to heaven in a sack." [1]

"They were playing on a terrace where there were seats and tables; so I ordered my breakfast at a table near them, and sat and listened, something like that Trowbridge policeman who knows the Róm'nimus, and hides behind hedges to hear what Gipsies say. They were jabbering away in Romanes; but their Romanes is somewhat different to ours, hard to understand till one gets used to it. By-and-bye, however, an old lady came by, a very ugly old lady, and '*Phúri chóhani,*' said Mr Coxcomb with the dulcimer."

"Why, I know what that was; 'Old witch,' he meant."

"Right you are, Plato; and I could understand that too. I just looked hard at him, and repeated his words, '*Tátchnes penésa, púri chovihóni si, béngeski púri chovihóni.*' Down went the fiddles, up they jumped, in an instant they were round me like a lot bees. '*Románo pràl*' (Gipsy brother)—'*Katár avés*' (Where do you come from?)—'*Besh téle ménsar*' (Sit down with us); their words poured out fast as the Swallow Falls. And when I was seated between chief violin and dulcimer, they fell to questioning, trying to find out what I really knew. One pointed to his hair ('*Bàl?*'), another to his eyes ('*Yaká?*'), a third to a servant girl who stood close by ('*Pórni minj?*')"—

---

[1] A reminiscence of the "Master Thief," of which hereafter.

"My father!"

"Ay, that I could understand; but there were many things they said that seemed to me upside down. What would you say they meant by '*Pi dràb, pràla?*'"

"'Drink poison,' to be sure. That was a funny thing to ask a man."

"'What'll yer pison yourself with?'—the Nevada invitation to a friendly glass. No; '*pi drab*' means 'smoke tobacco' with these Gipsies, just as *fogus* is 'tobacco' with highfliers, and 'poison' with some mumply Romané. And a bottle of wine they called a *tùshni mol.*"

"A 'basket of wine;' but that would be one of those wicker-covered bottles; you'll hear some English Gipsies use it for 'can.' But didn't the Gentiles stare to see the gentleman sit down with the poor dear Romani players?"

"They opened their eyes a bit, but then they think that every Englishman is mad; and besides, poor Romani players are often great people down in Hungary. I spent three days at Siklos, and was never better amused in all my life. There were a lot of Gipsies living in the place; but these men came out of Transylvania, as you come up from England into Wales, only they had left their wives and families behind. They could not speak much German, and I didn't know ten words of Hungarian, but we managed fairly well with Romanes. Very eager they were to know what I was doing: did I want any horses, and were there many Gipsies where I came from? for they

are terrible fellows for asking questions. These had
not travelled much; but some Hungarian Gipsies,
coppersmiths, think nothing of starting on a five years'
round through Germany, France, Spain, England,
Norway,—I can't tell where." [1]

"That's not much like my daddy. We had the
awfullest work to get him to come up into Wales this
summer, for he never likes intruding nowheres where
everyone doesn't know him, and where people don't
call him 'Master Lovell.' But really now, you'd think
they would be daunted going in countries and never
knowing the talk."

"Yes, but many of these Gipsies speak German and
French as well almost as they speak Hungarian, and

[1] Continental Gipsies are, as a rule, much greater travellers than their
English brethren. The *Weserzeitung* of 25th April 1851 announced that
one hundred Gipsies had passed through Frankfurt, on their way from Hungary to Algeria; and according to the *Magdeburg Zeitung* (1846, No. 16),
a singular movement had been for some time afoot among the Spanish
Zincali, many of whom were preparing to cross to Morocco, while Abd-el-
Kader's name was on every lip. England has had several visits from foreign
Gipsies, Turkish, Hungarian, and Italian; and Mr H. H. Howorth,
author of *The History of the Mongols*, tells me that in 1879 he en-
countered in Sweden a band of fez-wearing Gipsies, natives presumably
of the Balkan Peninsula. English Gipsies confine themselves, as a rule,
to English-speaking lands. Lately I read a letter from one of the
Smiths, who, having wandered through Canada and the States, was on
the eve of sailing for Australia. Perhaps the most travelled English
Gipsy was one Jones, a Cambridge knife-grinder. Having "left his
country for his country's good," in the old transportation times, he had
made his escape from Australia by stowing aboard a ship, and, the ship
touching at a Spanish port, had landed and fallen in with Zincali, with
whom he wandered for some time. "He was regarded," my informant
writes, "as a master of deep Romanes among the People round Cambridge."

have a smattering of other languages besides. Four
years ago I was in Halle, a German town where lives
Professor Pott, a very great man who has written a
very great book on Romanes. I had just been talking with him, and he had told me that once only in
his life had he spoken with living Gipsies, so I asked
him, 'Did they never come to Halle?' 'No,' he
replied ; and presently I came away. I was not two
hundred yards from his doorstep, when I saw a curious
sort of skeleton waggon, drawn by two little horses,
shackled together, just as you were describing. On
the top of this waggon sat a woman smoking a big
black pipe ; and round it three or four children were
playing, naked as ever they were born, or as your
father in his young Egyptian days. It's perfectly
true, Plato ; stark naked the Hungarian Gipsy children run till they are twelve years old ; and the story
goes, that if one of them grumbles at the cold, his
mother will give him a strap: ' Here, sonny, put that
on to keep the winter out.' The waggon was standing
outside an inn ; and entering the inn, I found two
Gipsy men seated at the table, eating soup and drinking beer. I greeted them with ' *Látcho dívvus* ' (that's
how they say ' Good day '), and they were not one bit
surprised, for these were travelled gentlemen. Three
years they had been away from Hungary, in France
and Germany ; and I only wish that I could speak
French and German as well as they. I remember we
compared passports (a sort of travelling licence, Plato),
and mine they pronounced an exceeding *shúkar lil*

(fine paper), the lion and unicorn seeming to take
their fancy. Every place they come to, they must go,
first thing, to the head policeman and show their
passes, and then he tells them where they are to stop.
They are allowed three days in every place, and
no one can meddle with them all that time. What
do you say to that, Plato ? "

" Why, I say it's a very good way indeed. Just
fancy the pretty hangmen ever giving you leave to
stop anywheres here. It's always, 'Move on ; you
must'nt be staying here ; it's against the law.' And
what then, brother ? "

" The women came in, two of them, and some of
the children. There was one, a little fellow of nine
or ten, as brown and pretty a thing as ever I saw, but
wild as a fox-cub. His father gave him a plate of
soup to finish, and he lapped it up just as a fox-cub
would, looking out at me now and again from behind
his mother. Then they paid their reckoning, the
women climbed up on the waggon, the children
shouted, and the men cracked their whips. 'God go
with thee, brother ;' and so we parted, they for Hungary, and I for England."

" They were'nt from that country, then, Garmany,
how d'ye call it ? You'd think there'd be Gipsies there."

" So there are, plenty ; but they are not half as
deep as those of Hungary. Just two days after I saw
that lot, I came on a company of German Gipsies.
There were three men, five or six grown-up barefoot
women, and a host of children ; but they had neither

horses nor donkeys, only two tiny carriages drawn by dogs."

"What! regular highfliers, like those poverty Crinks?" And Plato pointed to the tinsmith's tents, just visible from the bridge where we had been sitting for the last half hour.

"No, hardly as bad as that: but they mix up German with their Romani talk, much as the London Gipsies mix up English. You know how they always say '*Mándi jins*' for '*Jináva me*,' and '*Kei's túti jássing*' for '*Kei jássa tu.*' Well, these are not unlike the London Gipsies; and all the show-people know a little Romanes. There was one old woman I saw at Leipzig Fair, blear-eyed, toothless, frightful to look at, and she was singing 'I am so ticklish.' She could *róker* a bit; and so can the circus folk and keepers of the merry-go-rounds. No, the only really deep German Gipsy I ever knew, I met in Göttingen. 'Hermann Brandt, artist,' he calls himself; for he is a rope-dancer. I met him and his brother and little boy on the market-place one bitter November day, and said 'Good day' to him in Romanes, to which he answered '*Also ein Rómano chal*' (A Gipsy, then), and made as if he would press me to his heart. Hermann wore two gold watches, though he could not tell the time; and his boy had on a magnificent bearskin coat. We stood talking some time together, and, as we talked, a little old gentleman came by, in a white wide-brimmed hat (just like a mushroom), the kindest, merriest of little gentlemen, and the deepest of

Eastern scholars. He looked at us hard through his
spectacles, and then passed on. The three were going
off to Münden; so we went to the station, and spent
two hours in the refreshment-room, drinking *lager-
bier* and waiting for the train. Of course, we were
talking all the time, and really both brothers knew as
deep Romanes as your father Silvanus, or even as
old Sylvester Boswell. But they, too, used a lot of
words that no English Rómano would understand,—
buríka for 'donkey,' *shúkar shambóna* for 'pretty
pipe,' and *stacheléngro* for 'hedgehog.' And Hermann
actually had a hedgehog in his pocket; so you see
they were proper Gipsies. I met them several times
after that, and Hermann has sent me letters from time
to time. The finest thing was, that when I got back
home, I found a note from the Professor, saying that
he had just passed four Gipsies on the market-place,
and that he sent to tell me, knowing the interest I
took in Gipsies."

"He had'nt made you out, then. But there! you
might pass for a Romano with Romané, and have,
maybe."

"Thanks, Plato, for that very pretty compliment;
the greatest that heart of a Gipsy can devise. But no,
when I get among strange Gipsies, and they ask me,
'Romano, eh?' I shake my head, and gravely assure
them that I am the rankest gorgio ever walked the
road."

"Ay, and then of course they thinks the more,
brother; 'cause they knows if any one asks one of

we plump out, 'Are you a Gipsy?' we're bound to answer, 'No.'"

"Yes, something like old Mrs Lucretia Boswell. First time I saw her was when she came up with baskets to a house where I was staying. I saw her coming, went to the door and greeted her with '*Sor shan, déia? Rómani hoi?*' and she replied 'No, my gentleman, I am not a Roman woman.'"

"It looked like it. Now if you was to ask one of these here gentry" (we were passing the Crink encampment on our homeward way) "whether they were Gipsies, they'd be fast enough belike to tell you, 'Ay.' Just like Credit. To hear him talk, you'd fancy there was'nt a deeper traveller going. But tell us some more about your real originals."

"Well, I was walking one day in London, not so long ago, past the great church of Westminster, when I saw two men, and a look was enough to tell me what they were. One was tall, hook-nosed, and elderly, the other a slim good-looking young fellow, but both were as black as any tea-kettle; so presently I came up by them. 'How d'ye do?' said I, in Romanes; and the tall one answered, 'And how are you, brother? I haven't set eyes on you I don't know when.' Which was likely enough, Plato, because he had never seen me in his life. 'No,' I said, 'it *is* a goodish while;' and as we walked on talking, I learnt that they were two of the Smiths, staying at Battersea. By-and-bye hook-nose says, 'You'll take a glass, brother;' so we went into a public-house, and

first he paid for a quart, and then I paid for a quart ;
and then, 'You haven't been out long, brother?'
'No, not very long, brother.' 'Seven years was it,
brother?' 'Seven years it was.' 'About a horse,
brother?' 'About a horse.' And then I came away."

"Oh, very good! capital that was ; but they'd do it
better next time. You see, bor, they were trying to
draw you out, by making as how they thought they
knowed you, and that you had got seven years for
horse-stealing! Any more?"

"Let me see. You know a lot of the Gipsies up
by London keep cabs and horses. There is one,
Mark Davies, who, when first I knew him, had
hardly a penny he could call his own, and now he
has thirteen cabs, men under him, and money in the
bank besides. In the summer they take their cabs
and horses to fairs and races, and hire a meadow in
which to put their cabs and pitch their tents, so that
it costs them little for keep, whilst they'll be making
from two to five pounds a day. Ascot's a mighty
place for that, because of the Eton boys. This was
in London, though, that I'm going to tell you. I was
walking by Kensington Gardens, coming from Notting
Hill, when, passing a cab-stand, whom should I see
perched on a hansom but Albert Draper. I did not
know him then, but there was no mistaking the
breed of him ; so, thinking to play a merry jest, I got
into his hansom. Soon as I was in, he opened the little
trap-door at the top (you have seen the hansoms in
Birmingham, Plato?), 'Where to, sir?' he asked, and

'*Jal to Beng*' (The deuce), was my reply. Bang! down came the trap-door with a tremendous slam, and then I heard him scrambling off his perch. Then a scared face came peeping through the window, then peering very timidly round at the front ; and for the life of me, I could not keep the laughter in. He was as pale as any ghost, and, so he told me afterwards, made sure he had got the ' Old un'' for a fare. Yes, that was how I first came to know Albert Draper ; and a very good fellow I have always found him. He did me a kindly turn at Epsom once. Some rascally pickpocket stole my purse,—a greater loss to me than prize to him, for it held my return ticket to London, as well as all the little money I was worth. ' I was all by my own dear self,' as Mantis says, and what to do I hardly knew, when luckily I came across Albert by the station. He heard my tale, and with hardly a word, reached me an ancient leather purse, holding, I daresay, forty pounds or more, and left me free to take as much or little as I chose. Not many gorgios would have done the same."

"No, you may take your oath on that, bor, nor Gipsies neither ; though it would be a poor thing, too, if we would'nt assist a gentleman as had always been kind to we, especially if one was sure of getting his money back, with something maybe on the top of it."

"There you go spoiling a very pretty sentiment. But have you ever been taken for a gorgio ? "

"Oh, ay ; for a foreigner leastwise. Heaps of times people has asked me, when I and my brothers would be

talking in a public, 'What language is that, young
man?' 'Spanish,' I always tells 'em; and then they'll
say, 'Oh! I was a-thinking you was a Spaniel by your
beautiful dark eyes. What part of Spain might you
belong to?' 'Minjo,' says I; 'that's the town as I
comes out of.' 'Minjo! dear me! And is it a nice
place, Minjo?' 'Beautiful place,' I always answers
'em; 'there's nothing in the world comes up to Minjo.'
Dàbla! what fools folks are. But the laughablest
thing as ever happened to me was in an inn at
Swansea. I had taken an old horse of my daddy's
to the knacker's, and went to get a glass of beer; and
there were some of the Lees there, drinking and
quarrelling (just like Longsnout's breed) with a pretty
gorgio. And there were some more mumply, gor-
giofied-looking fellows, sitting the other side, and just
when the Lees got fighting, these sung out,—

> 'Well done, my gorgio,
> Del him adré the múi again;
> S' help mi dearie dúvel,
> You can mill kushtó.'

Some of the Prices they was; but to look at you'd
never have thought they had one word of Romanes.
That's the way, though, nowadays; every highflier
has got a bit of the talk, and you never know where
you are. If you want Romanes, you go to Gorselar,
nine mile the other side of Gloucester. A little bit
of a country place it is, all surrounded with nasty
poverty woods, and snakes scrawling about everywhere.
It's on the top of a bank, and there are two inns there.

And if any Gipsies goes in to take a glass of beer, and get talking where they shall stop, and saying there's not a bite of *chor* (grass) for the *greías* (horses), some ugly górgio as happens to be in, with a smock-frock on, will say, ' Oh, I can poóker you a kúshto poov to chiv your greías adré ' (tell you a good field to put your horses in). All the górgios talk Róm'nimus round there; they learnt it off Poggi-Bul's lot, for they're always round about. And Charlie Huggins, Lizzie's man, why he speaks Romanes as well as anybody, though he has'nt a drop of Romani blood in the whole of his scrape-pig body."

" I never knew a case like that exactly, not in the country, but up by big towns, where Gipsies stop from one year's end to the other (London, Bristol, Wolverhampton, Manchester, and so forth), there are scores of Gentiles who understand the talk, though they may not be able to speak it over well. The betting-men, too, have got a touch of it, and horse-dealers still more. I was coming by train once from Hungerford to Bath, and it was fair-day at Devizes, and three men from the fair got into the carriage I was in. Well-to-do farmers I took them for, till one of them said, ' It's a good job Mr Páni[1] was'nt there to-day ; ' and another answered, ' Ay, Críshindo's safe to cooper

---

[1] This speaking of the rain as "Mr Water," reminds one ot *Happy Thoughts*, by F. Burnand ; but the usage is of some antiquity. From Egan's edition of Grose's *Classical Dictionary of the Vulgar Tongue* (1823), we learn that canters, speaking of a person who was gone, would say, "Mr Nash is concerned," *nash* being Romanes for "run."

a walgóra' (The rain is sure to spoil a fair). I never
said a word to them till just as they got out at Trowbridge; then I remarked, 'Kairáw have kánas, and
prástermengré tei' (Houses have ears, and so have
railway-carriages). Another time I was staying in a
Peterborough inn, where a carpenter was busy on some
job inside the bar. I never took any notice of the man
(he was an ordinary enough fellow to look at), so you
may guess how surprised I was to hear him come out
one day, as the clock struck one, 'Hóbben chaíros,
mándi must lel kérri to my rómadi' (Dinner-time, I
must get home to my wife). Of course I got talking
with him, and found that he had married one of the
Smiths."

"It does make me angry, brother, to hear of Romani
women learning such nasty *kennicks* anything. Often
I swear I'll never speak another word of Róm'nimus;
and I'll tell you another thing as makes me wild, and
that is, to hear some of our own people ashamed of
their own tongue, making themselves. It was me and
my daddy went to Wolverhampton market with two
ponies and a donkey, and we saw two swellish-looking
women walking down among the horses, all covered
with falderals. They had red and green and yellow
coloured handkerchiefs round their necks, and red
velvet bonnets and green parasols, black dresses with
short black velvet jackets, and they had veils on too.
Lord bless us all, what a state they did make
theirselves! They were coming talking about their
husbands one to the other; it was all, 'My master

this,' and 'My master that.' Right by us they passed ; but I never took much notice, for I was quite a little chap, as it might be Dimiti, and hadn't no notions of women. But my daddy asked, 'Do you see those two ladies, Plato?' 'Devil's ladies,' says I ; and my daddy said, 'They're two monkey Gipsies, married to colliers.' And if you spoke to them in Romanes, they'd turn their noses up, make as they didn't know no such vulgar talk. Such women as them is never no good. They ought to be burnt."

"Mind you don't get burned yourself, Plato, for keeping Richénda waiting for her breakfast. It is close upon ten."

"That'll be time enow, the day is quite young yet. But you'll come in and take a bite with us?"

"Not this morning. I had my breakfast before I left the house, and I've got two letters to write, and then to catch the midday train to Barmouth. But, I daresay, I shall look you up again this evening. What racket are you up to, as highfliers say?"

"I! oh, I'm going over to Dina's about a horse; and Nathan is coming too, so we shall take our fiddles. And some of the others was talking of taking theirn to Pen-y-bonh, to play at the Tal-y-llyn inn ; and they'll get some fishing maybe in the lake. Well, take care of yourself."

Chapter Third.

TOOK good care of myself, as Plato bade me; and, returning from Barmouth safely, came again to the camp at five in the afternoon, to find it almost utterly deserted. True, Silvanus was there; but he was discussing glanders with the owner of the meadow. Two or three of the women had not gone out, but they were washing at the brook below; and the younger children were sure to be not far off, but where it might have puzzled Puck to tell. So I strolled about, and took a look at the tents.

The oddest tent I ever remember seeing was pitched in the middle of many-towered Prague, on a patch of waste ground not far from the Moldau's bank. It was simply a market-woman's white umbrella, sheltering the heads of some seven Bohemian vagrants, whose legs stuck out like *radii* drawn to an unknown circumference. In London I have looked on skewer-cutters' huts cheek-by-jowl with a red-brick church; and I have seen the Epping donkey-drivers crouching beneath an apron-covered bush.

54

The tents of the Lovells differed from all of these, as Gipsies differ from the non-gipsy tramp. For a description of their like I must go to Elias Boswell, and quote from a treatise of the old man's making:—

"The tents are of rough blankets. They are nearly always made of brown ones, because the white blankets are not so good for the rain. First of all, when they make up the tent, they measure the ground with a ridge-pole; then they take the kettle-prop, and make the holes exactly opposite each other. Then they take up the ridge-pole, and stick all the rods into the ridge-pole. Then there is a blanket that goes behind, that is pinned on with pinthorns. Next to that comes the large ones over the top of all, also pinned with the same pins. Now there are some very large, and others much smaller; but for my part I like a middling-size one quite as well, because the large ones are often cold."

Thus far Elias; and I, his commentator, remark that the kettle-prop is an iron bar, crooked at one end and sharpened at the other; that pinthorns are natural thorns employed for pins; and that the largest tents are 20 feet deep, 12 feet wide, and 10 feet high, the cost of such varying, with the materials, between £10 and £20. Tilt-like in form, they are sheltered in winter by "balks" or "barricades," a kind of fore-tent, where stands the hearthstone or the charcoal brazier, and which sometimes connects two tents pitched front to front. In summer, however, the balks are either dispensed with, or left as a rule uncovered; and in summer the fire is made, of course, outside. Some writers have said that Gipsies always build to face the

rising sun ; but herein they err, Gipsy castrametation
depending on the set of the ground and the quarter
whence the wind may chance to blow. These tents,
for instance, had a southern aspect, being pitched in
Indian file,—Lementina's first, Lucretia's next to hers,
and so on down to that which Loverin shared with
his two unmarried brothers. Complete the outward
survey by noticing a shallow trench, intended to carry
off the rain, and then glance into Lementina's "place."

Round its sides runs a kind of divan, of oat straw
spread with furs and brilliant rugs ; a daïs is formed
at the farther end by feather-beds, blankets, and
other bedding ; in the midst is a carpet, sure token
of Romani prosperity. A nosegay of wild flowers,
a bunch of withered hops, some peacock feathers, a
looking-glass, and two resplendent carriage lamps, are
all the adornments, but the effect is neither unhomely
nor inæsthetic ; there are thousands worse housed than
are the houseless Gipsies. Houses on wheels there
are none ; for cumbrous caravans are as little suited
for the hills of Wales as for Cyprus roads, where Sir
Samuel Baker tried them to his cost ; but yon two-
wheeled tilted carts cost £40 apiece, and Willy has
besides a light spring cart. What these will not
carry, in moving from place to place, is packed on
the horses' and the donkeys' backs.

Such are the tents, which I have here described with
some minuteness as a curious survival (in England),
in the nineteenth century. Older than cromlechs,
older than buried towns, older than the pyramids,

they take one back to that far distant time when
Jabal became "the father of such as dwell in tents,
and of such as have cattle." But were our Gipsies
always tent-dwellers? That is a question to which I
incline to answer, No. All the old chroniclers of the
fifteenth century are silent as to Gipsies' tents, though
they speak of their waggons, horses, hounds, and
outlandish garb. Korner's statement, "*Extra urbes in
campis pernoctabant*," and Rufus's, "*Se legen in deme
velde, wente me wolde se in den steden nicht lyden*,"
imply no more than that the Gipsy immigrants of 1417
were not allowed to pass the night within the walls
of the Hanseatic towns. Arnold von Harff, patrician
of Cologne, who about 1497 visited the great Gipsy
colony outside Nauplia, has much to say of the Gipsy
bellows, nothing of Gipsy tents. Nor are they mentioned in any of the documents and scattered notices[1]
relating to English Gipsies in the sixteenth century ;
nay, as negative evidence may be cited the letter of
Edward Hext, a Somersetshire justice of the peace,
addressed to the Lord Treasurer in 1596. We learn
from it that the Egyptians of a shire did "meet, either
at fairs or markets, or in some alehouse, once a week.
And *in a great hayhouse*, in a remote place, there did
resort weekly forty, sometimes sixty ; where they did
roast all kind of good meat" (Strype, *Annals of the
Reformation*, vol. iv. p. 410, Oxf. ed. 1824). The trial

---

[1] See Mr H. T. Crofton's exhaustive and admirable monograph,
"English Gipsies under the Tudors," in the *Papers of the Manchester
Literary Club* for 1880.

of the Browns and of James M'Pherson at Banff in
1700 (*Spalding Club Miscellany*, vol. iii. pp. 175-91)
shows Scotch Egyptians lying in kilns or temporarily
taking houses ; and tents were till recently unknown
to Gipsies of the Principality.   Mr John Roberts, in
a letter of 22d January 1880, writes :—" The Welsh
Gipsies was not known to camp out in those days,
but they always used to ask leave to lodge (*mong
lodybens*) in barns and other buildings, and they were
allowed to make fire in the buildings as well as outside
it.   I often heard my father say that it was him that
made the first tent that was made for them in Wales,
by the instructions of my grandmother.   She was
one of the Stanleys [English Gipsies], and she used
to praise my father for picking it up so soon."

It seems to have been about 1750 that the Woods
and Ingrams migrated from England to Wales ; and I
am disposed to believe that tents did not come into
general use among English Gipsies till after then, a
view supported by the celebrated case of Elizabeth
Canning in 1754.   Of course, at different times and in
different lands, Gipsies have taken to tents, just as in
England and on the Continent they have taken to
caravans, or as at Altrincham, in Cheshire, they live
in railway carriages.   As early as 1387 we read of
forty tents of Acigani in Wallachia ; and to-day, in
the Ottoman empire, the tented Tchinghianés far
outnumber their house-dwelling brethren.   But the
foregoing observations, coupled with the fact that
the name for " tent " differs in almost every Romani

dialect,[1] and is often a borrowed word, point to the
conclusion that tents are by no means so national a
Gipsy institution as is commonly believed ; and such
a conclusion has its importance in the problem of
the Gipsies' origin.　For writers have argued thus :—
Gipsies are a tent-dwelling race, and a tent-dwelling
race must always have been noticeable ; *ergo*, if in
Byzantine historians prior to 1000 A.D. no notices
occur of a tent-dwelling race, Gipsies cannot have
existed in south-eastern Europe before that date.
But, if the premiss be false, the argument also falls.
The vulgar opinion, that Gipsies cease to be Gipsies
by ceasing to live in tents, is not worth refuting ; it is
as sensible as the notion, that all who live in tents
are necessarily Gipsies.

My tour of inspection brought me to Sinfi's place,
an ambitious protest against the Tinklers' " dog-cubs ; "
and as I loitered, lost in admiration, a strain of music
fell upon my ear.　I will not, after Liszt, attempt to
analyse the Gipsies' music—" its sounding cataracts

---

[1] The Anglo-Romani *tan*, "a tent," seems to be identical with *tan*,
"a place" (Sansk. *sthāna*, Prakr. *thāna*).　Formerly I regarded it as a
distinct word, akin to *tent*, and so too Sansk. *tan*, "to stretch," whence
possibly *than*, "cloth," of German Gipsies ; and this view was somewhat confirmed by the likeness of the broken-Romani phrase, " *tanning*
all over the tem " ("pitching tents all over the country "), to the Vir-
gilian "legio latis *tendebat* in arvis."　But English Gipsies render *tan*,
"a tent," as often as not by "place" (*e.g.* "my mammy's *place*") ;
and in the sense of "tent" the word is unknown to all Continental
Gipsies.　True, Kogalnitschan gives " *tanya*, tent," in his would-be
Roumanian-Gipsy vocabulary ; but the "learned Sclavonian" quietly
appropriated this word, with *bouro, hotchawitcha*, and two hundred
more, from Samuel Roberts' *Gypsies* (Lond. 1836).

bursting in mighty din, its murmuring fountains glid-
ing o'er mossy bed." What chiefly struck me here
was an infinite sadness, weaving a threnody from
ballad and hornpipe and Offenbachian air. I guessed
the player to be Loverin, and Loverin sure enough it
proved to be.

You might sit and talk for hours with Loverin
Lovell, and, did you not know his story, could you
keep clear of all disturbing topics, might never take
him for the "innocent" he is. He is not altered much
from the handsome dandy lad of ten years back; his
hair is as black, his face as brown, as ever. Only the
eyes are changed. Some Gipsies have an ugly trick of
sleeping open-eyed, and Loverin's eyes resemble theirs
—big, dark, but blank, like shuttered windows of a deserted house. Yet his look was glad as he sprang up to
meet me; his voice had not lost the merry Gipsy ring.

"Why, Francis lad, come in and sit you down.
You're kindly welcome; for, faith! I was wondering
why you had never come anighst me. Plato was
bragging at breakfast how he'd been treating of the
rei to ale, and 'Winkles' was bragging how he'd
been swimming with the rei. It was all 'rei here, rei
there,' till I fetched Mantis a clout aside the head.
'Don't be so fast,' I said, 'talking 'bout what's got
nothing to do with you. He wouldn't be seen with
the likes of you black Gipsies.' You wouldn't, would
you, reía?"

"Certainly not, Loverin; unless they were very
particular friends."

"Now, isn't that just what I was tellin' em? 'He always was *my* Romani Rei,' says I; 'and I means to get a notice-board and stick it on him, warning as how all varmin 'll be persecuted that comes a trespassing on Squire Loverin's land.' I was thinking on you the very moment you come up, and found me 'musing myself with my dear little violin."

"Yes, I've been standing listening round the corner, admiring your brilliancy of execution. But how was it that you did not go with the others to Tal-y-llyn?"

"Oh! I don't know ; I never cares much for going with a crowd of rude young boys. And someone must stop and mind the place; and there were the sticks to get 'gainst Nora comes back from the town. She's down to the station after a lot of baskets, from Mr Joseph Burluraux's, you know, 29 Tavistock Street, Covent Garden London. Thank you, I don't mind if I do try a pipeful of your 'bacca."

My pouch was like a little woolly black bear, and Loverin eyed it with a child's delight, sagely observing, "It looks ondikelous pulling the 'bacca from under the tail, don't it now? Beautiful 'bacca, too. I wish I could offer you a cigar, refa; but they're all locked up, and miles and miles away, a matter I daresay of two or three hundred mile."

"Don't mention it ; I never smoke cigars."

"You used to ; and I would really have liked to have offered you one of these. Twopence apiece, and a black man smoking on the lid ; I won 'em raffling at the 'Bandon Arms.' But what's the use of talking, when

they're all locked up along of the other valuables. A
silver teapot, and three silver spoons, and a silver fruit-
knife that my mammy got off Mrs Scudamore, and a
beautiful horseshoe breastpin, and three gould studs
like flies, and Nora's coral necklace, and the earrings,
and more besides, if I could only mind it. Oh! we're
not so bad off, me and Nora ; but there! it would never
do go taking good things about where there's such
cattle as that Richénda. They'd never be safe a
minute. So we locked them up in the big black box,
and buried it ; I've got the place put down on a bit of
paper. I'll not mind showing it you ; but don't you
go letting on to none of the others. I know their
crafty ways."

From the pocket of a fly-book, Loverin, first glancing furtively around, drew forth a damp-discoloured
"death-card," bearing the words—

> "In Memory of LEONORA LOVELL,
> Who died at Clavering, February 26th, 1869,
> Aged 19 years.
>
> Farewell, mother and husband dear,—
> Don't weep for me, though I am not here ;
> Don't weep for me, nor neither cry,—
> I am gone to meet my Lord on high."

"Read it up," said Loverin cheerfully.

"Clavering, February 26th, 1869," I read.

"That isn't all of it. Read it right up from the
beginning: 'In memory of Leonora Lovell;'" and
Loverin repeated it straight off by heart.

"Can't you see, man, as that was just a screen to put
'em off their curiosity? 'Twasn't likely I should go

and tell them that I'd been hiding so and so; but now, if one of them was to see that paper—'What's that?' they'd ask; and I should answer, careless-like, 'Oh! nothing but a death-card; you're welcome to read it, if you has a mind.' And they might read it, but they'd never make nothing on it, never think as that was where I'd hid the treasure."

"I suppose not. And where the treasure is, there shall the heart be also?"

"No, no," Loverin ran on vauntingly, heedless of my self-communing remark; "I was a bit too old there for the Yorkshire jockey. She was always hankering after Nora's necklace, calling her 'Sister,' and wanting her to change for an old brass thing that wasn't worth picking up in the road. I can't abear such nasty fly-catching ways. And the boys takes after her, prodigal young ringtails! I gave it Mantis, though, this morning. Pretty fellow, to brag about convarsin' with *my* gentleman?"

"Never mind your nephew, Loverin; tell me about yourself. You were always a highly moral, well-conducted youth."

"That's the truest word ever you said, bor. I was the best out of all the ruck, never getting into no rows or contravartins, nor nothing of the sort. Wherever I goes I always manages to get a glass of beer, 'cause I'm so innocent, gorgios say. But Wisdom now, he always was a hard-faced one. You can see the badness in his very looks. We were stopping at Flashbrook onest, by a bit of a pond, along with Solomon's lot; and it was fearful cold that winter, and of course this pond was frozen over. Well, one fine frosty morning my mammy was plucking a chicken in the tent, and Wisdom got outside the place with nothing but his short shirt on, and a small clay pipe a sticking in his mouth that my daddy had brought from the 'Batchiker Arms.' I daresay he'd be about seven years old. My mammy kept shouting to him to come and be dressed, and he wouldn't. Sliding on that place he was the whole day long; and next morning he was took very bad, his head and his eyes swōll up fearful. And then we went away from there, and went to that place called Aspley, by Eccleshaw; and my mammy took him to the doctor there, oh! three or four times she had him to the doctor. And he was bad for a long time after.

"That was the same place where my daddy and mammy took the donkey to fetch a great dead pig from a farm about two miles off. I can't say what it was like, but it was bigger than the donkey. And he hung it upon a great old oak tree, on one of the lower branches; and I know Sinfi and me were awfully frighted of it. It looked like a ghost hung up. And a fox came hovering round the place—smelt it, I suppose; and the second night it come again, and caught hold of one of the legs and brought it down, branch and all together. He left it lying on the ground next morning, and went off immediately—got such a fright, I suppose; and then my daddy cut it up, gave some to Solomon's and some to Gilderoy's.

"Ay, bor; and then my daddy brought home a pair

of great old-fashioned flat scales, one night soon after
that; and Sinfi and me put 'em up in the tent, and
got in swingle-wise. We used to sit there, and weigh
ourselves backwards and forwards, bobbing up and
down like two young porkypines. And then my
daddy sold them for old copper. I mind my mammy
was fine and angry, 'cause Sinfi put little Ambrose in
them onest."

"Little Ambrose? I don't know the name."

"Oh! that was the dear little boy that died by
Norton, when he was only three months old. He came
atween Lance and Lina. Shúri was nursing him, and
she'd been angry just before; didn't want to hold the
child. And she was shaking him about on his stomach;
he was crying, and he had a fit,—died in it. Dear
little fellow! I remember that little child's face as well
as can be to this day. It was blue. And then my
mammy laid him out on the things, on the pocket, in
his short frock; and we took it down, and played with
it, as though it was a doll. My mammy took it off us,
and put it back on the things. Then next day the
man brought the little coffin down; and two little
girls come dressed all in white, and they brought two
great bunches of wallflowers, and put them all over the
child in the coffin. And to this day, whenever I see
those sort of flowers, it takes me back to that; the
very smell of 'em do. And I remember, we looked
upon it, me and Sinfi, as though it was something to
please us like. We had no sense; we were quite
little. And then, when they took the child away

E

to be buried, we wanted to go with them ; and my
mammy would not let us. She had to turn us back
twice, to make us stay at the place ; and we yelled as
loud as ever we could yell. And whiles they were at
the funeral, I wanted to go by myself somewhere, and
Lance would follow me. And there was a long drain
crossing the road, wide enough for any child to walk
up. There was no water in it ; it was all dried up.
And I took him underneath that drain, and thrashed
him well. I thought it would sound fine, for we used
to go there to hoot. And he did open his mouth
above a bit ! "

Loverin had been very near crying when he came to
Ambrose's blueness, but this last reminiscence seemed
to cheer him up. And the depths of his brother's
wickedness, contrasting with his own integrity, had
still to be laid more bare.

"That drain was something like another bridge ;
only there was water there. We were all stopping in
a beautiful road, called the Worcester Road ; and
there was the river running right across, and over it a
little foot-bridge. Patience and Shúri got washing
this bridge one day (little bits of wenches they was
then), and Nathan was walking round about with one
of those wooden hoop things round his neck. And he
would keep walking on the wet bridge ; and long and
by last he tumbled overboard, right into a deep mud-
hole. He swum down underneath the bridge, and
Uncle Perun's wife pulled him out, Lippi. Then
Pyramus made a fire in my Aunt Plenty's tub, and

baked cakes. We all sat round, and made a feast, until she come. Then we had to run all roads; and she did lay it on to him for burning the good wash-tub. It was a new one. But Pyramus's greed was past all bearings. There was him and Tilda onest. My mammy and the rest were all gone out; no one at the place, only just us children. And there was a whole field-full of Travellers, all sorts; and Pyramus and Gilderoy's Tilda got at my mammy's flour, and took the frying-pan and filled it, and begun kneading it up. And they'd neither matches nor sticks, nor nothing in the world to make a fire. They sat in the ditch, where they thought no one could see 'em; and just as they were about finished "—

"But how did they manage, if they had no fire?"

"Just kneaded it up, and ate it so like pigs. They'd got through the first panful, and begun on the second, and they were gormed all over, when they saw my mammy and all the others coming; and they scattered it all over the bushes, and a good way along the ditch where they'd been sitting. My daddy, when he seed it, burst out laughing; and Pyramus fell on his back in the ditch, thinking he was going to be beat. But Tilda ran off all down the field, and Gilderoy after her with a poking-stick.

"Another time it was Plato and a górgio lad; and we were stopping in a place called Shaybroom Lane, the place where the pigs ate up Seth Boswell's fiddle. He had a pistol, this monkey had; and he filled it full of powder, and he put a match to it, and it didn't go off. Then he laid it down on the grass, and put another match in it, and told Plato to stoop down and blow up it. And he blowed, and the moment he did so, the thing went off, and let fly right in the middle of Plato's face. Perfectly blind he was for some time; and my mammy went down to the fine woman, the lad's mother, and scold about it ; and the fine górgio beat the boy. And very next day Nathan hit my cousin 'Híngo-píri' on the nose with a tent-rod, made her nose bleed; and my Uncle Gilderoy came to hit Nathan, said he'd throw him in the middle of a gorse-bush. But Nathan runned off, got in the very furderest corner of my mammy's tent, and hid hisself."

"But what about the pigs and violin, Loverin?"

"The pigs ? Oh ! that was onest when we were stopping in Shaybroom Lane, along with Seth Boswell and his wife. And my daddy and him went off to Market Drayton, to the fair. We were all small children at the time. Their tent was made close to my mammy's ; and before Seth's wife went out in the morning, she asked us to take notice of her place, that the donkeys and things didn't get in. And we said we would. But we never did ; we were too much occupied in our own way, playing about. So, while we were all away from the place, two great big pigs come up the road from the little farm just by, walked into my mammy's tent first, gnawed two great big holes in the wallet, and rooked the straw all about. Then they went into Seth's place, and ate up one or two loaves of bread, and chewed a new violin all in pieces, left nothing but the head. A lion-headed fiddle it was. And when she came home she began to cry, and we told her how it had happened. Then she begged and prayed of us not to say nothing to him about it; and the very first thing she did when he came back again was to go and tell him it was me and Nathan had done it. There was a beast! And then we told him all about it; and then he beat her like anything for telling lies. And I don't think we ever stopped with them after that. But fancy her saying it we me."

"Yes, only fancy it; but conscious innocence upheld you, doubtless. The oddest thing to me is, Loverin, that the others never took pattern by your example. You never lit fires in wash-tubs, or blew up pistols, went sliding naked, or even hit your cousins with a tent-rod."

"No, if you'll believe me, reía, I never was 'dicted to no such nasty villainies. Worst thing that ever I did, was killing a gully [gosling] down by Dorstone onest. My mammy sent me to the farm after some milk, me and Lancelot. As we were coming back, there was a drop of water to cross, and all the geese and young gullies was on it. And there was a portly old gander came craning at me (I hadn't got no shoes on), and I picked up a dear little tiny bit of a pebble, was aiming to throw it at him; instead of that, it caught one of the little ones. And I never noticed the górgio, standing just over the hedge, watching. And the moment he seed me throw the stone, he got

over the hedge, and come running after us. We had
to go up a terrible steep bank to get to the tents, and
I didn't wait to look behind me. I started off as hard
as I could go, I pitched the can down ; and we all left
that place at onest, went right away across the hills
for miles and miles. And I didn't do it for a purpose neither, 'cause there's never no good of killing
poor dear animals. Look at that black tom-cat by
Shayshall yonder."

"What of him, Loverin? Was she a witch, or
rather was he a wizard ?"

"No, you don't understand me ; you go too fast.
There now ! I declare if you haven't been and put
it clean out of my head, just when I was going to
begin."

"About the black tom-cat at Shayshall," I suggest ;
and Loverin picks up the thread of his discourse.

"Ay, ay ; it was at Shayshall sure enough, and I
was quite a little tiny thing. And we were stopping
with my grandfather, and Gilderoy's breed was there.
And Sinfi was the baby at the time ; and my
mammy always kept a piece of bread by her head,
in case the child woke up in the night and wanted
some. And two nights running the bread was gone ;
she didn't know how it went. Ay, bor, so the third
night my daddy watched, and saw a great big black
tom-cat come in, an awful fierce-looking thing. It
stole the bread again, and bolted. Then my daddy
made a little bit of a snare out of a bit of wax-end,
and put it right in the middle of the balk, at a little

hole in the blanket. It come through again, and got into the snare. My daddy rose up in his shirt, and beat it like anything ; and the cat jumped up, nearly put his claws into my daddy's eyes. Then my Uncle Gilderoy rose up, and they took the poor cat outside, dashed its brains out with a piece of stake and a bill-hook. Long after they'd killed it, as they thought (they left it lying on the ground), and the poor thing groaned most awful. And then they made a hole close anunst the tent, and buried it. Then about ten o'clock in the morning, when we were having our breaksfast, the old man come by as owned the cat, and asked my daddy if he'd seen aught of it. ' No,' my daddy said ; ' I haven't seen it nowhere. The boat-men must have took it,'—for there was a canal close by. And the poor old man went round about, calling ' Puss, puss, puss ;' and he shaked all over, and kept crying, ' Oh my poor pussy !' He said he was awful sorry he couldn't find it ; it often used to go in and bring out the water-hens, and lay them down at the door. And he said the cat knowed as well as any-thing everything he said to it. No boatman, he said, couldn't have taken it ; she'd never allow anybody to touch her. Something dreadful must have happened to it ; and then he went off. Bless us all, how that poor animal did groan !"

While Loverin told his story of the cat, I was rummaging vainly for a pipe-light. My box was empty, but there might be some fuzees scattered loose in my pockets, whose contents I accordingly

turned out upon the grass. Among them was a
bunch of watercress, given me that morning by one
of the boys. Loverin espied it, and picked it up ; as
he did so, a curious change passed over him. His
dreamy indolence gave place to sharp suspicion ; his
face grew pale, or rather ashen-grey; his words came
quick and vehement :—

"That's watercress. Where did you get it from ?"

So sudden was the change, so commonplace the
question, that, vaguely reminded of Tweedle-dum, I
vaguely answered, " That ? why, Dimiti picked it out
of the brook when I went to bathe this morning. I
put it in my pocket, and had clean "——

"You're a liar, man. That never come out of no
Welsh brook. Do you think I'm a fool ? do you
think I don't know nothing ?"

" But, Loverin,"——

" Don't ' Loverin' me. Do you think I haven't got
no eyes in my head ? do you think as I don't mind
the Shawford cress ? Why I knowed it—— She
was lying in the tent, dear wench, deathly pale and
sick, for she was near her time (we hadn't been
together not a twelvemonth), and she was always
dalicate. We'd sent for the old woman to come and
nurse her, old Tryphi Gray, but she couldn't come ;
was in trouble about a fortune-telling. I can see it
now that place, Clavering, all down among the poverty
wet fens ; but it was a beautiful sharp bright morning
(Valentine's Day it was); you could see your breath
curling up like smoke, and the fog wasn't only half

lifted. And she says, said she, 'I'm sure I could relish a bite of cress, my Loverin. And she knowed that country; I'd never been there much afore. Just above the foot-bridge going to Mr Bowen's, she said, I was sartain to find it; across the meadow where the bull was kept,—and he was a size of a bull. Off I started, never put no hat nor jacket on, for I was fine and pleased as she could fancy anything; came to the brook, and found the cress just where she said it growed. And there was no one back at the place but her and Genty, and Genty was nothing but a half-growed maiden. And I come tearing back, was got as far as that great big oak tree, when Genty meets me, flying: 'Run, bor, run; there's a nasty górgio a speaking badness to my sister.' I didn't run, I fled, clean over the hedge, right into the road, never looked for no gaps nor nothing. There was his horse outside the place (a beauty he was, rale thorough-bred), and the gentleman, Squire Pomfret, a-standing right inside the balk, in his fine red hunting-coat, top-boots, his box-hat and all, puffing away with a cigar in his mouth, and a Bank of England note a-fiddling in his fingers. 'Damn you, you cursed rogue!' I shouted. I was on to him in a twinkling. He couldn't stand up against me not one moment, but I had him down atop o' the burning coke, and I beat him (Lord! how I did beat him!), and I kicked him and wrastled him, and I got at his throat and worried him, and I catched up the kettle-prop, and I — I —"

Expressionless, said I not, were Loverin's eyes?

Ah! better so, than burning as now with passionate
lust to kill; better those merciful tears that will wash
away the memory—stirred so unwittingly by a bunch
of cress—the memory of long-forgotten sorrow. I
know, for I have often heard, the story, whose sequel
is hardly known by Loverin. Enough, that he only
did not kill the scoundrel;[1] and, leaving him for
dead, fled forth a fugitive from górgio law. And Nora
died, and Loverin's people came and buried her;
and Loverin joined them after five weeks of wandering by himself. Where he had wandered, they
cannot tell; but he was famished, and footsore, and
as "tattered as a mawkin. All his rags," said
Lementina, "jumped for joy." The news of Nora's
death only made him an idiot. He is harmless,
tractable, and not unhappy.

"Look, Loverin, here is the little woolly black
bear again. It really is ridiculous to see how one
pulls the tobacco from under the tail, is it not?
That's right; laugh away, only don't get blackguard-
ing me, for you are a fine big fellow, and I am but a
little one. You frighten me, you know. Be a good
lad, and you shall hear the story of the Great Huge
Bear, and the Middle-sized Bear, and the Little Small
Wee Bear."

I began the tale, but it proved an eminent failure,
my hearer being fidgetty and absent. Native polite-

---

[1] To spare the feelings of that scoundrel's kinsfolk, I have altered
names; but the scoundrel himself, if he ever read these pages, will
know what "Pomfret," "Clavering," and "Shawford" stand for.

ness kept him for some time quiet; but just as I got to where the three bears come home, he started up, saying apologetically,—

"Dear heart, what a time that foolish woman do stop. Excuse me, reía, but I'll walk to the top of the hill, to look if I can't see her coming."

Chapter Fourth.

SO LOVERIN went to watch for Leonora; and passing down the camp, I came upon Silvanus, sitting with back against the wall and outstretched legs, a picture of placidity. I told him about "poor" Loverin, and the old man chid me for my pitying epithet :—" It's a sin to go *poor*-ing innocents and such like, for you know's it's my dear God's will, and you must leave it where you find it, refa." Then I asked who the farmer was, with whom I had left him talking.

"That was Mr Chamberlain, a very free nice gentleman."

" A Welshman ? "

"Oh, dear no; doesn't know two words of Welsh; he hasn't been up these parts more nor thirteen years. Deerhurst in Gloucestershire is his natival, so we're kind of 'sociates like. He's got one sister married back at Winchcombe; keeps a fine big farm, Mrs Cartwright, but we always calls her Madam One-Two-Three, 'cause, whenever we goes up fiddling, she's safe

76

to ask for the polka of that name. Christmas-time we are mostly stopping in her orchard, and she'll say to Lementina, 'Well, Mrs Lovell, and have you seen my brother, Mr Chamberlain, lately?' 'Oh yes, ma'am,' Lemmy tells her; 'and he sent his very kind love to you.' Then summer-time, you see, we come and stop in this here meadow, and Mr Chamberlain 'll say to me, 'Well, Lovell, have you seen my sister?' 'Oh yes, sir,' I answers; 'and she sends her duty and very fondest love.' So brother and sister always lets us stop, 'cause then we tells 'em all that's going on."

"But do you mean to say they never write to one another?"

"No, they never writes; leastwise if they do, it's unbeknown to we. But górgios are different to Gipsies. There was an Irishman at Malvern onest, I mind; he wrote to his daughter, and 'Send him his shirt' was all he put in it."

"Well, Gipsies, though frequent, are not very good correspondents. I hardly ever read a Gipsy letter that contained much more than loves and kisses, the next address, and 'Write back by return of post.' But it's chiefly, I take it, the fault of the people they get to write for them; for when Gipsies can write themselves, their letters are better as a rule than those of górgios. How many of the boys can read and write?"

"Oh! all of 'em knows their letters, 'cause Lementina learnt them that much; and Plato can read a fairish bit. But Wisdom and Nathan are regular scholards. They got it off their wives, for all Welsh Gipsies are terrible ones for larning."

"Yes; so I understand from old John Roberts. You know him, I suppose, Silvanus?"

"No; I never seen the old man himself, though lots of times these country górgios ask, Be I any kith to him? and I always tells 'em, Ay. He really is Rodi and Alabīna's kinsman. But I met the boys onest, playing up at the Kerry Beacon. Beautiful harp-players they are, though I stand up for the good old English fiddle."

"There are some good violinists among them, too ; but what I was going to say is that the father is a better scholar, and a man of greater intelligence, than half the farmers in the country-side.[1] Letters and letters I have from him in this old pocket-book, all written in the very deepest Romanes, letters that it would puzzle even you to understand."

"Ay?" incredulously.

"Ay, indeed. I can tell you they were worse than Greek to me, when first I tried to make them out. Come then, I'll put you to the test. Let's see, we'll try this one:—'Nevo Gav, yndra ow Welshanengo Tem, *18th* Me Dublesco *Month*os, *1877.* Meray *dera* parchana Semensa, Shom ma boinno te cerra caia chinamangery te bitchera to mengey te pena to

---

[1] How few farmers, in England at least, would dream of writing out a vocabulary of their native dialect, with tables of inflections. John Roberts compiled such, being ignorant at the time that any works on the Romani tongue existed.

mengey ta geyom cerray, ta llateyom saw meray *foky* mishto, ta comday te dicken man.'[1] No, that's too easy, Silvanus; I'll find you a stiffer bit than that. Here's something that must have been written expressly for your benefit:—

"Now for a bit of *rokraben*[2] in the English Gipsies' style, to a Welsh Gipsy man, meeting in a fair in Brecon. The English man has a lot of horses to sell, and the Welsh man has nothing but his harp or violin. The Welsh man takes a walk from the hotel or public-house where he is playing, to see the fair, when he meets two or three very tidy English men dressed like gentlemen. When all at onest the English sees something in the phizeog of the Welshman, and says to him, '*Sharsan*,[3] my *Pall?*'[4] when the Welsh one says, 'I am very well, thank you. I don't know who you are.' ENGLISH:—'*Maw didakai!*[5] he don't *jon*[6] who I am; he *kers*[7] himself like a *gorugho*.[8] Don't you *jon*[6] when *totes*[9] come to us where we were a *atching*[10] in de lane about three miles from here, on de Tal-y-bont road? don't *totas*[9] *jon*[6] the time when *mandays*[11] give you a butt of a fishing-rod, and *totas*[9] *deld*[12] *mandays*[11] a fiddle-stick? Where do you *atch*[10] in the *gav*[13] here? do you *jiv*[14] *akai?*[15] WELSH:—

---

[1] "New Town, in the Welsh country, 18th my God's month (*i.e.* Christmas month—December), 1877. My dear respected Kinsfolk, Am I (I am) proud to make this letter and send to you to tell you that I got home, and found all my people well; and they liked (were glad) to see me." [2] Talk. [3] How art thou?, [4] Brother. [5] Nay, look here! (a mere exclamation.) [6] Know. [7] Makes. [8] Gentile. [9] You. [10] Staying. [11] I, me. [12] Gave. [13] Town. [14] Live. [15] Here.

'Yes, I have my *boshamangary*[1] at the "Bell"; will
you come as far?' 'Yes, my brother, I will; look after
those hosses a bit, Josiah.' 'Don't be long, my
brother.' 'No, I shan't, my fellow; I am only going
to hear my Uncle John *kell*[2] a bit upon his *boshamangary*.[1] I haven't heard him, the Lord knows
when. I think the last time I heard him was somewhere in Herefordshire, on the borders of Shrop-
shire, the time when we got very *mateay*,[3] and you
had to go to some *filashin*.'[4] The two are now in
the 'Bell,' in a good big taproom. 'Now, my Uncle
John, what will you *lel*[5] to *pee*?[6] Play us up a
good hornpipe.' When presently in comes one of the
brothers, and just sold a horse for £20, and begins to
dance like a good 'un. When the harper praises the
dancer up by saying, 'Mishtoe,[7] *faith!* bau; kosko
kelamangero shan too. To shan ow fedader kelamangero ta dicttom may undray temorry *famaly*a.
Mero stiffo pal ses *very* kosko yeck, *but* to shan
fedadare *nor* yov. Repera may les te kellel saw e
parlochey *from* lesky chichaw yek rat, undray *some*
curchima in e Abergainaia; ta kordas ow fedadare
kelamangero en dova gav; ta, te pena ow tatchyben

---

[1] Harp.   [2] Play.   [3] Drunk.   [4] Mansion, gentleman's house.
[5] Take.   [6] Drink.   [7] "Capital, faith! lad; good dancer art thou.
Thou art the best dancer that saw I (I have seen) in your family. My
brother-in-law was (a) very good one, but thou art better nor (than) he.
Remember I him that (he) dances (I remember his dancing) all the
nails out of his boots one night in some inn in the Abergavenny; and
(he) was called the best dancer in that town; and, to tell the truth, was
called I (I was called) the best harper in the same town."

toky, kordom maia ow fedadare borrey boshymanero unray ow *same* ow gav.' 'Oh dear! Uncle John, please to speak a little plain. I can't understand all you said to me; it's a little too old for me.' When all at onest a gentleman comes to the harper, and asks him in Welsh to play a Welsh air called *Morfa Rhyddlan;* and the harper speaks Welsh to him. When one of the brothers says, ' *Maw didakai*,[1] he is *kerring*[2] himself like a *gougho*[3] now.' Now drink, my Uncle John ; we must be going, we have a long way to go, and the *chaves*[4] are by themselves. Good-night."

" There, Silvanus, what do you say to that? You wouldn't find many farmers who could so well describe a meeting with a friend at market."

" No, bor; I daresay not. But I didn't much like that part about the English Gipsies making as how they don't know nothing. And I'm sure some of the words were not good English Romanes at all. Why, a *boshoméngri* isn't a harp, it's a fiddle ; and if you want to say 'drunk,' you'd say ' They got *mótto*,' not *maatí.* That's like old Damhras's talk. You may depend upon it, they wasn't no real English Romané at all, but just some dealers."

" I don't think that; but of course John Roberts

---

[1] Nay, look here ! [2] Making. [3] Gentile. [4] Children. Here, as elsewhere, I have retained the exact spelling of the Romani words in the original MS., merely altering the punctuation slightly, and italicising the English words (*very, but*, &c.) that occur in the middle of a Romani sentence, and *vice versâ.*

holds that Welsh Romanes is deeper than the English, and there he is right enough, though there may not be all the difference that this makes out. But tell me honestly, was that bit in the middle too old for you or not ? "

" Oh, dear no ! I could understand it fast enough ; all of it leastwise that was written right."

" You are like Sylvester. I read it to him once, and he got very wild over it. All that he could understand, he said was right ; and all that he could not understand, he said was wrong. That is always the way, I find. The truth is, that Wester knows words that old John Roberts does not, and John Roberts knows words, and ways of placing words, that Wester has never heard. Yet to take their opinions of one another, one might fancy they were a couple of know-nothings, though—saving yourself, of course, Silvanus—they are the deepest Gipsies I have ever met."

" Is that Westaarus Boswell you'll be meaning ? Pyramus met him at Rhyl a fortnight gone, but I have not set eyes on him for donkey's ears [*i.e.* long years]. He's got a fine silver medal presented him, so Pyramus was saying, for larning gentlemen to speak the Róm'nimus ; *I'd* larn 'em anything."

" Even so, Silvanus ; and those two gentlemen, Dr Bath Smart and Mr Crofton, of Manchester, have written a book on *The Dialect of the English Gipsies,* which tells all that is to be told about the old-fashioned Roman tongue. Don't get blaspheming,

for blasphemy will do no good ; and, after all, there
were books written years ago, by Mr Borrow and
others, from which any. one could pick up all he
wanted, better in some ways than from Wester's
book. Very few but real scholars will ever dive into
that. It is too deep, and Virginia Water is more to
the taste of ordinary pleasure-seekers than Thirlmere
or Bala Lake. Joking apart though, I was as eager
as you once to lock the stable door, till I found, on
looking, that the steed was stolen. Sometimes, however, the thieves have got hold of some very curious
animals. What does *júvas* mean, Silvanus?"

"Why, 'varmint,' to be sure; *Scotch Greys*, the
highfliers calls 'em."

"Exactly; but many of the books on Romanes
make out that *júvas* means 'women,'[1] and that a

---

[1] The real Romani word for "woman" is *júvel*, pl. *júvia*. Substitute *pulex* for *puella* in a Latin poem, and some conception may be
formed of the curious effect of this confusion of two nearly homo-
phonous words. The following spurious or mistranslated Romani words
and phrases occur in the vocabularies of JACOB BRYANT (1784):—
Bauro beval acochenos, "a storm" (=*baúro bával*, i.e. "great wind," *a
catching us:* Pott connects *acochenos* with χολή); *adra pani paddee*,
"drowned" (lit. "in water they fell"); *borwardo*, "giant" (=*baúro
várdo*, "great cart"—the giant's caravan, probably); *covascorook*,
"laurel" (=*kóva si o ruk*, "this is a tree"); *Jasia vallacai*, "to command" (=*jas* or *vel akaí*, "go *or* come here," *cf.* Luke vii. 8); *plas-
tomingree*, "couch" (for "coach"); *porcherie*, "brass" (=*posh-hóri*,
"a halfpenny, or copper"); *redan*, "yellow" (=Engl. *red 'un*, "red
one"); and *sauvee*, "an eagle" (=*soov*, "a needle"). Of D. COPSEY
(1818):—*bildrrah*, "kettle" (=Engl. *biler*, "boiler"), and *kannélla*,
"bad food" (lit. "it stinks"). Of COL. HARRIOT (1830):—*achi-
paleste*, "bless" (=*atch apré léste*, "rest on him"); *chariklo*, "cage"
(for "bird"); *dein avai lova*, "charity" (=lit. "giving away money");

'young man' should be called a *júvalo mush*" (i.e.
homo pediculosus). "What would the boys say if
any one were to address them so?"

"They wouldn't say nought, they'd do; something
like I did at Llanigan onest. You see, bor, I was
fiddling at the public there, and some of the Lees
knowed I was going to play, went to Mr Bruntlow,
and tried to get the place. He wouldn't let them
have it, no fears of that; so what does these pretty
Júvalo Guné do but stop all night just out of aggrawa-
tion. Next morning I come down into the kitchen,
and Abel Lee begun upon me there. What does I do?
I offed with my shirt, right in the middle of the
kitchen, 'fore all the people. '*Kek ne júvalo shom mi
kúkero*,' says I, in górgiones, 'and I'll fight the lot on

Efage, "Irish Gipsy" (? Engl. *effigy*, i.e. scarecrow, tatterdemalion);
preopodus, "second story of a house "(=*pré o boŏrdas*, "up the stairs");
and *vail goro*, "fair in hue" (=*valgóro*, "fair, or market). Of S.
ROBERTS (1836) :—*chīvya*, "tongs" (for "tongues"); *delman*, "ask"
(=*del man*, "give me"); and *Sellitaree*, "take out" (=*Lel* it *avrí*,
"take *it* out," cf. his *Biggerit* "carry,"=*Rigger* it, "carry *it*;"
chinglet, "tear,"=*chinger* it, "tear *it*," &c., and the *kéravit*, "to do,"
dickavit, "to see," &c., of Mr Leland). Of Dr B. SMART (1863) :—
sorto-poov, "garden" (=sort o' *poov*, "sort of field;" omitted in 2d
ed.). Of MR BORROW (1874) :—*yarb-tan*, "garden" (=herb-*tan*,
"herb place"). Of MR LELAND (1873-79) :—*kris*, "mustard" (? Engl.
cress, cf.) "mustard and *creess*"); *gógemars*, "swampy places" (? Engl.
quagmires); and *pukkus-asa*, "monkey" (Engl. *pug*, disguised by two
common Romani suffixes, -*us* and -*asár*). These mistakes, which could
at least be quintupled, are due in some cases to mutual misunderstanding, in others to Gipsies' disinclination to "larn górgios anything."
To the latter class belong *boro fule*, "a steeple," and the statement
(found in Hoyland, Copsey, Hone, Crabb, &c.) that *Corrie* is a
common Gipsy name.

SYLVESTER BOSWELL

you for half-a-crown.' A great big portly man that
Abel is, but he was downright cowed; and, bless us!
how the people burst out laughing."

The point of which story, if point indeed it has,
is that a feud exists between the Lees and Lovells,
and that *Júvalo Guné* is a nickname of the former,
whose utterance by Silvanus was tantamount to challenge with unblunted lance. Its moral is, accost no
Gipsy lad as *júvalo mush*, least of all if he chance to
bear the name of Lee. But Silvanus had not done
with Wester yet.

"*Dádia!*" he presently broke out; "I can't get
over that old air-beater going and larning them two
gentlemen."

"Now, don't go calling Wester names, for he is a
fine old fellow, whom I hold in singular esteem.
How should I not so hold 'the most populated man
in Portingal, Lancashire, Timbuctoo'—how runs the
testimonial? I have a copy of the original, written
clear and big in Dr Bath Smart's own hand. Listen
to this, Silvanus, and own your master :—

"This is to certisfy that Sylvester Boswell, a well-known
and popalated Gipsy, now living in the parish of Seacombe,
Codling Gap, one of the best characters that ever was known
in the name of a Gipsy, which he is true bred and born,
and is a man which is most trustworthiest with any amount
of property in his care, also possessed of learning according
to what he has been taught, also knowing a little of *every*
profession in life according to honest industry, also thinks a
great deal of his time to come with care and not as people
thinks that Gipsies are or has been spoken of on their dis-

honesty, for I will assure any gentleman or any lady he is most worthy to be placed in any situation—respectable—according to his abilities in life.

"Although now sleeping under a tent that is called a Gipsy tent, but much to his profit as it is so—on the accont of health, sweetness of the air, and for enjoying the pleasure of Nature's life—this is to inform any of the Gentry in this country or any other that he is the most particularest man now on record of his fraternity or any other in the profession he is now placed in, and the more punctualer man in gentlemanhood cannot be found in the world, for he is able to converse in common learning with any Counsel, lawyer, or magistrate, or to give answers with good understandings in any Court of Justice in England, and now a free man (and has been all his life), free from all cares or fears of law that may come against him, and still an honest and industrious man and *well known to all nations* as a first-class well-known Gentleman Gipsy, and is now in Co. with some of the highest respectable gentlemen and ladies for his *grand* and good gentlemanlike conduct.

"Also his name is in force in popular printing, all parts abroad, France, Spain, Portingale, Asia, Africa and America, East and West Indies, Germany, Turkey also, and all other nations too tedious to mention, and is now at Seacombe in the county of Cheshire, which is much credit to the whole of the county to say that they are possessed of a man in their parish as they are now possessed of. The heads of the parish of Seacombe can boast of having in their sight at any hour and of seeing one that is a most noted character *to all the world*, with purity, and only a common so-called (by low-classed people) Gipsy man, and also now wears a most beautiful medal for his great knowledge in grammaring one of the ancientest langeges on record, one that has been lost for numbers of years. No other man found in no nation by proof of learned men can be found for his great knowledge of understanding and grammaring of the original Gipsy true langege.

"Composed by Sylvester Boswell, and taken down by Bath C. Smart, September 1875."[1]

"There, what say you to that? You haven't, by the way, got such a thing as a cough-lozenge about you?"

"Ah-h-h! and did this Dr What-d'ye-call-'um make all that 'stificate for Wester?"

"Yes; that is to say, he wrote it out, Sylvester telling him what he was to write. A very excellent way, for home-made testimonials should be as good as home-baked bread. None but ourselves can know how good we are; and even the heads of the parish of Seacombe may not, for all their gazing, have discovered all their prophet's worth. But Wester has besides a whole packet of testimonials from clergymen, lawyers, doctors, ay, and shopkeepers, whose shops he has taken charge of."

"I'd charge 'em. But that's the way. A man'll never hurt as long as he can praise himself a bit, or find anyone fool enough to do it for him. Why didn't you never write my testimonial?"

"Meaning me for a fool. Thanks for the compliment."

---

[1] Surely Sir Arthur Helps beheld, in mind's eye prophetic, this composition, when in *Realmah* he defined the "weighty sentence":— "Powerful in its substantives, choice and discreet in its adjectives, nicely correct in its verbs; not a word that could be added, nor one which the most fastidious could venture to suppress; in order lucid, in sequence logical, in method perspicuous, and yet with a pleasant and inviting intricacy which disappears as you advance."

"I never said nothing of the kind; and don't you go thinking thoughts, like Fox's pig."

"And what thought Fox's pig?"

"Why, thought they were heating the water to brew, and all the while it was to scald him in. No; but what I was going to tell you, when you come in with your 'meanings' and your 'compliments,' there aren't many Gipsy men like me, let 'em be who they will (I don't care nothing for their silver medals), but not more decenter or civil-spoken. It's not your falderals, but manners'll win the day; and I'll say that, bor, I'm fittin' to go before the world. *I* never had much dealings with magistrates and lawyers, for them is gentry as I couldn't tolerate; and the only trouble ever I was into, come all along of a dear little pinch of salt. It was at Farrington, close by Northleach, and me and Pyramus was going down the road (Pyramus warn't nothing but a novice— a perfect novice), and a butcher asked us if we'd have some lettuces. I said, 'No thank ye, sir;' but Pyramus was coming behind, and he'd take one, Cobham-like.[1] He axed the fine butcher for a pinch of salt first; and his wife came out, said she hadn't ne'er a bit in the house. Then he went to the other little cottage and axed for a pinch, and he stood at the door, and the pretty constable came out with a great knobbed stick and handcuffs; and Pyramus

---

[1] "Cobham" (or "Cob'em," perhaps) is the greedy dog of Romani nursery lore, who "gobbles his food without waiting to chew it."

runned back where I was standing up the road. And I asked the fine górgio where he was going in a hurry, and he said, 'Darn his young hide, I'll tell him where's *he*'s going;' and he made to put the handcuffs on to Pyramus. I pushed him off, and axed him what he meaned. Then he heft up the stick to hit me on the head, and he was going at Pyramus again. I told him, 'Get away,' and he said he wouldn't. Long and by last I hit him "—

"And gave him a fine black eye, cut his face, I think," said Christopher. "And the butcher was watching all the while." The boys had just got back from Pen-y-bonh; and Christopher, Dimiti, and Mantis, with half-a-dozen more of lads and girls, were squatting cross-legged in a ring about us. Christopher knew this oft-told episode in his father's boyhood, better perhaps than did his father's father; but Silvanus took no notice of his prompting.

"Long and by last I hit him, and he tumbled in a fit—it was a fit—trembling all of a dither. There he laid till I and the boy got a long way up the road; then he comed running after us again. Then he was going to hit Pyramus again with the great knobbed stick, and I told him to get away, else I'd give him a wusser one than what he did. And he said, he would take him. Then I hit him again, knocked him down. Then he got up, and went straight off into the fine Northleach; and the warrant was brought to the tents; near a week after it was when we got it. I went across in the boat, me and Pyramus did, tried to give him the slip, but he was in Northleach before us. Then I meet the fine hangman, and the fine hangman said to me, 'You've been pretty near killing that fellow.' Sly old monkey that Tompkins was; Lord! they all of them are. He said, 'You've gived him a fine pair of black eyes;' and I said, 'If I'd knowed as much as I know now, I'd have gived him ten times worse.' And, days after, I was going round by the 'Bull's Head' fiddlin', and we went through the fine Northleach; and as we was coming back, two pretty hangmen come and meet us, wanted to put the handcuffs on me. I told 'em neither them nor no one else should put 'em on, and they was going to lay hold of me. I said, 'Stand backwards, else I'll knock you over.' They never put 'em on, and I walked with them so right up the street. Well, then the fine hangmen said, 'Now you must have 'em on just before we gets there;' and I said, 'If I had a mind, neither you nor no one else could put them on me.' They put them on; and then when they took me in, I began fall kicking the door. The other fine head superintendent come to me (blue-face that was, for all the world like one of these blue monkeys!), and told me if I didn't stop it, he'd put me in the cell. Lord! how they can use poor dear people when they've got 'em in there! I waited till he went away, and told 'em to send me up some water. One of the pretty children brought me some; then I beginned fall kicking the door again. Then I told them to loose me out of that. No, he said, he wouldn't; he said he'd loose me out next morning. There I was all night, kicking the door, kicked all the nose of my good boots out. They keeped me there till twelve o'clock next morning, and then I had to pay five pounds."

Silvanus faltered, thoughts too deep for words arresting further progress; and Mantis, seeing his chance, took up the running instantly.

"Ay, bor, and *my* daddy was fined onest by Albrighton, only for stopping in the road. He was just going to shave himself, and my mammy had been making cakes to the fire, and there was two hedgehogs roasting, and a lot of potatoes baking in the ashes; when on turning round, my daddy saw the fine policeman coming. Pretty hangman said, 'Good morning, Lovell.' 'Good morning,' said my daddy, with the razor in his hand. 'You've got to go along with me,' he said. 'All right,' my daddy answered, 'we'll go anywheres you has a mind to,' thinking he was only joking. And then he pulled out the handcuffs, and put them on my daddy's hands, and took him off. About five miles it was he took him, to Shifnal, to have him tried, only for stopping in the road. And the magistrate there wouldn't say nothing against him; so then he took him to another magistrate's, where my mammy used to call; and after a deal of trouble my daddy got off with paying three half-crowns. And the pretty hangman was afeared to walk along the road with my daddy afterwards; he wouldn't go with him. And whiles they were away, Dimiti pulled the tent down, and took the two biggest tent-rods, and made himself ploughing up and down the road with them. And he drank a great big canful of milk, and ate up all the cakes. That was his day's work, when my daddy was took ; never paid the slightest notice. And that was the first and last time as ever that pretty hangman had anything to say to we. My daddy sold him a pair of breeches after that, and thrashed his brother."

"There! and I met him onest, and shouted 'Object!'" said Dimiti, jealous for his filial piety ; "and wasn't I troubled all that blessed day, pulling the tent down, minding you young children, and keeping an eye upon the animals ?   But the nicest policeman as ever I knowed, refa, was him as married Mrs Elliot's Susan. They were both quite young, and she always used to go with him every night upon his rounds, said she never liked to trust him by himself. And when they'd come by our tents, they'd stand and talk for ever so long ; and very often she'd come in and sit down, and he'd stand outside talking. He didn't bide there long ; górgios said he was too good for a policeman. He never took up nobody, and the pretty fine magistrates didn't like it."

"Wanting in zeal he doubtless seemed to them ; but what, Silvanus, really is the law about Gipsies stopping by the side of roads? In some few parts of England one sees every stretch of turf blackened with tent-places, in others Romané must hire fields, at least if they can't get them for the asking."

"The law? why that you mustn't make up your place within fifteen feet of the crown of the highway; but mostwise it goes by squire's or parson's liking, whether they're partial to our kind of people. Some places you are free to stop, and welcome; and some you durstn't stop at for the life of you, no, not if you was to make right off the road, a hundred yards and more. I never stops much in roads myself, fear of the horses and neddies getting pounded; nor it isn't often I pays for a field, 'cause all the highest gentry knows me where I travel. Now Pyramus was paying ten shillings a week, where he was staying up by London last December; and Plato was in a field by Brummagem, oh! two years gone, with some of the Hernes and Bucklands, and the lot of them were paying thirty shillings. Lord bless us all, how times is altered! If you'd told my grandfather, old Henry Lovell, of paying for a bit of ground to stop, he'd have thought the world was coming to an end."

"I daresay. But here, in Wales, at least, I suppose you never have much trouble?"

"No, not for the stopping; but it's a terrible bad part for straw; leastwise when none of the boys' girls aren't with us, to talk to the Crockans in their country gibberish. I mind, at Caen Office, when we were coming up, I went to a little bit of a farmhouse. There was the farmer, just like a common Gloucester ploughman; and, when I axed him for a truss of straw, he made as he didn't understand my meanings. 'Straw,' I bawls at him, 'straw, man,' and picked up a little wisp of it in one hand, and shows him a shilling in the other, and then he understood it fast enough. Oh! very uncultivated folks is hereabouts; but still it's nice."

"Nice! ay, and something more. For here, as Wester has it, you enjoy the pleasures of Nature, and yet are free from the annoys of inns. Often I have fancied how pleasant it would be to exchange my dingy chambers for a tent at the foot of Snowdon or Helvellyn, provided always 'it rained not hard and small.' And then I have turned to John Roberts' masterpiece, his picture of the days when he was young. By the bye, I must read you that, Silvanus, and you shall give me your opinion of it. You won't mind?"

"Dear heart, no! It does one good to hear a clever man. Head-piece is everything the whole world over. Now don't make no noise, children, but sit ye still, for the gentleman's going to read something will make you open your eyes."

And I read what has always seemed to me a perfect Romani idyll :—

"THE WHOLE FAMILY CAMPING OUT WITH HORSES, DONKEYS, AND DOGS.

"*On the first wakening in the morning.*

"*Mother (speaking to my Father in the tent).*—'Now, man, wake dem boys up, to go and gether some sticks to light de fire, and to see where dem hosses and donkeys are. I think I heared some men coming up de road, and driving de things out of de field. Now, boy, go and get some water to put in de kettle for breakfast.'

"*The Boy.*—'*I dawda!* I must go and do every bit o' thing. Why don't you send dat gal to do something? Her does nothing at all, only sitting down all de blessed time.'

"*Mother.*—'I am going to send her to de farmhouse for milk, Dog's Face,' when a brand of fire is flung after him, and he (the boy) falls over a big piece of wood, and hurts his knee. The girl goes for the milk, and she has a river to go through, when presently a bull is heard roaring.

"*Mother.*—'Dere now, boy, go and meet your sister. Dere's de bull a roaring after her. She will fall down in a faint in de middle ob de ribber.'

"*Boy.*—'How can I go to her, when I've hurt my leg, and am quite lame?'

"*The Old Woman.*—'Go, man; go, man, and see how dat poor gal is a coming. Dey do say dat dat is a very bad bull after women.'

"Strange men brings the horses and donkeys up to the tents, and begins to scold very much. The little girl comes with the milk, and begins to scold her brother for not going to meet her, when they both have a scuffle over the fire, and very near knocks the tea-kettle down, when the boy hops away upon one leg, and hops upon one of the dog's paws unseen, and the dog run away barking, and runs himself near

one of the donkeys, and the donkey gives him a kick
until he is whining in the hedge.

"*The Old Woman.*—'Dere now, dere now! here's
my poor dog killed.'

"Breakfast is over, with a deal of bother and a little
laughing and cursing and swearing. They strike the
tents.

"*The Old Woman.*—'Now, comrades, I'm off. I'm
a going another road to-day, and you will meet me
near de town. Be sure and leave a *pátrin* by de side
·ob de cross-road, if you should be dere before me.'

   .   .   .   .   .   .

"The old man and the boys pitches the tents, and
gets himself ready to go to the town. The old woman
comes up, and one of the girls with her, both very
tired, and heavy loaded with victuals behind her back,
enough to frighten waggons and carts off the road
with her humpy back. They intend to stay in this
delightful camping-place for a good many days.

   .   .   .   .   .   .

"To-day is supposed to be a very hot day, and a
fair-day in a town about three miles and a half from
there. The old woman and one of the daughters goes
out as usual. The old man takes a couple of horses
to the fair to try and sell. The boys go a fishing.
The day is very bright and hot. The old man soon
comes home.

"One of the prettiest girls takes a stroll by herself
down to a beautiful stream of water, to have herself
a wash, and she begins singing to the sound of a

waterfall close by her. When all of a sudden a very nice-looking young gentleman, who got tired fishing in the morning, and, the day being very hot, took a bit of a loll on his face, his basket on his back, and fishing-rod by his side,—the girl did not see him, nor him her, until he was attracted by some strange sound. When all of an instant he sprang upon his heels, and to his surprise seen a most beautiful creature, with her bare bosom, and her long black hair, and beautiful black eyes, white teeth, and a beautiful figure. He stared with all the eyes he had, and made an advance towards her; and when she seen him, she stared also at him. And approaching slowly towards her, and saying, 'From whence comest thou here, my beautiful maid?' and staring at her beautiful figure, thinking that she was some angel as dropped down; when she with a pleasant smile, by showing her ivory teeth and her sparkling eyes: 'Oh! my father's tents are not very far off; and seeing the day very warm, I thought to have a little wash.'

"*Gentleman.*—'Well, indeed! I have been fishing to-day, and caught a few this morning; but the day turned out so excessively hot, I was obliged to go into a shade and have a sleep, but was alarmed at your sweet voice mingling with the murmuring waters.'

"They both steer up to the camp, when now and then as he is speaking to her on the road going up, a loud and shrill laugh is heard many times. The

same time he does not show the least sign of
vulgarity, by taking any sort of liberty with her
whatever. They arrive at the tents, when one of
the little boys says to his daddy, 'Daddy, daddy,
there is a gentleman a coming up.'

"The gentleman sets himself down, and pulls out
a big flask very nigh full of brandy, and tobacco,
and offers to the old man. By this time that young
girl goes in her tent and pulls down the front, and
presently out she comes beautifully dressed, which
bewitched the young gentleman; and he said that
they were welcome to come there to stop as long
as they had a mind, so as they would not tear the
hedges. He goes and leaves them highly delighted
towards home, and he should pay them another
visit.

"The camping-ground belonged to the young gentleman's father, and is situated in a beautiful part of
Denbighshire.

"One of the little girls sees two young ladies
coming a little sideways across the common from
a gentleman's house which is very near, which turns
out to be the gentleman's two sisters.

"*The Little Girl.*—'Mammy, mammy, dere is two
ladies a coming here. Get up.'

"The young ladies comes to the tents and smiles;
when the old woman says to one of them, 'Good
day, me-am [ma'am]; it's a very fine day, me-am;
shall I tell you a few words, me-am?' The old
woman takes them on one side, and tells them

something just to please them, now and then a word of truth, the rest a good lot of lies.

"The old man goes off for a stroll with a couple of dogs. One of the young boys asks his mother for some money, and she refuses him, as says she has got none. The boy says, 'Where is the money you got from those two ladies?' '*Maw didacai!* I got none from them. They said they'd come again.'

"One of the other brothers says to him, 'Here, Abraham, I'll lend you five shillings.' 'Will you, my blessed brother?' 'Yes, I will; here it is. Now we will both of us go to the town together.' One gets his fiddle ready, and the other his tambourine; the harp is too heavy to carry. They got to call at the post-office for a letter. They both come home rather merry.

"The next day the boys go a fishing again, and bring home a good lot, as the day was not near so hot as the day before; and comes home in good time to play the harp and violin, and sometimes the tambourine, for the country górgios, as a good many comes to have a dance on the green. The collection would be the boys' pocket-money."

"There, Silvanus, is not that a pretty picture?"

"By Job, it's proper; better nor that other bit you read about the fair, for I didn't much care to hear the English Romané run down. But that's what I call something like; you can fancy you see 'em all a getting up in the morning, and the animals had

been over in the górgio's field ; and then the old
woman with her *de's* and *dere's*.[1] It took me back,
bor, to my young days, 'xactly how I remember our
old people. They'd sit, the old man and woman,
one each side the fire, and each of 'em would have
a poking-stick, and they'd be poke poking the whole
day long. And then some gentleman would come
riding by a horseback, and my granny would say to
one of us young children, 'Ask de gentleman what
time it is, my blessed child.' And then it would
be, 'What time did he say, sonny?' and we'd always
answer, 'Thirteen o'clock, granny.' 'Thirteen o'clock!
dear, dear, how de time do fly!' Ay, ay, there was
some rale old 'riginals sure-ly, and merry times them
was."

"Better than now, eh?"

"Better! ay, sure enough. You might go where
you liked, and stop where you liked: none of these
blue-coat gentlemen about. First time, I mind, as
ever we seen a policeman, was at Brompton Bryan
June fair. There was a lot of us going, twenty
belike or more, my grandfather and all the rest on
'em. And that was a curious thing, too, his own sons
would never call him 'daddy,' but always nothing but
plain 'Henry.' Forty pounds he'd brought with him
to spend on horses, and we had come up all the way
from Limer's Lane; but soon as ever he sees this

---

[1] Silvanus and his family, I may here observe, have hardly a *th*
among them. Throughout I have supplied their deficiency, of which
they are themselves unconscious.

mounted policeman (they all were mounted at first
starting), he turned back, wouldn't go anighst the
fair. We'd heard some talk of 'em before, but never
put much hearkenings in it. Why, you'd see the lanes
then crowded with Romané—Lovells and Boswells
and Stanleys and Hernes and Chilcotts. Something
like Gipsies they were, with their riding horses, real
hunters, to ride to the fairs and wakes on ; and the
women with their red cloaks and high old-fashioned
beaver hats; and the men in beautiful silk velvet
coats and white and yellow satin waistcoats, and all
on 'em booted and spurred. Why, I mind hearing tell
of my grandfather's oldest sister, Aunt Marbelenni,
and that must have been a hundred years and more.
She was married to a very rich farmer in Gloucestershire, so she was very well off; and one day some
of her brothers, Henry including, went to call on her,
and when. she seen 'em, she wouldn't allow them into
her house, for she said, ' Now that I am married,
I shall expect you all to come booted and silver-
spurred.' Gipsies ! there aren't no Gipsies now."

"What do you call yourself, then ?"

"What do I call myself? why a crab in a coal pit.
But what I mean, it's different from how it used to be.
All the old families are broken up, over in 'Mericay, or
gone in houses, or stopping round the nasty poverty
towns. My father wouldn't ha' stopped by Wolverhampton, not if you'd gone on your bended knees to
him, and offered him a pound a day to do it. He'd
have runned miles if you'd just shown him the places

where some of these new-fashioned travellers has
their tents."

"Yes, I have often thought what a poor exchange
brickyard or building-plot must be for lane or common.
I remember one patch of ground near the Addison
Road Station, close to London, that only five years
back was covered with tents and waggons, but now is
all built over. There were some of the Norths stayed
there; and one of them, a very old old woman, told
me a story about those Boswells you were speaking
of. How, when she was a little child, she fell over a
stile in Wales one day, and made her nose bleed;
and how two beautiful ladies, dressed all in silks and
satins, picked her up. Their grandeur awed her,
though they spoke to her in Romanes, for these were
two of the great Boswell tribe; and still she spoke of
them with deep respect, as I might speak of some
high-born stately countess. Yet górgios fancy all
Gipsies are the same—Lovells and Taylors, Stanleys
and Turners, Boswells and Norths. Nay, worse than
that, they take for Gipsies the Nailers, Potters, Besom-
makers, all the tag, rag, and bobtail travelling on the
roads. How do they make that out?"

"Easy enough, for what should low-bred people
know but lowness? Show a mongrel a mongrel, and
he's bound to call it a greyhound. I'll say and stick
to it, there's nothing worse than mumply górgios."

"What, nothing worse than all who have not had
the privilege of Gipsy birth? But, Silvanus, less than
one hundred years ago, in those good old times that

you just now were praising, you and the boys might have been hanged by górgio law, solely because of your Egyptian birth. And I myself might have been hanged for keeping fellowship with you."

"Now, don't that show the wicked górgios' badness. You mark my words, the breed of 'em is bad."

"And górgios said the breed of you was bad. It was something like the cruel old Norfolk gardener. He was hoeing one day, and a frog hopped out before him. 'I'll larn you to be a frog,' said crabbed Roger; and hoed it forthwith in pieces. So 'I'll larn you to be Gipsies,' said English lawgivers; and the gallows were their means of education."

Chapter Fifth.

AND I told Silvanus, to the best of my recollection, how at Aylesbury in 1577, Rowland Gabriel and Katherine Deago were, with six others, hanged " for feloniously keeping company with other vagabonds, vulgarly called and calling themselves Egyptians, and counterfeiting, transforming, and altering themselves in dress, language, and behaviour." How at Durham, in 1592, five more were hanged " for being Egyptians." How " it has been delivered down to us that in some distant time a gang of Gipsies used to haunt a dingle at Whiteford, Flintshire, and that eighteen of them were executed, after which the Gipsy race never more frequented that neighbourhood. I cannot learn their crime," adds Pennant ; " possibly there was none, for they might have been legally murdered by the cruel statute of the 1st and 2d of Philip and Mary." How, at Bury-St-Edmunds, thirteen Gipsies were executed shortly before the Restoration, and others at Stafford shortly after it. So late even as 1819, it was carried unanimously at the Norfolk Quarter Sessions, " that all persons wandering in the habit or form of

Egyptians are punishable by imprisonment and whip-
ping ;" and in 1827, a judge at Winchester announced
the determination of himself and his brother-judges
" to execute horse-stealers, *especially Gipsies.*" Yet a
pardon was granted in 1591 to Robert Hilton, and in
1594 to William Stanley, Francis Brewerton, and
John Weekes, for the felony of calling themselves
Egyptians ; and England throughout was almost
merciful compared with Scotland. Witness the following jottings from Scotch records. Four Faas were
hanged in 1611, two Faas and a Baillie in 1616, six
Faas and two others in 1624. In 1636 the sheriff of
Haddington passed doom on an entire company—"the
men to be hangit and the weomen to be drowned ;
and suche of the weomen as hes children to be scourgit
throw the burgh of Hadinton, and brunt in the
cheeke." Then in 1698 seven Baillies were executed,
as were two more in 1714; and in 1700-1 James
M'Pherson, James Gordon, and Peter and Donald
Brown, were hanged at Banff, the sheriff of Murray
further ordaining " that the three young rogues now
in prison this day have their ears cropt, be publictlie
scourged through the toune of Banff, be burnt upon
the cheek by the executioner, and be banished the
shyre for ever under paine of death." In all which
cases the crime was not murder or pillage, but the
being " callit, knawin, repute, and holdin Egiptians ; "[1]

---

[1] Even in 1770 these words formed *part* of the indictment brought
against Jamieson and M'Donald, whose execution on Linlithgow
bridge Simson describes in chap. iv. of his *History of the Gipsies*
(London, 1865).

and proofs in the last-named trial were, that the
panels spoke a language which the witnesses understood not, but which was not the Irish tongue,
and that they were suspected of inability to "re-
hearse the Lord's Prayer, the Belieff, and the Ten
Commands."

From sorry discourse like this, whereat the boys
twitched nervous ears, I passed to merrier themes—
to the entertainment that Thomas Earl of Surrey
gave to "Gypsions" at Tendring Hall, in Stoke-by-
Nayland, Suffolk, some time between 1513 and 1524;
to the dance of "Egyptianis" at Holyrood House
before King James the Fifth in 1530; and to the
Romani city of refuge, Roslin Castle. A pleasant
story that of Father Hay's, how about 1623 Sir
William Sinclair "delivered ane Egyptian from the
gibbet in the Burrow Moore, ready to be strangled,
returning from Edinburgh to Roslin, upon which
accoumpt the whole body of gypsies were, of old,
accustomed to gather in the stanks of Roslin every
year, where they acted severall plays, dureing the
moneths of May and June. There are two towers
which were allowed them for their residence, the one
called Robin Hood, the other Little John" (p. 136
of Father Richard Augustine Hay's *Genealogie of the
Sainteclaires of Rosslyn*, edited by J. Maidment,
Edinb. 1835). Drummond of Hawthornden may
well have beheld those plays; but Royal Ben, his
guest, came some five years too soon.

In the very trials there is much that is comforting

to Gipsy pride. After the bloody fray of Romanno[1] in Peeblesshire (1677), did not the Edinburgh Council claim for itself "the money, gold, gold rings, and other things which were upon the persons of the Faas and Shaws, likewise the weapons with which they fought?" and had not M'Pherson, who suffered at Banff, been leader of twenty-seven men in arms, with a piper playing at their head, as befitted the son of a Highland gentleman by a beautiful Gipsy mother? His great two-handed sword (the relic of an earlier day) is shown at Duff House, the residence of the Earls of Fife ; his fiddle-neck is an heirloom in the family of Cluny, chieftain of the M'Pherson clan. Burns tells us how—

> "Sae rantin'ly, sae wantonly,
>   Sae dauntin'ly gaed he :
> He play'd a spring and danced it round
>   Below the gallows tree ; "

and relics more precious than either sword or fiddle are his rude reckless *Rant*, and the beautiful air to which he set the same. He played it as he walked to execution, and at the foot of the gallows proffered his instrument to who would take it, but no man venturing, snapt it across his knee. Strange tales, indeed ; but could Silvanus tell me who one Stanley was,

---

[1] It has been thought that Romanno, or Romano (both forms are used), was called so from this famous Rómano battle ; but the name is as old at least as 1591. The spot had probably become a favourite camping-ground with Romané, from the chance likeness of its name to theirs ; much as, if a suggestion on p. 25 be true, the κίγκλος, or water-wagtail, became *the* bird of Cingari or Gipsies.

executed at Ilchester, for crime unknown to me, in
1794? He might have been Lementina's grandfather;
but I only knew "that about three years before he
had been elected King of the Gipsies,[1] and that his
wife and daughter, who attended at the place of
execution, were not more remarkable for the beauty
of their persons than for the very costly appearance
of their dress."

No; Silvanus knew nothing of this Gipsy king,
who led us to speak of Gipsy potentates generally, a
dynasty dimmer than that of Pharaohs or Ptolemies.
And first of one, concerning whom the Malmesbury
Abbey register contains this curious memorandum :—
"John Buclle, reputed to be a gypsie, deceased
September 21, 1657, at John Peryn's house upon
the Ffosse, in Shipton parish, in Glocestershire; and
was buried in King Athelstone's chapell by King

---

[1] "Elected King of the Gipsies."—The words agree with John
Lee's statement made to Lieut. Irvine, aboard the *Preston* East India-
man in 1805, that "the Gipsies' king is, strictly speaking, elective,
though usually chosen out of one opulent family. He receives presents
at stated times from his subjects, and has been known to impose and
exact a tax upon watches. His royal style is, the *Ry, Bara Ry,* or *Ry
of the Roomdichil.*" So, too, the *Adventures of Bamfylde-Moore Carew :*
"Their king is elective by the whole people, but none but such who
have been long in their society, and perfectly studied the nature and
institution of it; they must likewise have given repeated proofs of their
personal wisdom, courage, and capacity : this is the better known, as
they always keep a public record or register of all remarkable (either
good or bad) actions performed by any of the society; and they can
have no temptation to make choice of any but the most worthy, as their
king has no titles or lucrative employments to bestow, which might
influence or corrupt their judgment." Observe the mode—by ballot—
of election, set forth in that veracious history.

Athelstone, and the Lady Marshall, within the abbie church, at Malmesbury. This buriall was September 23, 1657. Howbeit, he was taken up again by the meanes of Thomas Ivye, esq. ; who then lived in the abbie, and by the desires and endeavoures of others, out of the said chappell was removed into the church yarde, and there was re-buried neere the east side of the church poorch, October 7, 1657, in the presence of Thomas Ivye, of the abbie, esq.; Pleadwell of Mudgell, esq.; Rich Whitmore, of Slaughter, in the countie of Glocester, and Dr Qui, of Malmesbury, with very many others."—Moffatt's *History of Malmesbury* (Tetbury, 1805), pp. 71–72.

Next on the roll stands " Henry Boswell, a Gipsy king, who died in affluent circumstances, and was buried at Wittering[1] in 1687," early enough *perhaps* for us to recognise his widow in Lyson's extract from the Camberwell register :—" June 2, 1687, Robert Hern and Elizabeth Bozwell, king and queen of the gipsies, married." *Perhaps* this last couple reappears

---

[1] Whittering, near Stamford, is meant more probably than East or West Wittering, Sussex. For, though the registers for 1687 of Whittering and West Wittering are equally defective, the Northamptonshire churchyard is known to contain the graves of three members " of the tribe called Gypsies," viz., Varto Lee, who died in the Lane near to White Water, and was buried 12th Nov. 1804; a Henry Boswell, who died, *æt.* 90, in the Lane near the Barnack Ford, and was buried 8th Oct. 1824; and Traynet Smith, who died, *æt.* 20, in a camp erected on the Old Oundle Road, and was buried 22d Nov. 1851. " There is a very good stone," adds the Rector, " to Varto Lee's grave, which must have been rather an expensive affair, evidently proving that he occupied some conspicuous place amongst the Gipsies."

in two entries in the register of Stanbridge, Bedfordshire, viz., " Mⁿ Hearn a Gypsey Queene was buryed
ye 20th of August 1691 by me Ed. Hargrave *(Vicar
of Leighton-Buzzard)* and no affidavit made ;" and,
on the following page, " A warrant was granted by
Sʳ ffr. Wingate, to distrain on ye king of the Gipsys
but no distress to be found."   What might not a
Serjeant Buzfuz make of these last six words?   But
I pass on to a third *perhaps*, that it may have been
a daughter of Elizabeth, who figures in the register
of St Mary the Great, Cambridge :—" 1720. Edw.
Bosvile, of Yowarave [Youlgreave], Derbyshire, &
Lucy Hern, of Witchford, marᵈ Sept. 23."

Which brings us back to Boswells, or Bosviles
(according to the North Country spelling of their
name), one of whom was buried at Rossington, near
Doncaster, on 30th January 1709. An iron-railed
stone, to the right of the choir door, long marked
his grave ; but the stone was gone when the villagers
told the Reverend Joseph Hunter, Historian of South
Yorkshire (1828), how Charles Bosvile[1] "established a
species of sovereignty among that singular people, the
gypsies, who before the inclosures frequented the moors
round Rossington. His word with them was law, and
his authority so great that he perfectly restrained the

---

[1] E. Miller, in his *Antiquities of Doncaster* (1804) calls him *James*
Bosvill, which reminds me that my friend Sylvester claims Johnson's
biographer as "one of our fraternity;" while the Stanleys, he thinks,
" origined in Lord Derby over there [*there* being Knowsley] about two
hundred years ago."

pilfering propensities for which the tribe is censured,
and gained the entire good will for himself and his
subjects of the farmers and the people around. He
was a gentleman with an estate of about £200 a
year; and his contemporary, Abraham De la Pryme
of Hatfield, describes him as 'a mad spark, mighty
fine and brisk, keeping company with a great many
gentlemen, knights, and esquires, yet running about
the country.'" Thus Hunter; and Miller tells besides,
that "for a number of years it was a custom of gipsies
from the South to visit his tomb annually, and there
perform some of their accustomed rites, one of which
was to pour a flagon of ale upon the grave."

Turn we from ale to prayer. For on the north
side of Little Budworth churchyard, near Delamere
Forest, Cheshire, there is, or was, a large stone on the
ground, bearing inscription : " Here lies in Hopes of a
joyfull Resurrection the Body of Henry Lovett. He
departed this Life the 27 Day of January 1744 aged
85 Years. He died a Protestant." Cole, no great
lover of Protestants, records this epitaph in vol. xxix.
of his MS. collections, now in the British Museum,
and adds two notes. *The first :*—" The Oddity of the
last Line excited my Curiosity to enquire who this
good Protestant might be, who thus professed his
Belief on his Tomb Stone ; and Mr Tonman told
me that he was the King of the Gypsies ; that he died
at a Place called Beggars Bank, in this Neighbourhood, a famous Rendezvous for this Sort of People ;
that his Companions gave him, the Curate, at his

Funeral, one of the most ample offerings he had met
with ; and that they still came to his Grave to pray
once a year: this looks as if the Subjects were
Papists, tho' the King died a Protestant: we want
some of their own Historians to clear up this important Part of their Egiptian History." *The second :—*
" This day I had at my Door, being Blecheley Feast,
Monday, Sept. 15, 1766, a grandson of this Henry
Lovett ; as he called, with a wife and 7 Children, all
as black as Egyptians, but clean-limbed well-made
people, who lived, as they said, at Risborough in
Bucks, and were Fidlers."—(*New Monthly Mag.*,
1819, p. 334 ; *Notes and Queries*, May 29, 1880.)

What, then, would Cole have said to a Gipsy
re-edifier of ruined churches? Yet at West Winch,
Norfolk, is a tomb, once raised, now level with the
sod and broken into three pieces, which the present
Rector has had cemented together, " out of respect
to the memory of a Gipsy king who is said to have
aided in repair of *East* Winch Church." The stone is
inscribed, " Here lieth the Body of Abraham Smith,
who died Feb. the 16. 1748, Aged 60 Years ;" and
the register contains a corresponding entry, " Bury'd
Abraham Smith a Stranger, Feby. ye 20th. Affidt.
made by Elizth. Bailey." Now Baillie is a Scottish
Gipsy name ; and another noteworthy circumstance
about this grave is, that so late as 1841 it was visited
by two fine young Gipsy men, whom the Rector saw
but did not accost, not knowing then the story of
its inmate. Hardly so strange, though ; for less than

twenty years before that date a Smith was living,
who might have often talked with Abraham. This
was the subject of the following epitaph, in Turvey
churchyard, Bedfordshire :—

> "IN MEMORY OF
> JAMES SMITH
> WHO DIED MAY 10TH 1822
> AGED 105 YEARS.
>
> I lived beyond a hundred years,
> A wanderer through this vale of tears :
> The time seemed long, but short 'twill be
> Contrasted with Eternity.
>
> O mortal man, arise, beware,
> Sin spreads around the dangerous snare ;
> Then pray, or perish, seek thy God,
> And trust thine all in Jesus' blood.
>
> WIDOW
> ELIZABETH ROBINSON
> DIED JANUARY 20TH 1825
> AGED 105 YEARS."

Elizabeth was James's mother-in-law, herself a Gipsy,
though Robinson is not a common Gipsy name ;[1]
and the lines upon James were written by Legh

---

[1] It was borne by several of Bunyan's descendants; and those who
hold that Bunyan was a Bedfordshire Gipsy may here, perhaps, find
confirmation of their theory. To me that theory seems neither established nor disproved; but everything connecting Bedford with the
race has certainly a special interest, *e.g.* two entries in the register of
St Paul's Church, Bedford :—"1567 Robartt Ane Egiptic bapt. same
daie" (viz., "Marche xxxth daie"), and "1567 Aprill—John, Ane
Egiptn bapt. xxvith daie." Only three Romani baptisms during the
sixteenth century have heretofore been placed on record—of Joan, at
Lyme Regis, Dorsetshire, 14th February 1558; of William, at Lan-
chester, Durham, 19th February 1564 ; and of Margaret Bannister, at
Loughborough, Leicestershire, 2d April 1581.—(Crofton, *English Gipsies
under the Tudors*, p. 16.)

H

Richmond, rector of Turvey, and author of *Annals
of the Poor*, as also of this vigorous quadrain, well
known to every Turvey villager :—

> " Here lies Jim, the wandering Gipsy,
>   Who was sometimes sober, yet oftener tipsy ;
>   But with the world he seemed to thrive,
>   For he lived to the age of a hundred and five."

" Stuff ! " says some follower of Sir Cornewall
Lewis, "they never would both have reached the same
abnormal age, nor would the son-in-law have been
the older." Perhaps not, perhaps yes ; but Gipsies
are a singularly long-lived race. I know myself two
Gipsy great-great-grandmothers, and have spoken
with Betsy Letherlund, the " Elizabeth, daughter of
Thomas Horam (Heron), Travailer," who was christened at Chinnor, Oxfordshire, 24th April 1763.
Samuel, her eldest son, was fifty-nine when he was
drowned at Hadlow, Kent, 20th October 1853 ; and
Betsy survived him by one-and-twenty years, dying
at Tring towards the close of 1874. Read, O incre-
dulous one, the paper that Sir Duncan Gibb, of the
Westminster Hospital, addressed to *The Lancet*,
January 30, 1875 ; then ponder the case of that
" noted old tinker," Robert Oglebie, who began life
at Ripon, November 16, 1654, to end it at Leeds,
November 15, 1768. Or of Tinkler Billy Marshall,
who was born at Kirkmichael, Ayrshire, in 1672, and
died at Kirkcudbright, 28th November 1792. This
" miracle of longevity," Easton [1] tells us, " retained his

---

[1] In *Human Longevity* (Salisbury, 1799).

senses almost to the last hour of his life, and remembered distinctly to have seen King William's fleet riding at anchor in the Solway Firth, and the transports lying in the harbour. He was present at the siege of Derry, where "—and here I allow a grain of salt—"*having lost his uncle, who commanded a king's frigate,* he returned home, enlisted into the Dutch service, went to Holland, and soon after came back to his native country." Anne Day, who was buried at Arlsey, Bedfordshire, in March 1799, was young comparatively, only 108 years old. " Bent almost double, and nearly blind, she travelled the country on an ass, attended by three females of her fraternity, and was well known in most parts. She had not slept in a bed for seventy years, and for the last forty years had not a tooth in her head, and only a faint sight but by one eye, having lost the other when young. She lost three of her toes but twelve years before by the frost, being obliged to have them amputated, and at the same time lost the use of one of her arms. She died under a hedge near Henlow, and her funeral was attended by a vast concourse of people from the neighbouring villages, but by only two of the people to which she belonged, who called themselves her son and daughter, the former eighty-two, and the latter eighty-five years of age, each having great-grandchildren."

And Gipsy longevity leads back to Gipsy royalty, —to Margaret Finch, queen of the Norwood tribe, who was born at Sutton in 1631, travelled through

England nearly a hundred years, then settled at
Norwood Forest, whither crowds of visitors were
drawn by her great age and skill in palmistry. Long
sitting with chin bowed upon her knees so contracted
her sinews, that, when at last she died, they had to
coffin her in a deep square box. She was buried at
Beckenham, 24th October 1740, her funeral being
attended by two mourning coaches, and a sermon
being preached on the occasion. And Bridget,
Margaret's niece, reigned in her stead, during whose
reign "the Prince and Princess of Wales, with Lady
Torrington in Waiting, Lady Middlesex, Lord
Bathurst, Mr Breton, and I [Mr George Bubb
Doddington], went in private coaches to visit the
Norwood settlement," 28th June 1750. Bridget herself "died in her hut, worth above £1000;" was
buried at Dulwich, 6th August 1768; and was in
turn succeeded by a niece, whose name is lost,—
deservedly, as that of a degenerate house-dweller. As
such, though, she perhaps escaped her subjects' doom,
when in 1797 "about five o'clock in the morning,
twenty police officers came to Norwood in three
hackney-coaches, threw down all the gipsy tents, and
exposed about thirty men, women, and children in the
primitive state of man, whom they carried to prison to
be dealt with according to the Vagrant Act."

Exeunt Norwood Gipsies, naked and chattering
like a flight of daws ; but there were other Gipsies,
dead, or to die, as she thus mentioned in the *Annual
Register* for 1773 :—" The clothes of the late Diana

Boswell, Queen of the Gipsies, value £50, were burnt in the middle of the Mint, Southwark, by her principal courtiers, according to ancient custom ; it being too great an honour for subjects to be clothed in robes of state, and too great a disgrace for her successor to appear in second-hand royalty. Her remains were interred the day before in Newington churchyard, at which ceremony more than two hundred of her loyal subjects were present." Again a Boswell! and at Calne, in Wiltshire, a handsome monument to Inverto Boswell, son of a Gipsy king, bears date of erection, 1774. Ashena, daughter of Edward and Greenleaf Boswell, was buried in the north aisle of Stretham church, near Ely, 2d April 1783. And likewise *in* Ickleford church, near Hitchin, were buried Henry Boswell, King of the Gipsies, aged 90 years, 11th February 1780 ; his wife, Elizabeth, aged 70, 18th March 1782 ; and their three year old grand-daughter, Elizabeth, daughter of William and Hannah Boswell, 15th October 1796. Close to the south side of the chancel of the old church at Eastwood, Nottinghamshire, deep under the foundations of the present building, three more of the Boswell family were buried—King Louis, aged 42, 26th January 1835 ; Frampton, his son, aged 20, 28th December of the same year ; and Queen Vashti Carlin, his daughter, aged 25, 20th April 1839. The latter was married to a górgio from the neighbouring parish of Greasley, " but could not brook the confinement between four walls of a house after the freedom

of a tent. The funerals were attended by an enor-
mous concourse of Gipsies on each occasion ; the
graves were watched for many nights ; and periodical
visits were made to them. Even now," the Rector
writes in 1880, " I hear they come to look at them."
Then in one grave at Beighton, Derbyshire, are
buried "two Gipsy ladies," mother and daughter probably [1]—" Matilda Boswell, died 15th January 1844,
aged 40," and "Lucretia Smith, Queen of the Gypsies,
died 20th November 1844, aged 72." These lines are
cut upon their tombstone—

" Happy soul, thy days are ended,
    All thy mourning days below ;
Go, by angel guards attended,
    To the sight of Jesus, go."—

a better epitaph than that upon King Dan Boswell's
headstone at Selston, Nottinghamshire, which headstone was broken by an irreverent cow—

" I've lodged in many a town,
    I've travelled many a year,
But death at length hath brought me down
    To my last lodgings here."

In many a quiet country churchyard one comes on

---

[1] In nothing is Gipsy family love more visible than in the closeness
with which one death in a tent is followed by another. During
1870-75 one grave received King Studaveres Lovell, Yourégh his wife,
and his sister Emily, in Guide Bridge churchyard, near Ashton-under-
Lyne ; where also are the graves of Moses Herring and of Josiah
Boswell (died 7th July 1873, aged 48). "Each grave is neatly kept,"
and, when Mr Crofton visited the spot in 1876, "some fresh flowers
beneath a glass shade told a plain tale of unforgotten grief."—(*Papers
of Manchester Literary Club for 1877:* " Gipsy Life in Lancashire and
Cheshire.")

these sepulchres of Little Egypt : at Loders, Dorsetshire, an altar tomb, simply inscribed, " The King and
Queen of the Gipsies ; " at Sandford, a headstone " to
Mistress Paul Stanley, who died November 1797 ; "
at Belbroughton, Worcestershire, an oblong stone
structure, " erected to the memory of Paradise Buckler,
who died 8th January 1815, aged 13 years." Concerning which last burial a long account appeared in
Truth (28th August 1879), how, " being an unmarried
girl, this heir-apparent was to be carried by nothing
but white pocket-handkerchiefs, and the coffin was
to be covered with the same. Every Gipsy of the
tribe also wanted a white pocket-handkerchief for
his own use on the occasion. They went round and
' borrowed ' these commodities ; and the villagers and
gentry gave them up in much the same spirit as the
Egyptians did when the Israelites borrowed of them,
not liking to incur the enmity of the tribe by refusal.
But when the ceremony was over, each handkerchief
was duly restored to its owner, beautifully washed
and bleached. In one or two cases where the borrowed articles had been slightly injured, they were
replaced by others of the finest cambric. To this day
some of the ' oldest inhabitants ' tell of the spectacle
of that funeral of the Gipsy child-queen, and how
the Gipsies gathered by hundreds from the country
round to attend the ceremony; and most of all, how
astonished the parishioners were at the honesty of
the Gipsies on the occasion. Besides the scrupulous
return of the borrowed handkerchiefs, there were

no complaints of thefts during the inroad of the tribe for the ceremony. They seem to have felt themselves in the light of guests, and under obligations for the loans made to them, and returned the compliment by a temporary regard for *meum* and *tuum*." The passage less illustrates Gipsy honesty than a górgio's ignorant estimate thereof; but, forbearing comment, I only ask its author, if he is in the habit of attending funerals to pick the pockets of his fellow-mourners. Those who will, may recognise in the white handkerchiefs the "mysterious handkerchief of cambric," emblem, as Mr Borrow explains, of chastity amongst the Spanish Gipsies. Unfortunately white handkerchiefs are not peculiar to Gipsy funerals, but are used in Worcestershire at all the funerals of children and young persons of both sexes.

Again, Crabb tells us that, " in his tent at Launton, Oxfordshire, died in the year 1830, more than a hundred years of age, James Smith, called by the public the King of the Gipsies. By his tribe he was looked up to with the greatest respect and veneration. His remains were followed to the grave by his widow, who is herself more than a hundred years old, and by many of his children, grandchildren, great-grandchildren, and other relatives; and by several individuals of other tribes. At the funeral his widow tore her hair, uttered the most frantic exclamations, and begged to be allowed to throw herself on the coffin, that she might be buried with her husband."

And in the neighbouring county of Wiltshire, and the same year, a Gipsy woman, "wife and mother for nearly threescore years and ten," died in a lane at Highworth, on 5th August, and was followed to the grave by her venerable husband and numerous offspring, amid a pitiless storm. Hone's *Year Book* gives a full and interesting description of her burial, how " in the coffin with her remains were enclosed a knife and fork, and plate ; and five tapers were placed on the lid, and kept constantly burning till her removal for interment ; after which ceremony the whole of her wardrobe was burnt, and her donkey and dog were slaughtered by her nearest relatives, in conformity to a superstitious custom remaining among her tribe."

This custom has often been described, most vividly by "Cuthbert Bede," in *Notes and Queries*, June 6, 1857 :—" The following particulars relative to the death and burial of a Gipsy were communicated to me by a trustworthy informant, who had been an eye-witness of some of the incidents. The man, who was an ordinary member of the tribe, was ill of pleurisy. A surgeon was called in from the nearest town, who bled him, after much persuasion, the Gipsies being much averse to blood-letting (so said my informant). The man became worse, and the surgeon's assistant came to see him, and proposed to bleed him again ; upon which the assistant was forthwith sent about his business, and the surgeon's bill was paid, his further attendance being dispensed

with. The man then died. He had expressed a wish
to be buried in his best clothes, viz., a velveteen coat
with half-crowns shanked for buttons, together with a
waistcoat with shillings similarly prepared for buttons;
but a woman[1] who had lived with him ran off with
these garments, so he was buried in 'his second best,
without a shroud, and in the very best of coffins.'
He was buried in the churchyard of the nearest
town. 'They had a hearse and ostrich plumes; and
about fifty Gipsies, men and women, followed him;
and when the church service was over, and the clergyman had gone, the Gipsies stayed in the churchyard
and had a service of their own.' What follows is (to
me at least) very curious. According to my informant,
when a Gipsy dies, everything belonging to him (with
the exception of coin or jewels) is destroyed. At any
rate, thus it was in the case now mentioned, as my
informant was a witness of the destruction. 'First,
they burnt his fiddle—a right down good fiddler
he was, many's the time I've danced to him at our
wake; and then they burnt a lot of beautiful Witney
blankets, as were as good as new; and then they
burnt a sight of books—for he was quite a scholar—
very big books they was, too—I specially minds one of
'em, the biggest of the hull lot—a book o' jawgraphy,
as 'd tell you the history o' all the world, you under-

---

[1] If the clothes' owner were really old Henry Clisson, according to
Silvanus's conjecture, this woman was a Brummagem Delilah, of górgio,
not of Gipsy origin. In that case she had *run through* five silver teapots, before she *ran off* with coat and waistcoat.

stand, sir—and was chock full o' queer outlandish
pictures; and then there was his grindstun, that he
used to go about the country with, a grindin' scissors
and razors and sich like—they couldn't burn *him!* so
they carried him two miles, and then hove him right
into Siv'un [*i.e.*, the river Severn]; that's true, you
may take my word for it, sir; for I was one as help'd
'em to carry it.' "

Another note on Romani funeral rites was communicated to *Notes and Queries* by Mr John E. Cussans,
15th May 1869 :—" For many years they [Shaws,
Grays, and Dymocks] interred in a field belonging to
Mr Nehemiah Parry, a farmer residing at Strett Hall
[Streethall], four miles from Saffron Walden, though
it was no uncommon thing for bodies to be buried at
the road side. A labourer told me that, about forty
years ago, an old Gipsy woman died near Littlebury,
Essex. The body was swathed in cloths, and laid
upon trestles by the encampment. Over the head
and feet two long hazel twigs were bent, the ends
thrust in the ground. From these hung two oil
lamps, which were kept burning all night, while two
women, one on either side of the corpse, watched,
sitting on the ground. The following day the un-
coffined body was buried in Littlebury churchyard
by order of the local authorities ; not, however, without great opposition on the part of the deceased's
friends, who wished to bury her elsewhere."

This almost solitary notice of Gipsy burial in uncon-
secrated ground is curious, but needs corroboration,

which is not forthcoming from the present rector of Streethall. "No one," he writes (March 1880), "has the slightest recollection of Gipsies being buried within the parish. Skeletons have been dug up at various times, the last about thirty years ago; but whether they were Gipsies or not it is impossible to say, as no one seems to know anything at all about them, and there is no record of Gipsies coming to visit the graves." But he adds, what is rather significant, that "the last Nehemiah Parry, who died in 1861, married a Gipsy young woman, one of the Shaws."

According to *English Gipsy Songs* (1875), p. 31, "In the old times, or till within fifty years, the Gipsies buried their dead in lonely and remote places; but now they manifest great anxiety to secure Christian burial, and incur considerable expense in funerals." The statement is partly at least disproved by the foregoing pages; of its possible part truth, I can only say that I have never met a Gipsy whose forefathers to his knowledge had ever had other than decent Christian burial.[1] Silvanus scouted the notion with

---

[1] I speak of English Gipsies; but Crusius's *Annales Suevici* (1594) also records three emblazoned monuments of Gipsy chieftains buried in Christian churches, within the century following the Gipsies' westward immigration. The first was reared at Steinbach in 1445, "to the high-born lord, Lord Panuel, Duke in Little Egypt, and Lord of Hirschhorn in the same land;" the second at Bautma in 1453, "to the noble Earl Peter of Kleinschild;" and the third at Pforzheim in 1498, "to the high-born Lord Johann, Earl of Little Egypt, to whose soul God be gracious and merciful." In Weissenborn churchyard, Saxony, is another

infinite contempt. "The time appointed for his burying being come, he is carried to the burying place, and thrown into the grave as dog Lion was, and there is an end of Wully,"—these words, from *A Modern Account of Scotland* (1670), convey no measure of his indignation. To soothe him, I recounted how, in the summer of 1878, "the Gipsy Queen of the United States was buried at Dayton, Ohio, the headquarters of the American Gipsies, representatives of every clan and tribe scattered over American territory being present at the funeral. Red was the predominant hue in the funereal trappings; each mourner wore a scrap of crimson, and the hearse was decked with red plumes. Queen Matilda and King Levi Stanley emigrated to the States in 1860." Of course they did; why, Levi is son to Lementina's cousin, and Goliath and Patience were probably among the red-trapped mourners. Yes, that was something like; and here I had ceased, had not

---

interesting inscription:—"Here rests in God Dame Maria Sybilla Rosenberg, Gipsy, and wife of the honourable and valiant Wolfgang Rosenberg, Cornet in the Electoral and Brandenburg army, who died at Weissenborn, 9th October 1632, aged 42, to whom God be merciful." To Weissenborn church this Gipsy cornet presented a silver flagon. His descendant, Friedrich Rosenberg, was serving in the Blücher Hussars in 1837.—(Liebich, *Zigeuner*, p. 26.)

Burial in Christian churchyards was first conceded to the Montenegrine Gipsies under Prince Danilo (1851-60), and it had probably been likewise denied to the forefathers of those Gipsies who made their appearance in Western Europe in 1417. If so, one can understand why Gipsies should to this day set such high store on Christian sepulture, token of their escape from the degradation—it may be from the bondage—of untold centuries.

America suggested one more epitaph, from the
churchyard of St Kea, by Truro :—

"IN
MEMORY OF MEZELLEY
THE DAUGHTER OF
PLATO AND BETSY BUCKLAN,
*born in America
and died 21st Novr. 1862*
AGED 2 YEARS.

Farewell, thou little blooming bud,
Just bursting into flower ;
We give thee up ; but oh, the pain
Of this last parting hour."

There I did really stop, though half the Romani
graves upon my list remained unnoticed. At Cogges-
hall, Essex, of Casello, or Celia Chilcott,[1] "one of a
company of Gipsies, who died at the White Hart
Inn," 29th September 1842, aged 28. At Beaulieu,
Hampshire, of King Joseph Lee, who died 6th September 1844, aged 86, and who some years before
had given his grandchild Charity one hundred
spade-guineas and much silver plate for dower. At
Balsham, Cambridgeshire, of "Old Charley Gray, who
chose a grave close to the church door, because he
thought it would be lively on Sundays when the
folks gossipped there." At Linlithgow, of Captain
M'Donald, who, towards the middle of last century,
was shot dead in his attempt at highway robbery,
and whose "funeral was very respectable, being

---

[1] *Query*, was Mary Chilcott, who died at Ponghill, Devon, in 1797,
aged 101, a member of this Gipsy family?

attended by the magistrates of Linlithgow, and a number of the most genteel persons in the neighbourhood." *Et cetera, et cetera;* but the longest lane must have a turning, and the turning here was Lementina's summons to our tea.

Chapter Sixth.

AT TEA I asked how things had gone with every one that day. The boys, I learnt, had prospered mightily at Pen-y-bonh, there having found a picnic company from Aberystwith, who had danced to their fiddling, and paid the fiddlers well. The only pity was that none of the women had been there, for the ladies perchance had crossed their hands with silver. Not that the women had done so badly, for a country where money is scarce though victuals are plentiful; Sinfi, at least, had certainly struck *ile*. She had called at a Scotchwoman's, a gauger's wife, and had sold her two "fanciful baskets" and a destiny for ten shillings in money, a dress, two cheeses, and three stone of flour; which last she had not lost, like Aunt Kiómi.

"That was by Ledbury," said Lementina. "We were stopping, about six miles from Ledbury, in a beautiful little lane (an awful place for hangmen walking about the roads). It was just when we had finished hop-picking; we were coming from close by

Bosbury. And old Kiómi stayed behind at a great big gentleman's house, and got telling the girls' fortunes; and they gave her a lot of cider, made her drunk. And a bagful of flour they gave her, and she had forgotten to tie the mouth of the bag up, just put it into the *mónging-gúno*, the mouth of the bag hanging out. And for nearly six miles she let the flour drop all along the road, right to the very place. She wouldn't have noticed it then, only one of the boys went to her, and asked her if she'd been making a track for the policeman. Then she turned round, and saw it; and when she looked in the bag, there wasn't a morsel of flour into it."

" Yes," added Ruth ; " and then she tumbled in the hedge and burst out laughing. But you should tell the rei about Catseye Trainette, as has got my Aunt Kiómi's eldest son. It was off by the Black Mountains, reía, and she went out one Wednesday, got drunk (for, bless us all! they are a nasty, vulgar, drunken lot), and come home late at night. All the children had been crying for bread. And she never took the slightest notice of them, pulled off the *mónging-gúno*, and spread it open right in the middle of the place ; and she sat a bit like Longsnout, and she forgot clean all about it. The children went and helped themselves; and then she turns round suddenly, and began to make the bed right atop of the *mónging-gúno ;* and she never remembered till morning that they had been sleeping on the bread and the meat and everything else that was underneath the bed."

Silvanus struck in choruswise: "If there is one thing scandal ashamed, it is to see a beastly drunken female. Such cattle as they ought to be shot. They be a nuisance to the road."

·And Lementina, with (I fancied) a side-thrust at some one, averred that *she* had sworn against strong drink this ten years past, had vowed that sooner than touch one spot of beer, she would go to Winchcombe churchyard, and drink the blood of her dead brother Perun. Was this weird pledge a remnant of vampire superstition?[1] It might be so; but before I could follow up the question, she was telling of Tryphi and her pound of butter.

"That was off by the Black Mountains, too, just in Llanthony Bottom, and she bought a pound of butter, and put it into the tea-kettle full of cold water to keep it cool; and old 'Lijah made a fire, and put the kettle on to boil. And when it was boilt, Tryphi poured the water out on to the tea, and found it just for all the world like broth. And that was the 'dentical place where we were stopping onest along with old Israel Draper and Chicken Lee; and we were just going to have our tea, and old Israel had put the kettle on, but his two daughters were not come back yet. Presently they come, and as soon as ever they got to the tent, he asked them if they'd

---

[1] The *chóvehóno*, "wizard," of English Gipsies is the *tchovekhanó*, "*revenant*, or spectre," of their Turkish brethren; and *The Fiend*, a vampire story in Ralston's *Russian Folk-Tales*, pp. 10–17, is *O Clohanó* of Constantinescu's Roumanian Gipsy Stories, pp. 52–58.

j

brought anything. They said, 'No, daddy, not even a bit of 'bacca.' Never said a word, he only gave a grunt; he got up there and then, took the kettle off the fire as it was, pitched it right in the middle of the road. And then sat down again quite quietly, and said, 'There's your kettle in the road, gal.' Although the rest of the people were so astonished, they couldn't help laughing at him; and his daughters had to go up to the shop at once, and get some victuals for him. He was quite an old old man, a very oldfashioned man; and you might not think that they would allow him to have such authority over them, for they were quite old women themselves, Rodi and Lani. They never married, and they used to make baskets and clothes-pegs. I don't know where they'll be now, but the old man died about a twelvemonth back; they say there was a sight of people to the burying. More than a hundred he was; and when he was quite an old old man, he'd play most beautiful on the violin."

"So poor old Israel's gone. Yes, he must have been close upon his hundredth year. I met another of his daughters, the youngest one, in Lancashire last autumn. She is wife to a Boswell, Sylvester's brother, and mother of a largish grown-up family: her eldest son has married the landlady of a Workington public-house. I forget this daughter's name, but she was asking after the old man and her two maiden sisters, whom she had not set eyes on for twenty years and more, these Boswells always stopping up round Liverpool. I told her all I knew of them, but it was not much; indeed, I thought that Israel was still alive. Hers seemed a very well-to-do family, and her sons and daughters have all had capital schooling; but I shouldn't say that Lancashire was altogether a pleasant country for Gipsies,—the *Píro-délin-tem*, 'kicking country,' as Gipsies themselves have named it."

"No," said Silvanus, "Lancashire's too much eaten up with low-bred Irish. Why, two of 'em nearly killed my cousin's boy by Manchester, five year ago come next November; knocked him down and kicked him shameful. I seen Louis at Congleton two weeks after, and he walked quite lame then, and he had to go back to appear against them at the 'sizes. I never heard how it come off, but he said the country was in a perfect uproar; and some more of these nasty outscouts had pretty nigh murdered four of the Boswells, chucked whole cartloads of bricks at 'em, and broken the women's skulls most awful. Lord bless us! they was cut all to atoms, you couldn't see their faces for the vounds." [1]

---

[1] This must have been the "Murderous Assault on Gipsies," reported in the *Preston Herald*, 31st October 1874. It was bad enough, if scarcely so bad as by Silvanus's telling. Some Manchester men paid a Sunday visit to a Gipsy encampment in a brickyard at Sale, and proceeded to pull the tents down. "On being remonstrated with, Sumuel Roe picked up two bricks, and threw them at Gilderoy and Mrs Homer Boswell, inflicting a frightful wound on Gilderoy's eye, and almost smashing in the woman's forehead." Mr Roe got four months' hard labour, and "seemed surprised at the verdict."

Plato just then came back from Dinas Mowddy. He had looked at the horse, but bought instead a retriever, whereat Richenda scolded : " A good lover of dogs, faith ! A perfect ratcatcher. I'll go and steal you a dead sheep to keep 'em with. As if I hadn't got trouble enough already without your bringing more rubbish to the place. Catch me going along the road with such a lot of poverty curs. Well górgios might say, ' You can't want nothing, if you can keep a pack of hounds like that.' "

" By Gum," Silvanus made haste to interpose, " I think you're all a pack of hounds together, for everlasting gnawing and tugging at one another ; especially when a gentleman like my friend here has done us the honour to come and drink a sociable cup of tea. Sure it's a poor thing if the lad mayn't buy himself a bit of a puppy ; and dogs are valuabler hereabouts than horses. *Mollekó*, boy ! go and get yourself a ten or twelve shillings by your 'trievier, and then she'll be crying to have it back again, for I'm sure he's a pretty creature, prettier by a precious sight nor our old Kill-a-chick. That was a shepherd, refa, come up to my daddy's tent, and we were stopping at Alice's Green, near to Dymmock in Gloucestershire ; and he saw the dog. It was one of those long-haired dogs, as old as could be, and hard of hearing too. You might bark at it for everlasting, and it would never mind you. There was only me and Gilderoy to the place, mere lads as if it might be Wanselo, and we told him it was a ship-dog [sheep-dog] ; and then

the man axed, ' How owld is it ? ' ' Two month old,'
we told him ; so we sold it to the man for a ship-dog
two month old for half-a-crown.   That was while my
daddy and mammy was out ; and with the half-a-
crown we'd got for it we went and bought a loaf of
bread, a quarter of butter, and I can't tell you how
much tea.   Well, bor, and when we took the dog
to the house and tied him up, we made the rope
big enough as he could jump out of it, but he was
that old he wouldn't stir.   So when my daddy and
mammy got home, they made a row about it (for it
had been poor Sago's dog, my sister that is dead and
gone), would make us go and fetch it back again.
But when we come to the farm, the man had just
done hanging his young ship-dog in the barn ; he'd
found it was no mannerable good, soon as we'd left it,
for he'd holla'd to it and it never took no hearkenings.   And then the man's fowls went into the barn
to it, and it killed a bantam, for we had always called
it Kill-a-chick.   So there was Kill-a-chick hanged,
and my daddy was perfect furious, was going to beat
us, but we runned away."

   " *Dábla!*" quoth Lementina ; " there was a way to
do, to use the poor dear dog as they'd had for long
and long.   I'd sooner hang my Tiny, than mumply
górgios should have it ; and I'm sartain the dog would
just as lieve be hanged as go and live with *kennicks*.
No górgios can never get Gipsies' animals to bide
with them ; and if Romané and górgios come up to
the tents at the same time, they'll smell out górgios

before they will Romané. They can't abear górgios, but'll go snifting round. And they understand the Róm'nimus as well as the children. That poor old Tiny of mine, she knows a constable the moment she sees him. And if ever we want to hide her, she'll know as well as can be what we want to do. She'll lie down like a Christian, and be as quiet as anything, if we just say ' Here's górgios.' And once when we were coming by Leominster, and we stopped along the road to get something to eat, and just when we were packing up again to be off, she went with one of the boys along the fields, and then she ran away from him. And we were gone far enough from the place then, and I had to go back and look after her, and found her sitting on the tent-place yelping. And before then, before I went to look after her, I had put *pátrins* in the road for some of the children, and when I found her, she started off, and went straight on along the road, and smelt her way right to the tents by the *pátrins ;* about six or seven miles it was, and she went through a great big wood, and was at the place long before ever I got there. And often when we're going along the roads, and she hears the boys playing up to some gentleman's house, she'll sit up in the middle of the road, with her head cocked up, listening."

Pyramus stopped feeding his brother's new acquisition to remark : " Ay, Romani's animals are never like górgios'. Look at the very neddies. There was old Tinker, as I called my neddy after. We'd had him about eight years, and at last my daddy sold him to a man to work down a coal pit; and the boy took him away, and we went off from there. And about three weeks we were back again; and old Tinker got loose from the house, and come straight down to the place. Poor old neddy. Lord! that was a shame, really. And he lay down close to the place among the other neddies, and the fine górgio had hard work to get him away. He'd kick like anything, and back into the hedge; and if you went to get on him, he'd carry you to the tent, and there lie down. But I never in all my life saw a neddy like him, to be so shy of the slightest bit of thing. If there was only a dear little drop of water shining in the road, he'd never pass it, without you was to blindfold him.'

"And there was that colt. Quite a little foal he was when my daddy bought him. By Job, he was stiff too; what legs he had. Five shillings my daddy gave for it at Talgarth. And he'd never stand any other place, only just behind my mammy's tent; and going along the road, he'd always be right between the tent-rods, same as if he was ploughing. And my daddy made a hole in the blanket behind, where he used to push his nose through"—

"Like our little brown Peggy," put in Mantis, "a chicken Dimiti had out of Wales; and she'd never sit anywhere else, only right atop of the balk, over the fire, and you couldn't see the colour of her for smoke. And she went off among some bushes one day, and we looked for her, and couldn't find her;

and found out afterwards it was the pretty górgio stole her."

"I do wish you'd learn your children better manners, Richenda," said Pyramus testily, "not to go poking in afore their betters. What's a chicken to make so much talk on? let alone the gentleman not wanting to hear a lot of little rude young boys. But what I was a saying, bor, my daddy kept this colt like that till he growed a great big thing, then he sold him to the blacksmith at Rindleford Mill for twenty pounds. And whenever we'd go that way (the man kept him in a little orchard, close to the road), he'd know the neddies as well as could be; he always come to the gate and begun to whinny. *Dórdi!* my daddy has had some nice horses."

With curly head nestled against his shoulder, sat Pyramus's only daughter, Leah, a bonny little piece of bright-eyed mischief, who, knowing she was free to speak unchecked, began—"And I had an old neddy once, Black Moses, refa; my daddy gave it me, and there! it wasn't worth picking up in the road. You couldn't get it to stir nohow; and we were going all along the road with Silverthorn's breed, and young Silverthorn offered me threepence for it, and Christopher said he'd give me fourpence, and I let it go. And the Saturday after, my daddy took that one and one of Silverthorn's to Guildford market, and sold them both for half-a-sovereign; and you may depend I was pretty angry after. Then I had another after that, another Moses; and my daddy swapped it

away for little Jessie, and got seventeen shilling
besides, from a gardener at a great gentleman's
house, so I didn't do so bad after all.   Then I
thought to myself, ' Now, won't I dress myself up?'
and I went and gave five shillings for a beautiful
straw bonnet.   It was a thing about the size of a nut-
shell, trimmed with a bright green ribbon, and a big
red rose stuck right on the top.   And when my
mammy saw it, she snatched it off my head, and
ripped it all to pieces.   And I bought a pair of red
shoes at the time, with thin elastic sides ; five shillings
I gave for them, and they only lasted me about a
fortnight.   *Dôrdi !* and I thought I was so grand."

"But you should tell the gentleman," said Pyramus,
"about the lovely Leghorn hat your mammy bought .
you against the Ascot races. You know, reía, Lucretia
couldn't abear to see the child with nothing vulgar,
like a little wench belonging to the shooting-galleries.
And tell him, Daughter, about your brother's foal, and
how they both was put in the pound together."

"What, that little donkey foal you gave a shilling
for, daddy, and Christopher used to ride it ?   Oh,
such a pretty little thing !   And my daddy sold it to
a parson, for his children to play with.   It was when
we were going along, and the parson had no place to
put it in just then, and he told the man to lock it up in
the pound.   And Christopher said he wouldn't let it
go, and he clung round its neck, and got locked into
the pound with it ; and he was roaring like anything,
both for the fear of being left locked up, and having to

leave his little foal behind. Long and by last he got out over the wall, and followed us."

" Donkeys should be cheap," I said, " if you can buy them for a shilling or fourpence. And horses, too— what was it, Pyramus, you said your father gave for the colt that always stood behind the tent ? "

" Five shillings, bor ; but that was years ago. Horses was cheap then, and no mistake, specially up in Wales, at Huntingdon, Talgarth, Knighton, and all them fairs. My daddy didn't need then go far up into Wales for his horses, only just round the Black Mountains. Onest we were by Albrighton, when he started off and went to a farm called Pen-y-Mawr (Powell, the people's name were), and he bought two nice young colts. And the man said he'd break 'em in a little for him before starting away ; and my daddy stayed there three days a purpose. They'd never been handled till he got them. And the groom pulled its neck out of place ; and the fine gentleman and all of them, they knew of it, and wanted to hurry my daddy away from the place, and made him pretty near drunk, so as he shouldn't take no notice. He started off, and the son went a goodish way with him ; and just when the son left him, my daddy saw that the horse began to reel about. He never took much heed, but went on with them, and they got to a place where the people were making hay ; and one of the farmers on the top of the hayrick shouted to my daddy, asked him what was the matter with the horse. My daddy said, 'Nothing.' He said, 'There

is, though;' he said, 'its neck ſs out of place.' My
daddy was perfectly struck, didn't know what to
think of it. And there was the poor young thing
with its neck all on one side, hanging down you
know. And my daddy asked him if he'd let him
turn 'em both in the field, till he went back to see
about it. And he did go back, told the fine farmer all
about it (a long long way he had to go), and he swore
that the colt's neck was never broke when it was there.
And while my daddy was away, there come a pretty
keeper up the road, and he saw it lying there; and he
stuck it, and had it taken home and skinned, and
hanging up in the apple-trees. Then my daddy
come home with the other pony, and told my mammy
all about it; and the next day we come right back
again to near Leominster, and my daddy and mammy
went off again. They went and told the magistrate
about it, and he said he couldn't do anything; it had
been left too long, he said. And thirty pounds my
daddy had paid for the two; so there was half of
his good money gone."

"Ay," said Silvanus, "and I told the fine Powell,
'None of your family will ever prosper, for serving me
this dirty trick.' They were supposed to be one of
the greatest farmers anywhere about there; and in
the same year his wife died and two children, and all
his cattle and stock was taken from him. And he was
turned out of the farm, and no one knew what become
of them. The Lord would never let such rascals
prosper, for cheating of a poor dear person so."

To us discoursing of the brute creation, Wisdom and Lancelot discoursed sweet music; Wisdom as first, and Lance as second fiddle. The tender *Shepherd of Snowdon* formed their theme; and Rodi presently taking up the words, the rest chimed in, in Welsh, or Welsh-besprinkled gibberish. So song became the order of the evening, and Grandmother was called upon to sing; who, in a voice thinned like her face by years, gave us this fragment of an old-world ballad:—

   " ' Cold blows the wind over my true love,
    Cold blows the drops of rain ;'
   I never, never had but one sweet heart,
    In the green wood he was slain.

   " ' But I'll do as much for my true love
    As any young girl can do ;
   I'll sit and I'll weep by his grave side
    For a twelvemonth and one day.'

   " When the twelvemonth's end and one day was past,
    This young man he arose :
   " ' What makes you weep by my grave side
    For twelve months and one day ?'

   " ' Only one kiss from your lily cold lips,
    One kiss is all I crave ;
   Only one kiss from your lily cold lips,
    And return back to your grave.'

   " ' My lip is cold as the clay, sweet heart,
    My breath is earthly strong ;
   If you should have a kiss from my cold lip,
    Your days will not be long.'

   " ' Go fetch me a note from the dungeon dark [?]
    Cold water from a stone ;
   There I'll sit and weep for my true love,
    For a twelvemonth and one day.

> " ' Go dig me a grave both long, wide, and deep,
>   I will lie down in it and take one sleep,
>   For a twelvemonth and one day :
>   I will lie down in it and take a long sleep,
>   For a twelvemonth and a day.' "

What a lovely old air she sang it to, as old most likely as the words themselves, but printed in no known collection. Yes, gatherers of old songs and melodies may go further afield than Little Egypt, to come back emptier-handed than if they had loitered an hour beside the tents. Myself, I know the tunes but not the notes, so am just as serviceable as an inkless pen; but let the first musician that lights on Boswell, Stanley, Lovell, or Herne, secure this air and those that followed it. For knowing the Lovells' repertory, I could pick and choose at will, so next demanded of Ruth that plaint of a forsaken one, each verse of which concludes, "As an orange grows on an apple-tree;" and then of Starlína the following homely ditty :—

> " ' A brisk young sailor come courting me,
>   He stole away my sweet liberty;
>   My heart he stole with a free good will,
>   He's got it now, and he'll keep it still.

> " ' There is an alehouse in yonders town,
>   Where my first lovier is sitting down,
>   And he takes another lass on his knee ;
>   Oh ! don't you think it's a grief to me ?

> " ' A grief to me, and I'll tell you why,
>   Because she has more gold than I ;
>   But her gold will flash, and her beauty pass,
>   And she'll become like me at last.'

" Her father came home, it was late one night,
Inquiring for his heart's delight ;
Upstairs he went, and the door he broke,
And found her hanging by a rope.

" He took his knife, and he cut her down,
And in her bosom this note he found,
And on the note these few lines was wrote,—
'O Johnny, O Johnny, my heart you have broke.

" ' Come dig me a grave both wide and deep,
And marble stone from head to feet,
And on the top then a turtle-dove,
To show the world that I died for love.' "

Silly words enough, but the buzzing, quavering tune calls up a vision of alehouse and smock-frocked drinkers, oak settle and mugs of cider, better at least than the glare and din of music halls. "A regular ploughboy's song," said Anselo ; and chanted forthwith, concerning that same ploughboy, how—

" — he ploughs and sows the land,
And his skin's as white as snow ;
Here's a health to every labouring lad
That ploughs and sows the land."

Then came *The Leather Bottél*, roared out by Pyramus with a voice that almost shook the Chair of Idris ; and then from Sinfi this Scottish ballad, which she had learnt of Jocky Neilson's wife :—

" There were three sisters going from home,
All in a lea and alony, oh !
They met a man, and he made them stand,
Down by the bonny banks of Airdrie, oh !

" He took the first one by the hand,
All in a lea and alony, oh !
He turned her round, and he made her stand,
Down by the bonny banks of Airdrie, oh !

" Saying, 'Will you be a robber's wife?
    All in a lea and alony, oh!
Or will you die by my penknife?
    Down by the bonny banks of Airdrie, oh!'

" ' Oh! I won't be a robber's wife,
    All in a lea and alony, oh!
But I will die by your penknife,
    Down by the bonny banks of Airdrie, oh!'

" Then he took the second by her hand,
    All in a lea and alony, oh!
He turned her round, and he made her stand,
    Down by the bonny banks of Airdrie, oh!

" Saying, 'Will you be a robber's wife?
    All in a lea and alony, oh!
Or will you die by my penknife?
    Down by the bonny banks of Airdrie, oh!'

" ' Oh! I won't be a robber's wife,
    All in a lea and alony, oh!
But I will die by your penknife,
    Down by the bonny banks of Airdrie, oh!'

" He took the third one by the hand,
    All in a lea and alony, oh!
He turned her round, and he made her stand,
    Down by the bonny banks of Airdrie, oh!

" Saying, 'Will you be a robber's wife?
    All in a lea and alony, oh!
Or will you die by my penknife?
    Down by the bonny banks of Airdrie, oh!'

" ' Oh! I won't be a robber's wife,
    All in a lea and alony, oh!
And I won't die by your penknife,
    Down by the bonny banks of Airdrie, oh!

" ' If my two brothers had been here,
    All in a lea and alony, oh!
You would not have killed my sisters two,
    Down by the bonny banks of Airdrie, oh!'

"'What was your two brothers' names?
   All in a lea and alony, oh!
One was John, and the other was James,
   Down by the bonny banks of Airdrie, oh!'

"'Oh, what did your two brothers do?
   All in a lea and alony, oh!
One was a minister, the other such as you,
   Down by the bonny banks of Airdrie, oh!'

"'Oh, what is this that I have done?
   All in a lea and alony, oh!
I have killed my sisters all but one,
   Down by the bonny banks of Airdrie, oh!

"'And now I'll take out my penknife,
   All in a lea and alony, oh!
And here I'll end my own sweet life,
   Down by the bonny banks of Airdrie, oh!'"

This, surely, was the "werry lonesome death-song, about a yard and a half long," of which the old Gipsy spoke to Mr Leland. Only that "had no tune in pertick'ler," while this was sung to a kind of monotonous chant, sad and suggestive as a river's flow. And Lancelot played a masterly accompaniment, that pled for the murdered, raved at the murderer, and moaned for his remorseful suicide. Next Sinfi's Scottish ballad started Lucretia off on a song of Scotland, the version of *Hugh of Lincoln*, namely, familiar to most London Gipsies, with its own quaint air, all runs, and trills, and "grace-notes." I heard it first at Shepherd's Bush, in 1872, from little Amy North, who, having "heav'd deep sighs," began—

   " Down in merry merry Scotland,
      It rained both hard and small ;
   Two little boys went out one day,
      All for to play with a ball.

K

" They tossed it up so very very high,
　　They tossed it down so low,
　　They tossed it into the Jew's gardén,
　　Where the flowers all do blow.

"Out came one of the Jew's daughtérs,
　　Dresséd in green all,—
' If you come here, my fair pretty lad,
　　You shall have your ball.'

" She showed him an apple as green as grass,
　　The next thing was a fig,
The next thing a cherry as red as blood,
　　And that would 'tice him in.

" She set him on a golden chair,
　　And gave him sugar sweet;
Laid him on some golden chest of drawers,
　　Stabbed him like a sheep.

" ' Seven foot Bible
　　At my head and my feet :
If my mother pass by me,
　　Pray tell her I'm asleep.' "

Here it abruptly ended. Nor did Lucretia get
thus far ; but, breaking down, called upon me to sing
"that Romani gílli, reía," of all things in the world.
So I, a górgio, gave to a Gipsy audience one of two
Macaronic effects, made years ago to meet the literary
want [1] that Miss Janet Tuckey, "Hans Breitmann,"

---

[1] The Anglo-Romani muse is dead, if indeed she ever lived ; but
on the Continent collections have been formed of genuine Gipsy poetry,
e.g., in Hungary by Reuss (edited by Pott in *Zeitschrift der Deutschen
Morgenl. Ges.*, 1849), Friedrich Müller (Vien., 1869), Miklosich (Vien.,
1874-78), and Meltzl (Klausenb., 1878); in Gallicia by Isidor Kopernicki
(ninety unpublished songs); and in Wallachia by Barbu Constantinescu
(Bucharest, 1878). The seventy-five specimens of this last collection
are strikingly regular in rhyme and metre ; but all, however rude, are
as much more valuable than any Songs of the *Afición*, as Sophocles' *Ajax*
than Lord Lyttleton's *Comus*. Pity that the "great Pharaoh Lay, of
epic character," is known to us only by one unintelligible stanza.

and Professor E. H. Palmer have since arisen to supply. Meant for a rendering of "See the smoking bowl before us," in Burns' *Jolly Beggars*, it goes to the tune of *Billy Taylor*:—

"Dórdi the toóvin' tátto-páni,
   Dórdi the tátcheno Rómani chals !
With the bóshoméngro kéllin'
   Muk us giv our gílli, Pals.
      Júkel's ful for prástaméngros,
         Mas for Kaúlos on the drom ;
      Kóngeris was but kair'd for ráshis,
         Stáribens 'cos dínlos kom.

"What's a púknius, so si wóngar,
   What's to be a bóro rei ?
So as we lels a kúshto jívoben,
   Why should we késser sar or kei ?
      Júkel's ful for prástaméngros, &c.

"Adré the dívvus pénnin' húkabens
   All about the tem we jas,
And adré the raáti in a gránzi
   Choómer our ráklis opré the kas.
      Júkel's ful for prástaméngros, &c.

"That the rei's várdo with its kístaméngros
   Prásters féreder, who might pen ?
Or that the wúdrus of the rómer'd raúni
   Diks any féreder kómobén ?
      Júkel's ful for prástaméngros, &c.

"Jívoben's kair'd o' dósta kóvas,
   Méndi 'll kek késser how they av ;
Muk them róker about decorum
   Who are atrásh for their kúshto nav.
      Júkel's ful for prástaméngros, &c.

"Then kúshto bokh to tan and sásta,
   Kúshto bokh to Kaúlos sor,
And kúshto bokh to the nóngo chávis :
   Muk's pen sor on us *Amusháw.*
      Júkel's ful for prástaméngros," &c.

Holes held by rags together, but chorus and third verse are not so bad. Anyhow, having had one, my hearers were bound to have the other, a perversion of Goethe's *King of Thule*, at least the tune whereof was Romanes, picked up from my eight fiddler friends of Siklos :—

> "There jiv'd a Rómano krállis,
>   And a tátcheno rei was he,
> 'Fore yoi múlli'd a kúrruv o' sónakei
>   Del'd lésti his pírini.
>
> "There was chíchi yuv kom'd so míshto,
>   Sórkon chaíros he haw'd he would pi
> 'Vri adúvel, and out o' yuv's yókas,
>   The páni nash'd avrí.
>
> "And when lésti vel'd to múllaïn',
>   Yuv pen'd as how sórkon gav
> Yuv del'd to the krállis arter him,
>   But kek o' the kúrruv a láv.
>
> "Yuv besh'd by the krállisko hobben,
>   With his kístaméngros sor,
> 'Dré his dádus's bóro kamóra,
>   Odoí by the dóriove shore.
>
> "Kek-kómi the púro píamóngro
>   The jívoben's yog should pi,
> For he wússer'd the kómelo kúrruv
>   Right alé dré the dóriov's zi.
>
> "Yuv dik'd lis pélin', pórderin',
>   Jal alé dré the páni loon,
> And his yókas pánder'd their kókoré.
>   And yuv was a gíllo coon."

What the Pott of the future will make of the closing line it were hard to say ; but my hearers took it all in excellent good part, applauding to the very echo. Rather an Irish echo, though, their "*Mishto, mishto,*"

JOHN ROBERT'S

returning from the darkening lane as " Bravo, capital,
very good indeed ! " and also rather an ironical echo,
to judge from its intonation.

" Górgios ! " said Lementina, standing up ; and
out of the twilight came a white-bearded figure, clad
all in black, topped by a broad-brimmed, tasselled,
clerical hat, and bearing on its back something that
looked like a one great folded wing, but was really
a harp cased in its oilskin cover. Talk of an angel
and you'll see the tip of his pinions ; this was. no
other than the old John Roberts, discussed by us
barely two hours ago. None but myself appeared to
recognise him, and, leaning back in Lementina's tent,
I purposely escaped a quick shy glance that he cast
on the firelit group, as, setting down his instrument,
he proceeded leisurely to fill his pipe. Silvanus, thereon, curious to throw some light upon the stranger,
bade 'Lina "give the gentleman an ember ;" and,
" Burn his beards, girl," whispered irreverent Dimiti,
and got a cuff from Pyramus for the suggestion.
No, the light revealed only a hale old man of middle
stature, with keen grey eyes, sharp-cut intelligent
features, and snowy hair, who, to look at, might
be a divine, a poet, or a legislator—anything rather
than a "stancient Romani chal." His voice, too,
high-pitched and voluble as any Welshman's, helped
him, though not for long, to keep up his incognito in
the ensuing discourse :—

John Roberts (condescendingly).—" You seem to be
enjoying yourselves, good people. I was on my way

to the hotel yonder, when I heard you singing and
violin-playing, and I couldn't resist halting, being a
bit of a musicianer myself."

Lementina.—"Yes, sir; it's a poor heart never
rejoices, sir; but often I say there's too much singing
and playing. Scrape, scrape, scraping from morning
till blessed night, till I can't hear my own ears sometimes; and after playing weeping comes next, you
know."

John Roberts.—"What would you say then if you
had nine great cubs like mine, all playing away at
once in one little tiny house, a practising some new
operatic pieces? *Do-da, do-da* they go for hours and
hours on end, and making all the horriblest noise you
can imagine, and do keep at it, till they are stopped
by me, by reason of the great annoyance they cause
to me, when I am writing to some high nobleman or
other patron. There's Lloyd and Madoc with English
pedal harps; Johnny, Albert, and Ernest with the
Welsh triple-stringed instrument; James flageolet;
Reuben the double-bass; Charley violoncello; and
little Willy solo violin. The Original Cambrian
Minstrels, there you have 'em."

Lementina (aside).—"Shoonta! sor górgiokono
náviaw, hoi?"

John Roberts.—"But what was that beautiful song
you were singing, one of you, when I came up; as
I did not understand the words very clearly, but it
seemed to be in some sort of a foreign language—
Italian?"

Lementina.—" No, sir ; that was Spanish, I think they call it, sir ; as a friend of ours was just obliging with. (Mollekó, bor ! Rómano si, penáva mánsar.) But sit you down, my gentleman, and rest yourself, for sure that thing must be an awful load to drag about. Ruth, fetch a chair down out of your sister's cart ; for you won't be used, sir, to sitting on the cold hard ground, like us poor people."

John Roberts (sitting down cross-legged on the grass).—" Oh, never mind chairs, my dear good lady ; pray don't put yourself out the least for me. I have been an old soldier in my time, and the sight of the tents and all your smiling faces puts me in mind of my young days when I served as a drummer in the 23d Royal Welsh Fusileers."

Lementina (scrutinising his easy attitude).—" So you've been a soldier, have you, sir ? Well, of course the tents would seem natival-like to you ; still I should just like to inquire (if you'll excuse my freedom), did you never chance to *dik* any of our sort of people on your travels ?"

John Roberts (falling headlong into Lementina's trap, "dik" being Romanes for "see").—" Yes indeed ; I always had a funny partiality for them ; and many's the time when I was quartered down at Portsmouth, I liked to go and have a chat with some of the Lees " (*this in a tone of interrogation*).

Silvanus.—" Oh, very good ; you did know some of the Lees then, did you ? Rather a rubbishy lot, they

Lees![1] Why, you might have seen the rale old
'riginals, Lovells and Ayres and Stanleys, by crossing
just over t'other side Southampton Water."

John Roberts (relieved).—" Well now, do you know,
but I was saying to myself that you were some of
the Lees yourselves."

Lementina.—"Oh, bless your heart, man, no. We're
nothing whatever to do with the *Júvlo-Gúne.*"

John Roberts.—" Ha! ha! ha! that'll be some
comical nickname that you've given them ; but, to
tell the truth, I never had much liking for those
Lees myself. There are a good many of them about
this country (very fair violin players), and one time
in May 1847 they came to a fair held in Llanfyllin,
Montgomeryshire, where I was keeping company with
an old Welsh harper called Evan Jones, in a parlour
at the Eagle Inn. I had a kinsman with me at the
time of the name of John, a skewer of a little fellow,
a playing the fiddle in the kitchen, when in comes
these Lees, and takes hold of the fiddle out of his
hands without asking leave. When all at once I
could hear my fiddle have a fall on the screen, and
made a great noise, that it attracted my ear to go
out of the parlour to see 'what was the matter, when I
could see John Wood holding one of the Lees with
his back on the fire. I went to separate them (but,

---

[1] Be it understood that I by no means endorse Silvanus's estimate
of the Púrums, being acquainted with many worthy members of that
black-faced, curly-locked family. IIe, too, referred not to the main
English, but to a minor Welsh branch of the tribe.

oh dear! e'er a one of them was fit to kill us both, if it was to come to that), and I tried to make friends between them as well as I could ; and through that it always used to make me to be afraid to go by a English Gipsy camp, as I used to think it might be some of them."

Alabīna. — " Sure that was my uncle, Eleazar's father ; and deárie Devél ! thinkesáva mi te kaía si váver kóko tei, dóva yek as rómer'd mi púroder bíbi. (*To John.*) And how did you leave your good lady, sir ? "

John Roberts. —" There, now you're making game in that funny gibberish of the poor old man, the oldest Welsh harper in the world at the present time ; and Mr Thomas Griffiths, the Prince of Wales's harper, is the next. But, ' my good lady !' Why, don't I set here, poor Pill Garlick, all by own dear self? and isn't it a beautiful young lady I'm wishing, and never able to find her, unless it's yourself will accept of the situation ? "

Lementina.—" Ay, sir ; that's the thing to do, sir. She'd better make up her mind to it at once, for very like she'll never have the chance again of taking such a nice young fashionable husband."

Thereat all laughed, Nathan and Alabīna leading off ; and through the laughter I threatened to " tell Perpínia," Perpínia being Mrs Roberts, mother of two daughters and twelve sons. And John, now making me out for the first time, remarked, that if they'd got that Wise Man with them, he gave

it up; so joined in the laughter, and entered upon
explanations.

"Really and truly," he assured them, "I made
certain you were some of the Lees; and they are
gentry I am always rather nervous of, because of
what I was telling you just now. But dórdi, dórdi!
who ever would have thought of falling in with kinsfolk so promiscuous like. Why, it isn't six weeks
that I met my cousin Feophilus in Brecon, when he
was telling me how two of his girls, Alabīna and,
I forget the other one's name (for I hadn't seen him
before since blessed goodness knows), were married
to two tiptop English Gipsy men, some of the Lovell
family; and my own mother's mother was a Stanley,
and everyone knows that Stanleys are kith to Lovells.
Oh dear! oh dear! what a story I shall have to carry
back to Newtown. But you were crafty, trying to
catch the poor old innocent man, noting his funny
bits of Romani way, but making as if he wouldn't
understand your _rók'raben_. And then Mr Groome
must needs come striking in, and spoils it all, just
when I meant to surprise you by bursting out: 'Shom
ma te penna to mengey ta Romano shom may, ta
mankey java mangey _away_, dava ma temen borro
parchyben _for_ te morro camlo drom ta sigaday
mangey cuddeyvess,'" &c., &c., &c.

The speech rolled forth with all the greater vigour
for having been long kept in, and its effect was really
considerable, especially on Silvanus, who followed it
better than the younger people. Its peroration

ended, Rodi said, " Now, my dear uncle, here have
you been sitting all this while, and we never as much
as offered you a bite of victuals, thinking of course you
were some fine gorgeous górgio, and would be above
eating with the likes of we. But what shall I make
you now a bit of something before you go to your
inn ? There's steak or bacon, and a nice few trout."

John's heart seemed set on a good plump Romani
hedgehog ; but, hedgehogs unluckily being out of
season, his demand called forth a little good-humoured
banter from the Lovells, and a lament from himself
over his fallen house-dwelling estate : " Whatever
would you have the old man know then, living stuck
up in four stone walls ? Often and often when I go
down the fields to take a stroll (which is near our
little house at Newtown), I am very near crying,
thinking how I am deprived of all my dear Romani
way, what I used to delight in when my poor old
mother was alive. Why, if you'll believe me, I would
sooner have tasted hedgehog again, than e'er a bit
of the very finest beef. However, just do me something the nearest way, though I'm downright shamed
to put you to so much inconvenience."

While this something was doing, the children
petitioned for a tune upon the harp ; Lancelot
brought it up from the gate, against which it was
leaning ; and John, as he stripped and tuned it,
recounted somewhat of his harping exploits. How
this particular harp was a very ancient one, " presented to him with a richly-engraved silver plate

affixed to it, bearing the names of Lady Florencia Hughes of Kinmel, Lady Buckley of Plas-yn-dinas, and other patrons, as a token of their esteem for his exertions in adhering to the national instrument of his country." How he had also carried off the Tredegar and other prize harps at the Abergavenny and Cardiff Eisteddfods ; and how he had " had the distinguished honour of playing by special request before His Majesty the King of the Belgians, His Grace the Grand-Duke Constantine, the Dukes and Duchesses of Bedford and Marlborough, and numerous other members of the Royalty, Nobility, and Aristocracy of Europe, England, and Wales." Then there were the triumphs of sons at ten different Eisteddfods, and the story how Johnny won only the second prize at Birkenhead last year, when " he ought to have had the first if he had fair play, for the one who played against him was a good player but made many mistakes, when my son did not make one, but played with better execution, better time, and with very marked expression. Which was plain to be seen that he was wrong dealt with by Mr J. Thomas ap Thomas, harpist to the Queen. And by Mr Thomas serving him so, I went there and then over to Liverpool, and challenged in the papers, that I would play him upon the real Welsh harp for any sum he would wish to mention ; but he was afraid to accept of my challenge, nor has he done it yet. For one thing, you will allow me to tell you quietly, that he is not able to do so. I could

say a great deal more upon that subject, but, to tell
you the truth of the matter, it's because we are
Romani Chals, and he wants to keep us under if he
can ; and as long as I know that he can't play the
Welsh harp, I shall try to stop him from judicating
upon it as long as I live."

This was lofty talk for lowly Romani tents, but the
strains that it preluded were loftier still. We had
them all—*The Bells of Aberdovey, Llwyn Onn, The
Rising of the Lark*, I know not what besides ; and
when he came to *The March of the Men of Harlech*,
our bard uplifted a lusty voice and sang :—

> "Around the hearth with noble cheer, the bowl of *meth* begun
>   the part,
> When deeds of warriors charmed the ear, and warmed the
>   Welshman's heart.
>   O'er his native mountains, with some noble chieftain,
>   For his Prince, his mighty Prince, his noble race for to
>   maintain,
>   He marches on with patriot's strides, relating tales of
>   Welshmen's tribes,
>   The deeds of old that charmed the ear, and warmed the
>   Welshman's heart.

> "England when to battle went the sons of liberty to save,
> She fought, she conquered, where she sent the sons of Britons
>   brave.
>   When the trumpet sounded, every heart rebounded,
>   Full of fire, that warlike fire, that every foe confounded ;
>   The deeds of honour valiant stood, reminding them of
>   their noble blood ;
>   They fought, they conquered, where she sent the sons of
>   Cymri brave."

"By Job," said Silvanus, "that's grammar ; and if I
could do as much as that, I'd wear a black coat too,
and a cocked hat atop of it. Scores on scores of

harp-players I've heard at fairs and races, but never a one could compromise to that.   It would be *thrum-thrum, thrum-thrum,* neither sense nor reason into it ; and the very next one I sees, I'll tell him put his instrument on his back and ·be off to Newtown, to take a few lessons off my uncle here.   You see, reía, I was bound to be right in what I was a telling you, it takes us Romané to larn the górgios anything."

This from Silvanus, after his late disparagement of harping, was praise indeed ; and the rest were yet louder in their approbation.   Of course they wanted more, and Nathan the Wise suggested *pennillions.* But it is not so easy both to sing and accompany *pennillions;* and the steak besides was in danger of growing cold, and Anselo had fetched up whisky from the inn.   So music gave place to ·supper, Lementina remarking that "one should not work the willing horse to death."

Chapter Seventh.

HEN John went off to his supper, the children fell to asking riddles, not modern conundrums, but good old-fashioned "sense-riddles," like the *zagádki* of the Russian peasantry. Ancient they must be; for who, without the leisure of Methuselah, could ever discover that "a nettle" is meant by "In the hedge, and out of the hedge, and if you touch it, it will bite you?" or that "Under water, and over water, and never touches water" signifies "a woman crossing a bridge with a pail of water on her head"? But the answers now-a-days are always known beforehand, and the children were charmed to find the Rei more ignorant than tiny Dona, who shouted "Blowbellows" to "The bull bulled it, the cow calved it, it growed in the wood, and the blacksmith made it;" and "Fiddle" to "It plays in the wood, and sings in the wood, and gets its master many a penny." "As I was a-going along the road one day, I met a man coming through the hedge with a lot of pins and needles on his back" was clearly

159

our Romani friend "the hedgehog;" but "a cherry"
was less obviously suggested by—

> "Riddle me, riddle me, red coat,
> A stick in his hand, a stone in his throat;
> Riddle me, riddle me, rōti tōt."

Stories succeeded riddles; and Leah led off with
"Happy Boz'll," well known to all Gipsies of the
Eastern Counties :—"Onest upon a time there was a
Rómano, and his name was Happy Boz'll, and he had
a German-silver grinding-barrow, and he used to put
his wife and child on the top, and he used to go that
quick along the road he'd beat all the coaches. Then
he thought this grinding-barrow was too heavy and
clumsy to take about, and he cut it up and made
tent-rods of it. And then his dickey got away, and
he didn't know where it was gone to; and one day he
was going by the tent, and he said to himself, 'Bless
my soul, wherever's that dickey got to?' And there
was a tree close by, and the dickey shouted out and
said, 'I'm here, my Happy, getting you a bit of stick
to make a fire.' Well, the donkey come down with a
lot of sticks, and he had been up the tree a week,
getting firewood. Well then, Happy had a dog, and
he went out one day; the dog one side the hedge,
and him the other. And then he saw two hares.
The dog ran after the two; and as he was going
across the field, he cut himself right through with a
scythe; and then one half ran after one hare, and
the other after the other. Then the two halves of
the dog catched the two hares; and then the dog

smacked together again ; and he said, 'Well, I've got 'em, my Happy ; " and then the dog died. And Happy had a hole in the knee of his breeches, and he cut a piece of the dog's skin, after it was dead, and sewed it in the knee of his breeches. And that day twelve months his breeches-knee burst open, and barked at him. And so that's the end of Happy Boz'll."

"That's a regular Lucas's tale," said Dimiti; meaning by Lucas a Romani Munchausen who flourished half a century ago, but is still remembered for his marvellous powers of romancing. And I capped " Happy Boz'll " with the Gipsy lying-tale from the Bukovina,[1] of the man who clambered up a willow-tree to heaven, and descended by means of a rope of barley-straw, which proving too short, he kept cutting off above and tying on below. Then Dimiti himself recounted the story of " Dootherum Jimmy," which deserves preservation only as being singularly widely-spread among our English Gipsies. Ask a Buckland of the south or a Herne of the north if he can tell the story ; he will answer, "Ay," and give it you in nearly these very words, pronouncing the *th* as *d*, whether he does so naturally himself or not :—

" Dere was an old Gipsy woman, and her name was old 'Licia Boswell. 'Old Galled-eye,' 'Licia used to be called ; and her had a fine son called Jim Boswell,

---

[1] Published in the original by Miklosich in part iv. of his *Beiträge zur Kenntniss der Zigeunermundarten* (Vien. 1878).

'Old Dootherum Jimmy;' and he had many fine sons
and daughters. So one day dere was a bit of *para-
mísin*"—canting or quarrelling ; Plato's παραμυθία,
argumentation—" between dem, as Spencer Lovell
and Cornelius Smith was going to fight. Jim's
daughter, named Genty, said to her father, 'Daddy,
ain't you going to see de men fight?' 'Ah, my
child, we'll go;' and dey went to see de men fight.
So when dey seed de one man knock de oder down,
Genty said, 'Dere, my daddy, dat is not fair; dey
will kill de poor child.' So den old Dootherum said
to Genty, 'Dere, my child, do you think I am going
to pick a thorn out of another man's hand, to put in
my own? I could eat and drink wid de man, and
toss him over the hedge de same time.' As de fight
was ended, so Jim and his daughter Genty went
home and had a good supper of dead pig. Dat is
what all Gipsies like, hedgehog and roasted potatoes."

"Yes, indeed," said Leah, " I wish I had some here;
but how would you go to cook a hedgehog, refa?"

"I can't say, Daughter; how would you?"

"Why, first take a stick and crawl him out; then
hit straight on the nose; then pitch him on the fire,
and let all the bristles be first burnt off. Then take a
knife, and scrape it nice and brown ; then cut open
the back, and wash it well; then put plenty of pepper
and salt inside. When all this is done, the hedgehog
is ready for cooking, which you can either boil or
roast it. It is very beautiful either way. And I'll
tell you another thing, refa ; it is very strange to see

how the hedgehog builds his nest. You would think now that the two companions would live together in one nest, but it is not so : the father has one nest all to himself, and the mother with all her young hedgehogs in another nest to herself. There is a regular path from one nest to the other, which any górgio might see thousands of times, and never know what it meant. The nest is made of grass and leaves very thickly put together ; and the strangest part of it is that they do not leave their nests during the winter-time. They have been found with all sort of birds, crab apples, and mice in their nests ; for they always pervide for the coming winter." [1]

"What's 'hedgehogs' in Romanes, brother?" Mantis asked.

"Why, *hótchiwitché*, I should rather think."

"Ay ; but there's another way you might put it— *Romané's baulé*, 'cause they are pigs the górgios can't deny us Gipsies. And *boúris*, snails—*Romani-górgios* they are, handsome-looking people ; for don't they live in walls like górgios, but always keep moving about like we ? "

"And a wren," added Christopher, "is a *chúvion*, witching bird, 'cause if ever you hear one chattering in the hedge close by the tents, you're bound to be drove from the place where you are stopping at. And a *táltordiro* is a crow ; and I can give you

---

[1] Leah knows more about hedgehogs than did White of Selborne, who "could never find that they stored in any winter provision."

something deeper than that, reía, and I'd lay a penny not one out of all you children can tell what a *fúlano chúmba* is. That's a blackbird, that is ; *muckheap*, don't górgios call it ? "

"Ah-h-h ! " galdered Dimiti ; " that's never no true word. You might say *kdulo chíriklo*, if you like now ; but what I'd like best would be another good long story." So I told them the *Master Thief*, as given by Constantinescu, with fourteen more Roumanian-Gipsy folk-tales. The original Romanes occupies eight pages, of which the following is merely an epitome.

A town thief once fell in with a country thief, and was challenged by him to steal the eggs from under a magpie without her noticing it. He achieved the feat, but during it was himself robbed unawares of his breeches by the other, with whom he then entered into partnership. They went to the King's treasure-house, and, making a hole in the roof, descended and stole two hundred purses of money. The King on the morrow, discovering his loss, took counsel with an old thief in prison, and by his advice found out the hole at which they had entered, by lighting a fire in the treasure-house and noting where the smoke escaped. Under this hole he set a great jar of treacle, in which next night the country thief was caught. To spite the King, he cried to his comrade, " Come and cut off my head, for I a dead man ; " so the King in the morning found only a headless corpse. " Hang it up on a gallows outside the gate," was the old thief's advice, "and set soldiers to watch it, for he that stole the head will come to steal the body also." Sure enough, the town thief, disguised as an old man, came driving by; and just as he reached the gallows, his waggon broke down, and a jar of drugged wine rolled out. The soldiers helped him, and for their trouble he let them have a drink, asking meanwhile what they had got up there. "A thief." "Hullo! I'm off then, else he'll steal my mare." "What a fool you must be, old fellow; how will he manage that?" "He will, though; isn't he a thief?" "Bah! he'll never steal her, he's dead; and if he does, we'll pay you for the loss." "All right, if that's the case." So the old man sat down by the watch-fire, and pretended [*lit.* made himself, just as with English Gipsies] to doze, while the soldiers finished the wine. It made them drunk; where they fell, they lay, without thought or heed of anything. Then the thief arose, put the corpse in his waggon, drove away to the forest, and buried it; then came back to the fire, leaving his waggon behind, and again pretended to sleep. In the morning the soldiers awoke, and seeing neither corpse nor waggon, wondered and said, "The old fellow was right, comrades, that the thief would steal his mare;" and they paid him four hundred piastres not to say anything about it. Other feats the thief performed; among them he stole away one of a yoke of oxen, and, cutting its tail off, put it hanging half out of the other ox's mouth. The owner came back and began to weep, when the King called him and asked what he was weeping for,

"Because, O King, while I was away at the play, one of my oxen has eaten up the other." Then the King laughed fit to kill himself, and promised the thief his kingdom and his daughter if only he would steal the priest out of the church. Then the thief went into the town, bought three hundred crabs and three hundred tapers, and going to the church where the priest was chanting, let out the crabs one by one, each with a taper fastened to its claw. "So righteous am I in the sight of God," sang the priest, "that he sends his saints to summon me. But how am I to go?" "Get into this sack," the thief answered; and the priest got in; and the thief drew the sack tight, and dragged it down the steps. *Tronk, tronk* went the priest's head against the steps; and the thief carried the sack to the King, and tumbled it down before him. The King burst out laughing, and there and then he gave the thief his daughter, and made him king in his stead.

Versions of this tale occur in *Strapparola* (Venice,[1] 1550), Dasent's *Tales from the Norse*, Campbell's *Tales of the Western Highlands*, and other collections. One, not the least curious, is given in vol. iii. p. 399, of Mayhew's *London Labour and the London Poor* (1851), as having been told by the boy inmate of a London Workhouse. Herodotus' story of Rhamp-

---

[1] Venice, one is reminded, as mistress of Corfu from 1386 to 1797, must have been the first Western State that was brought in close contact with Gipsies, one hundred of whom (children not reckoned in) have constituted the *feudum Acinganorum* in that island since 1370.

sinitus has often been called their prototype, and it is curious that the Gipsy and Gaelic versions resemble it far more closely than do the Italian, German, and Scandinavian. Nor can this resemblance be accounted for in the Gipsy as Campbell accounts for it in the Gaelic version, by supposing the Herodotean details to have been grafted on the folktale by some university scholar, since wherever the Gipsies got their stories from, it was not out of books.

Now, a noteworthy feature in Campbell's collection is the number of tales that he either obtained from, or found known to, Highland Tinklers ; from a London Gipsy he heard a version of *Oh, if I could but Shiver!* By itself the circumstance has no great value, since the stories belong to the " common stock of European folklore," and Gipsies in their wandering from the South-East to the uttermost West of Europe might well have picked them up, just as they picked up Greek and Slavonic, Magyar and German words. *Stĭfo-*, in *stĭfo-dad,* "father-in-law," of Anglo-Romanes, one readily refers to German *stief-*, because one knows that the forefathers of our Gipsies reached England by way of Germany ; but none would identify *ard,* "earth," of Syrian and Egyptian Romanes, with German *erde.* And so of Romani tales. If one heard Grimm's *Faithful John* from the mouth of an English Gipsy, one might reasonably class it with *stĭfo-* as a loan ; but how, when it is told by a Gipsy professional story-teller of Constantinople (Paspati, pp. 604-16), how when a Gipsy crone at Adrianople recounts the *Follower* of Ashbjörnsen, on which Andersen founded his *Travelling Companion* (*ib.*, pp. 600-4)?   Similarly, one meets in the Roumanian-Gipsy dialect with the *Valiant Little Tailor*, the *Twin Brothers*, the *Crows*, and other stories familiar to every folklore student.   Observe that these Gipsy stories can often be proved to be of some antiquity by their retention of old Romani words, and that variants of the same story have been obtained by different collectors, Miklosich's i. and xi. from the Bukovina corresponding to Constantinescu's xii. and iv. from Roumania.   Then ponder these statements relating to górgio folktales:—" They [*i.e.*, stories like Ashbjörnsen's No. 63] are as undoubtedly of Asiatic extraction, and they are as little affected by accidents of locality, as are the Gipsies, whose faces and figures at once betray the secret of their origin, however long they may have been naturalised in Western climes. . . . In every European land, however copious may be the references to its early religion preserved in the songs, the traditions, and the brief anecdotes current among its peasantry, the 'fairy-stories' which flourish along with them seem to afford but little information on the subject pointing, as they appear to do, to a different form of life, with strange doctrines and with alien gods " (Ralston, on " New Tales from the Norse," in *Frazer's Magazine*, Nov. 1872) ; and, " When the Empire had passed away, and with it the stock of literature which had satisfied the general craving, and the taste even for reading had degener-

ated, the want was supplied by professional story-
tellers, who, travellers by necessity, carried their
talents and repertories to all countries " (H. C. C. in
Notes and Queries, Feb. 1, 1880). Is it not possible
that these itinerant story-tellers were often Gipsies,
to whose late Asiatic origin our fairy-tales owe their
Asiatic type?

I ask the question, not to answer it myself, but to
submit it to folklorists' consideration. For one thing,
the Romani stories hitherto published are far too few
in number, and taken from too narrow an area, for
anyone to come to satisfactory conclusions. Friedrich
Müller's *Beiträge zur Kenntniss der Rom-Sprache*
(Vien. 1869) gives five from Hungary; Paspati's
Études sur les Tchinghianés (Constant. 1870) six from
Turkey; Miklosich's *Zigeuner* (Vien. 1874-78) sixteen
from the Bukovina, one from Roumania, and one from
the Hungarian Carpathians; and Constantinescu's
Probe de Limba si Literatura Tsiganilor (Bucharest,
1878) fifteen from Roumania. Dr Isidor Kopernicki
of Cracow has not yet published the thirty Romani
stories collected by him in Galicia (1875-77), so that
the above are almost the sum total of our available
materials; we are absolutely ignorant whether the
Gipsies of Scandinavia, Russia, Siberia, Armenia,
Syria, Egypt, and Persia, have similar tales or not.

From Catalonian Gitanos encamped near Paris in
1869, M. Bataillard obtained two legends, which he
communicated to me by letter. In one of them
Christ sends St Peter to find a sheep, and, bidding

him cook it, goes to heal a sick person, who rewards
him richly.   Peter begins by eating the sheep's
liver and kidneys ; and Christ, when he comes back,
asks where the liver and kidneys are, " for Jesus, who
is God, knows everything."   Peter replying that the
sheep had none, at the end of their meal Christ
divides into three heaps the large sum received from
the farmer whom he has healed.   " For whom are
these three heaps ? " asks Peter.   " Firstly, for each of
us," Christ answers ; " and then for him who ate the
kidneys."   " That was I," says Peter.   " Very well,"
Christ answers, " take my share too ; I return to my
own ; " and then it is that Christ takes the cross, &c.
" You see," the narrator ended, " that it was God
Jesus who at the beginning of the world (*sic*) founded
all the estates of men, first doctors, for he healed for
money ; and he it was who taught the Romani Chals
to beg and to go barefoot, while St Peter instructed
them how to deceive their like."   A curious story
this, thoroughly Romani in its application, yet clearly
identical with Grimm's *Brother Lustig*, and with *The
Pope with the Greedy Eyes* in Ralston's *Russian Folk-
tales.*   Compare, too, a legend in the latter collection,
of the Gipsy who learns of the Lord, through St
George's asking, that his " business is to cheat and
to swear falsely," so opens business by stealing the
Saint's golden stirrup.   The fellow to the Gitano
legend closely resembled it, as did others, told M.
Bataillard by Gipsies of Alsace, but never, unfortunately, taken down.

English Gipsies have no great store of folk-tales.
Mr Leland, in his *English Gipsies and their Language*
(1873), gives two Christ legends, the story of the
Seven Whistlers, and five beast fables, one of which,
accounting for the flounder's crooked mouth, I have
myself heard told about the plaice.   And one catches
an echo of forgotten stories in sayings such as " going
to heaven in a sack," "selling one's blood to the devil,"
" Get up, Seven Sleepers " (Silvanus' rousing cry ;
dormice being also so named), " The seven stars are
the Seven Gods," and, " What a face I've got, it
shines like Seven-Cheeks ! "   Welsh Gipsies, on the
other hand, are fairly rich in folklore, as I hope to
show briefly here, more fully hereafter ; though
whether their stories have anything distinctively
Gipsy about them is a difficult question that I leave
for critics to decide. " Come into my *tan*," words
spoken by a king, has certainly a Romani sound,
but *tan* may mean merely " place " as well as " tent ; "
and I would sooner lay stress on the episode where
the hero, lying down to sleep by the roadside, ties his
horse to his leg, that so it may not stray.   Still
harder were it to attempt to discover Romani features
in górgio tales ; I will only remark, that the common
request of a criminal to play one last tune on his
fiddle (*cf.* Grimm's notes on *The Jew among Thorns*)
is strongly suggestive of Macpherson's *Rant*, and that
the *Hedgehog's Race*, current both in Germany and
Northamptonshire, and alluded to in an old Greek
proverb, sounds very Gipsyfied.   I told it to Dimiti

once, and he instantly localised the field where it was run.

Such thoughts as these vexed not the Gipsy children, who, however, applauded my *Master Thief;* and the priest in it started Dimiti off on a legend, that certainly has no claim to Gipsy origin, though it reminds one of the Fisherman in the *Arabian Nights :*—

"It was at Chetwynd End, near Newport, just by the parson's house ; and there was a young lady, Miss Pigott, out hunting ; and the horse run up a great big sandy bank, and threw her off his back, and killed her. And they said she used to come night and day, and squeak awful. It got so terrible, that people couldn't go along the road for fear of her, but then they laid her, threw her into Chetwynd Pool. And somehow the bottle they'd put her in got broken (somebody skating, I think it was); and she come as bad again after that, and got jumping on the men's horses. It seems she would run after everything, carriages and all ; so long and by last they got twelve priestés, and they were all round a table with the bottle on it, and candles lighted all round. And they all begun to pray as hard as ever they were able, and they kept on till it seemed no mannerable good, and they were very near giving it up. But the oldest of them told them to stick to it, and their candles went out all but his ; and he prayed till the sweat dropped off his hair. All the rest, you know, were so afeard ; and if his candle went out, the devil would have fetched them, and

she would have scratted them all to pieces. Ay,
bor, and as fast as they lighted the candles, they
were blown out, all but this one; and the priest as
belonged to that, he prayed and prayed; and at last
they saw her come in between the candles, drawing
to the mouth of the bottle; and they kept on praying
hard as ever they could. Long and by last they got
her in. And then she begged of them not to be
thrown into the Red Seas; but the priest he wouldn't
hear of it. And so they threw her in, and the place
has been in quietness ever since. Why! you can
see the palings in the road, put in the wall right
again the pool where they laid her first."

"Ghosts and sarpents is things I can't abear,"
said Leah reflectively; "and Wanselo dreamed last
Monday night he swallowed a frightful sarpent, and
Granny said it was the devil, showing himself because
of my uncle's badness."

"Oh, because of his badness, was it? And have
you, Daughter, been troubled much by ghosts?"

"Not I, reía; for the only thing that ever I mind
of seeing I can't remember now. It was by Waltham,
and my mammy had been out (in the winter it was)
a long way round that day, and Christopher went
with her. I was a little one in her arms, a dear
little tiny baby. And coming back to the tents,
she had to go through the great big wood, and it
was that dark she couldn't see which way she was
going, and she'd been wandering about in the Forest
ever so long, got off the road you know. And at

last she come to one part of the wood where she had never been before, and they had to get over the hedge ; and just before she come to the hedge, in a open place underneath the trees, she saw standing what she thought was a man with a sheet thrown right over it, and no head on. She stood and looked at it for two or three minutes, and Chris saw it at the same time, but was too much scared to say a word ; and when they got over the hedge, my mammy asked him, Did he see it ? and he said 'Ay.' And then my mammy asked him if he thought he knowed what it was, and he said 'No ;' and she hurried back to the place as hard as ever they could get. And my daddy went down that way next morning, and couldn't see nothing."

"You never have seen nothing," said Dimiti, with some disdain ; "but if you want ghosts, refa, you go to Dosia ; she's the boy for ghosts. They were stopping onest in a lane by the Black Mountains, Gilderoy's breed was ; and there wasn't no houses there not for a long long way except one cottage. And Gilderoy was just pulling down the things, and a woman come by from working in the fields. It was towards evening, you know ; I daresay it would be about four o'clock. And she stood looking for some time before she spoke ; then she said, ' I wonder how you can stop in this lonesome place ;' and they asked her, Why ? ' Oh,' she said, ' there's supposed to be ghosts walk about this lane at night.' And they said, ' Oh, indeed !' And Gilderoy said,

'I daresay, woman, there's a good many live ghosts
walk about here ; but we don't mind 'em, we're used
to 'em.' Then she went on, never said no more. It
had been beautiful and fine all day, and then a wind
begun to get up, and it begun to rain. They made
their tents up, and had their supper, and then they
went to bed. I daresay it would be about seven or
eight o'clock when they went to bed. And about
midnight Dosia saw something get over the gate,
like an old woman ; and it come and stood close
by her tent, looking down upon her as she was lying
abed. And she stared at it for a long long time, and
at last she said, 'You wáfedi púri grásni [wretched
old jade], what are standing there for? Go away.'
There it stood, never took no notice, kept staring at
Dosia all the blessed while. Long and by last it
moved away towards her mother's tent, and they
heard a sort of groaning noise, come with the wind,
you know ; and all at onest a tremenjous gale of
wind tore right upon the place. Kiómi saw this old
woman (as they thought she was) standing just at
the front of their tent ; and then she waked up Old
Gilderoy, told him look what was that. And at the
same time they heard the ghost go away and say,
'I'll take the two, I'll take the two ;' and that very
instance Old Gilderoy and his son was dragged right
out of the place behind. They couldn't help themselves, they said ; and the tent was blown clean up.
And he said they couldn't stop themselves ; and she
got up to look, and found them lying breathless on

the ground some distance from the tent. And I
suppose they packed up 'mediately soon as it come
morning, and went off. They told some górgios
about it. Górgios said there had been a young
gentleman killed there not very long before ; he was
supposed to be very drunken, and the devil had
fetched him from leading a prodigal life. So they
never went back to that place, nor we never stopped
there neither."

Ruth and Starlína, weary of the elders' gossip,
had joined the younger story-telling circle, and were
watching my interest in Dimiti's ghost tale with a
look like that of the boy-librarian whom I asked one
day for Kingsley's *Water Babies*. " Perhaps you are
not aware that it is a mere child's book ? " the youth
inquired ; and Ruth seemed wondering what on earth
I could find in this children's rubbish, which yet, being
kindly, she was pleased to supplement :—

" It's perfectly true, my brother, every word of it ;
for we met the whole ruck of them only two days
after, and such a talk of it there was, you never saw
the like. We were stopping by the Black Mountains,
too, oh! a good way that time, but Gilderoy's were
right the other side, near to Dorstone ; and all of us
went to the Welsh Hay fair. What a beautiful day
it was, I remember ; and I was all in white muslin,
with a scarlet shawl ; and Trainette was there, dressed
up in green silks. And she got drunk—oh ! what a
spec she looked. That was the time when she was
going to fight the what's-his-name's wife, Abraham

Buckland's. He was playing in the same public
where we were, and she with a tambourine. And
my daddy and Old Gilderoy had been up the fair;
and Gilderoy had bought two little ponies, and my
daddy had sold an old mare. And we left the two,
and all we young people went down into the town
among the shows. We wasn't away very long; then
we turned back and went to the same public again.
My daddy and my Uncle Gilderoy was dancing, and
this Abraham Buckland was fiddling, and Old Gilderoy
with one shoulder higher than the other. This pretty
Buckland's wife used to be one of my daddy's sweethearts, you know; and then we all went in and sat
down, some dancing and some singing. And my
daddy and my Uncle Gilderoy sat up in a corner,
and my daddy begun to sneeze"——

"Ay," said Starlína, "we knew perfectly well what
was going to happen when he begun sneezing so, and
his eyes would twinkle; that's always old Chicken's
way when he gets a drop of cider into him."

"Sneeze most awful; and then they caught hold of
one another's hands, and begun talking how they used
to be when they were little boys, and about their father
and mother that was dead, and then they begun to
blubber as loud as ever they could. And all the fine
górgios staring, you know. And I told Plato and
Wisdom to take them out into the road, away from
the houses, you know. They were that drunk they
were obliged to be led all down the road; and my
daddy wouldn't walk with anybody, only catching

M

hold of Old Gilderoy's hand. It was like the Twins.
They opened their mouths more when they got out ;
bless us all, how those two did hoot ! And the pretty
hangman followed us some distance to hear what we'd
say ; and you might as well talk to the stones in the
road as talk to my daddy at that time. And then
they sat down side o' the bank ; and Trainette somehow was left behind in the public ; and when we went
back to look for her, she was standing up in the middle
of the kitchen, with a jug in her hand and her nose
bleeding, looking nine ways for Sunday. And Buckland's wife begun upon her, because Trainette told him
that she [Mrs Buckland] used to be my daddy's sweetheart. He went out crafty, and called a lot of górgios
in, and told the fine górgios to begin upon our young
men. They went out into the road, and stripped off
their coats ; and the same pretty hangman that followed us along the road come back again to the
public, and said if they didn't put their coats on
immediately, he'd take 'em all to prison. And then
we were obliged to go, out of the town altogether.
And then my daddy and my Uncle Gilderoy they
got much better while they were sitting out, and then
my daddy wished Old Gilderoy good-bye, blubbering
above a bit. Then we couldn't get a word out of my
daddy all the while after that ; never spoke, but just
kept boring on like some old hedgehog. That was
pretty well the last time I ever saw Old Gilderoy, and
I don't know how long ago that was, a goodish time.
Just as we were getting up by the mountains it come

on awfully misty, and Plato and Wisdom said they
w.eren't going on all in that rain, and they turned into
a barn. My daddy went on and left us behind; and
just on the top of the bank there was a big farm and
another old barn close to the road. And me and
Nathan and Loverin and Lancelot and Shuri and
'Lina, we all went in there; and it was so dark we
couldn't see what was inside. And I felt so dreadfully tired and sleepy, and Loverin dropped down
just inside, where there was not a bit of straw nor
nothing; and I lay down just by him, just at his
feet like. And the others were *gozveró* [artful], they
got where there was plenty of straw. Lord bless us!
what a fright I did get. I smelled some horrible
odour (and Loverin was as drunk as ever a pig),
and I felt something, I couldn't think what it was,
and I got up and strained my eyes to look. And
there! you can just fancy what a surprise I got, to
find that we were both lying on an old dead horse.
I started up and said, ' Oh *dórdi!* oh get up! we've
been lying on a *múlo grei.'* And when we went
into that barn first, we could scarcely scrawl; as
soon as ever they heared that, we were all out in a
moment, didn't even turn round to shut the door
behind us. Then we went on a little bit further,
and found my daddy sitting on the top of a gate
fast asleep. And we went into a shed close by,
where there were a lot of carriages, and got into
one of the carriages "——

"A little basket carriage," Starlína explained; "and

Lancelot and Nathan pulled it right out of the shed, and wheeled it up and down with all of us in it, and then the dog began to bark."

"And we made such a frightful row the fine gentleman came out, and asked us what we were doing there. 'Only resting a bit, Sir;' and he said he thought we'd better be off. Then we went on again, and got my daddy off the gate with a deal of grunting; but the best of it was my daddy had lost his coat, he had no coat on. Then we went on up the road, as ill-tempered as anything, never spoke to each other all the way, but kept walking in the hedge. And then we turned out of the road to cross the hills; and again' we got up them, we couldn't find the way, we lost ourselves. And we were going round and round the same corner all night long, not a bush nor nothing to shelter one from the rain; and soon as ever it begun to get morning, we saw that all the while we hadn't really been very far from the tents. And we were just like drownded rats for all the world; and when Plato and Wisdom come back to the tents, how they did laugh at us, said, What fools we were to go racing on, that we might have turned back with them. And next day, you know, it turned out most beautiful and warm."

"You forgot," said Starlína, "how, to encourage us my daddy would keep on saying to me and Shuri, 'Come on, old mares;' but it wasn't very encouraging, and *dórdi!* I was angry, frightful. It's a mercy we didn't all catch our death o' colds by that, but we

felt quite well, only dreadfully sleepy.   And that was
the last time ever I was at the Hay fair."

"Well, yes; that would almost be enough.   But
what had your daddy done with his coat, then?"

"Oh, chucked it down anywheres.   He's such a
funny old Chicken, whenever he get the leasest spot
to drink.   But tell the rei, Ruth, about how when
Lance was born."

"When Lance was born? why, we were stopping
at a place called the Links by Hinstock, and my
daddy was playing at the Cock.   My mammy had
been out calling that very day ; then she came home
and was feeling very bad, got worse and worse.   My
daddy had never been at home all day ; I think it
was the Gawby Market.   And then about one o'clock
Patience woke up me and Wisdom (I don't know
where Nathan was, I think he was with Gilderoy's
breed), to go up the road and meet my daddy.   And,
you know, my daddy might have come the other road
for all we could tell ; and we neither of us had any
shoes or stockings on, and no hats.   Up the road we
went whistling, because we were afraid of the ghosts.
It was a very bright starlight night, quite frosty ; and
we went on up till we got to the bend of the road, all
shivering and shaking, and sat down under the hedge
on a big round stone.   We never ceased whistling,
and waited there a short time till my daddy came
puffing and blowing up the road.   We told him to go
after the *dívi gaíri* [lit. mad wife].   He said we were
to go back, and gather some sticks to make a fire, and

I mind how we tore down the hedges, Wisdom and me, as we went down the road. And again' we got to the place Lancelot was born. The little dog we had then was out at the back of the tents, catching rats. Poor old Spot, from morning to night she was at those ponds. But when my daddy left us, he went off as hard as he could go ; and the new velvet coat he had got on, with silver buttons, pulled it off and pitched it in the road, and left it there till he came back. He had very hard work to drag the old woman along the road, she was that fat ; and he was back to the tents before she was. And when she come, all she did was to drink a bottle of brandy, and then lie down and go to sleep."

"And another time," Ruth went on, "we were stopping by Tenbury, at the Owd Measter's ; and it was on a Saturday, and my daddy said he'd walk up as far as the Lion. That was a public, on the top of the hill, about three miles from the place. He took his fiddle, and my mammy went out calling quite a different road (Gilderoy's breed and Perun's breed was with us). And when my mammy come home, we were waiting a good while, thinking my daddy would be back before we had our supper. Then when we saw he didn't come, we had it ; and my mammy kept on saying (she sat up a good long time), '*Mistügga!* where can the man be to?' and about twelve o'clock she heard him come singing along the road, in a way, you know, about *My Nan*.

Never any more, only just that. And just before he got to the tents, there was a little farm close to the side of the road, and the garden was just to the side of the road too, a little low hedge. It was just when the new onions and the new potatoes was just coming about like; and he had on a big brown velveteen jacket, with two great deep coat-pockets inside. And he stumbled over this little hedge into the garden, and stuffed both his pockets full of young onions, cabbages, lettuces, and potatoes. Then he took out his fiddle out of the bag, and filled that too. He cleared the whole of one little square bit of plot like; and my mammy couldn't see when he come, whatever he had got, and he emptied them every one out close down to the tent. Then he forgot all about them, till my mammy minded him next morning. And there was an old thick ash tree close to the place, with the inside burnt out; and when he saw what a lot there was, he clambered up and put them all inside, so that he could take them out just as we wanted any. And the pretty górgios made a row about it, and said to my mammy, ' I'm sure it's some of you Gipsies been into my garden' (he had knocked all the bank down); and my mammy said, ' No, ma'am, we weren't this way that night.' ' Oh,' she said, ' but I heard the dog barking;' and that same day that she was telling my mammy about it, my daddy and one of the boys went up to the house playing, and bought a donkey."

" Why, Ruth, you turn your stories out as glibly

almost as Dimiti, though you were laughing at my listening to his just now."

" I wasn't laughing, my brother; only you did look rather comical, perched up among the little children, as though you were playing cat's-gallows or sugar-candy."

" Sugar-candy! what's that ? "

" Now, didn't I say so ? You to have gone roaming about these years and years like a Wandering Jew, and never know what sugar-candy was ! "

" Not I; except as a sweetmeat."

" You show him, Daughter ;" and Leah began with all due gravity, suiting her action to her exposition :—

" Put your two hands on the top of one another, like that, reſa, and then somebody else puts theirs on the top of yours. And then you ask them what's in their hands, and they say Sugar, or anything, or dirt. Then you say, 'Take it off, or I'll knock it off;' then if they don't, you knocks it off—so. Then they ask you what's in your hands ; and you say anything, you know, it doesn't matter what, pudding perhaps. Then they say, ' Where's my part ? ' ' The cat's got it.' ' Where's the cat ? ' ' The dog's killed it.' ' Where's the dog ? ' ' Run into the wood.' ' Where's the wood ? ' ' The fire burnt it.' ' Where's the fire ? ' ' The water squenched it.' ' Where's the water ? ' ' The oxen drunk it.' ' Where's the oxen ? ' ' The butcher's killed 'em.' ' Where's the butcher ? ' ' Be-hind the church door, cracking nuts. You shall

have the shells, and I'll have the kernels.' That's
sugar-candy, reía."

"Oh, that's sugar-candy, is it? It bears a strong
family likeness to the pig-driving old woman who
couldn't get home to-night; and it strikes me forcibly
that neither shall I get home to-night, unless I look
sharp about it. Why it's half-past ten now."

"I don't care if its twenty," Anselo answered; "and
there you speak like a górgio, brother, having to get
back home. The night's young yet, and the time
that Pyramus joined us at Llangefni we never went
to bed at all till morning, and then were up again by
eight, or sooner. But sometimes we'll go to bed, even
in summer-time, about half-past six, when its broad
daylight, so you can fancy what a long time it is to
lie. And yet we sleep, and the górgios 'll come by in
the morning about eight or nine o'clock. There they
find some of us with our black heads sticking out
underneath the tent-blankets fast asleep, and they'll
say, ' Why, you lie abed till deäy, till the sun burns
your eyes out.' Or they'll say, ' Hanna ye gotten
oop yet?' And then sometimes my daddy will rise
up quite early in the mornings, and go off and look
for the things (neddies and that), and bring sticks to
the place, and often he'll have two or three hedgehogs. When he comes back and finds us still
sleeping, he'll be awfully angry, and he'll rip the
tents down, pull 'em right down."

"Yes, but often," said Starlína, "when I've been
walking all day, and am tired, then we come late at

night to a place; and when we've had our supper
and gone to bed, I often get up again in my sleep,
not the slightest notion what I'm doing. There I'll
be sitting, gaping at nothing in the darkness; then
when I wake up, I find that I'm pulling my bed
all about, trying to make it again. Often it will be
at places where górgios say there's ghosts to be
seen; and when I remember where I am, I'll be
awfully frightened. Then I get back into the things
anyhow, never trouble; cover my head over, then I
am all right."

Now was Ruth's time, from her vantage-ground of
eight years' seniority, to take a sorrowful retrospect
of bygone days. "Ah," she observed, "you're young,
girl, very young, and can hardly mind when there'd
be a whole lot of us stopping together, and the beds
would be made quite early like in the evenings, and
some of the boys used to put nettles and stones into
the others' beds. Then when we found it out, we'd
go and pull their beds all about, throw the things all
about the road, amidst a good deal of laughing and
jumping about. Then we used to have battles with
the blankets; and often when we'd got into bed,
we'd go to sleep for a short time, then get up, and go
and play about till we tired again. And my daddy
would always call us Hellhound's Breed, say we'd
walk about all night. Then very likely we'd be
going a long way the next day, and then my daddy
would say, 'I'll take pity on you to-morrow, I will.
You'll grunt all along the road, you'll never be able

to walk.' Then we wouldn't mind him one bit, we'd make as much row as ever we could ; then we'd get on the neddies, and ride them up and down the road. And you know Dilli at that time was more than thirty years of age, and she was quite as bad as any of the rest. And then my daddy would get frightfully angry, when we'd ride the neddies about. He'd get up with a bit of stick, and say, 'Stop a bit, I'll make you knock my poor dumb animals about.' Then the moment we'd see him coming, we'd be off. Then he'd shake his fist at us down the road, and say he'd give it us as soon as ever we'd come back. And so we'd keep on all night long ; even when we were in bed, we'd be never asleep scarcely, giggling and laughing. We'd ask one another riddles, then there'd be an explosion of laughing from all the places ; then my daddy would burst out laughing too at something that had been said to amuse him. Then Old Marchy she'd begin and laugh, and then Old 'Lijah would say very likely (he'd be wanting to sleep), 'De good talkers, dey will talk all night.' Then Old Marchy would be heard saying to him, 'Old Sal Shaw shall get his sleep, if nobody else does.' We'd try, you know, and stop ourselves from laughing, and silly things *would* come into your mind, make you laugh. Ah, well! poor Old 'Lijah sleeps sound enough now ; but they were something like merry times ; there's nothing like that now."

"No, dere's nothing like dat now," mocked Dimiti ; "why, my Aunt Ruth, you puts me in mind of Old

Munch-it yourself, you do. Ha! ha! ha!" and his laughter proved that, changed as the times might be, laughter at least was no lost Romani art.

"Was Old Marchy," I asked, frowning the scoffer down, "that little old woman who was with you when you were stopping on Chester race-ground, the first time we met, you know? She asked me for some tobacco, and I gave her a couple of cigars, and I remember she told me the Romanes for *a pail.*"

"Yes, that was my granny, Margery Pétuléngro. Really, you know, she was my mammy's grand-mother, but we children always called her so; and I was her favourite out of all our lot, used to travel with them for months and months together. Once I mind I went to stay with her by Newnham, when my great-grandfather had been dead about two months; and she knew an awful lot of people about there, gentlemen and ladies. There was one rei, a Mr George Badcock, who had got all her money, and kept it for her, oh! for a long time. And while I was there, they asked us to come and spend Christmas Day with them. *Dôrdi!* I thought it a great thing; I had never been in such a grand big house before. The lady sent me a hat, a nice hat; and my old granny cut up a black silk dress, and made one for me out of it, all frilled and flounced, and a little black silk Indian shawl. *Dôrdi!* and I thought I looked so smart. And she had a black silk dress on too, and one of those old-fashioned red silk Indian shawls,

and a yellow silk handkerchief round her neck.   And
then when we went along the road, I was walking on
before her, and she said all at once, 'Walk straight,
child, don't stoop so ;' and she'd say, 'Watch me.'
And there she'd walk along the road like a ramrod
for all the blessed world.   Then we got to where
there was a little bridge acrost the road, and a little
brook running down ; and she told me a story about
a man hanging himself there ; and I remember how
dreadfully 'fraid I was ; and whenever after I'd go
that way by myself, I'd walk with my eyes shut.
Then we went up to the house, to the front door,
and the lady and the gentleman come out; there
was a deal of shaking hands and wishing Merry
Christmas.   Then my old granny said to the rei,
' I wish ye a Merry Christmas, George.'   'Same to
you, Margery ;' then we were taken into the drawing-
room.   Then the lady begun talking to me, and I
forget all what she said, it being such a long time
ago ; but I stared about above a bit.   Then the
little young lady come in, and the lady told her to
take me into the garden ; and there was a little
wooden horse with a lot more broken dolls and
things, thrown underneath the bushes ; and I know
I was awfully pleased to look at them and play
with them.   Then we soon got great friends, played
about, and was quite happy, till we were called in
to the dinner.   And, dórdi! what roast beef and
plum puddings ; I never saw such a lot of victuals
in all my life.   Then after dinner the gentleman

asked my granny to go and have a smoke with him; ay, I remember the long black pipe that she took with her in her pocket. There they sat and smoked for a long while, and talked about my grandfather. And sometimes she'd cry, and then sometimes she'd laugh."

"I suppose you can remember quite well what your great-grandfather was like?"

"Dear me, yes; he was very black, and he always wore spectacles. And when he went out to see gentlemen, he'd always dress up, and he'd always wear a high hat. He used to say he never wore it, only when he went to see the company. And he'd always wear gloves too, brown ones; I should say it was to match the colour of his flesh. I remember once when my daddy and my mammy was angry with me (I think it was for breaking a plate, I'm not sure, a china plate), and I started off; it was about two miles and a half where I went, and I was quite a little tiny thing. I knew where my granny was stopping; it was on a Sunday. And before I got to the place, I saw my grandfather in the road with the horses; sitting under the hedge he was. And when he saw me, he got up and stood in the middle of the road, and held his arms open, for me to run in as though I was a rabbit. So I did, and clung round his neck. And then he carried me right down to the place; he kept talking to me all the while, and asking what they'd been doing. And how I used to be so pleased to get my mammy's doll to play with for two or three minutes. I was never allowed to have it for very long, for it was one that my mammy had when she was a little wench—a beautiful old-fashioned doll, one of these made of morocco, and it wore blue earrings, and a cap with artificial flowers in it and oh! such beautiful gowns, made of old-fashioned silks, pieces of my granny's frock. My mammy's great-aunt bought it to her, for my grandmother died when my mammy was quite a baby, and so Old Marchy had always had the bringing up of her. And when Old Marchy died, my mammy got her doll again, and she admired it then just as much as ever, I suppose. She seemed as if she did, and I asked her for it, and she wouldn't give it to me. And she dug a hole in the ground, and put the doll in it, and set it on fire, and burnt it all to bits. Then covered the hole over."

"But you never told me how your visit to this great gentleman's came to an end."

"Oh, Squire Badcock's! The lady put a lot of things, victuals and that, into a great basket; and it was late at night when we got back home, and the lady said I was to call every time I went by there. And so I did, but very seldom that I saw the lady. The pretty servant girls would come out, and say that she wasn't in."

"So that was your great-grandmother. A very deep old woman she seemed to have been; though, when I saw her, she was half childish. I suppose that her husband's death was a terrible shock to her."

· "Ay, she'd sit down on a little low stool at the
bottom of the waggon, and always the pipe was for
ever in her mouth; and she'd rock herself to and
fro, and always call him by his name. 'Ay,' she'd
say, 'my poor old man;' and then the moment she'd
hear any one playing (the boys or any one), she'd say,
'Ah, you'll never play like your grand-dad.' And,
I suppose, when she was young, she was a most
splendid player on the tambourine, and a capital
dancer; and every morning, soon as ever she'd get
up, she'd call me to kneel down by her and say my
prayers, after her reading out of a great big Bible;
and she'd never touch a morsel of anything till she'd
said her grace, and she'd never cook anything on
Sunday.   And all the great gentlemen at the big
houses all about knew them so well, they'd always
allow him to go and shoot anywhere about their fields,
and once he was asked out (pigeon-shooting it was,
you know) to Squire Cootes's of Cooton Hall, and a
good many of the fine gentlemen said he was the best
shot that was there.   Great people they were there
about that time for pigeon-shooting.   And then he
used to go to these houses at Christmas; he used to
play the harp, you know, but different to that one [*i.e.*
John Roberts'], and dulcimer; and he was liked
everywhere, and now the górgios would talk about
him just the same.

"And the night before he died, he dreamt that
he was making baskets, and that he'd finished them
all but one.   And that's quite true.   He had been

making a basket the day before, and it wasn't finished.
Then he thought he was out picking mushrooms
with a lot more górgios, and the mushrooms turned
to frogs, and jumped out of the basket ; and then
he thought he was *práster'd* [pursued] by the fine rei
that owned the field. And every word and thought
that he dreamt came true. Next morning about six
o'clock two fine górgios come up to the waggon, and
asked him if he wouldn't go along with them to get a
few mushrooms, about three miles out from the place
where they were stopping. He said, 'No, he wasn't
going to be bothered going ; ' and they said, ' Oh,
you'd better come ; it'll be a nice walk.' It was on a
Sunday morning. He said, ' I've got nothing to put
'em in, if we got any ; ' so then he thought him of the
basket that wasn't finished. And he got up, and
dressed himself, and left my granny still abed. They
went off to this field where the mushrooms grew, and
the fine rei that owned the field was, oh ! such a
rogue ; nasty, cruel man he was. Well, they'd only
just got three or four, when they saw the fine rei
coming across the field. He'd been up, watching the
mushrooms all night long, because it's a great country
off there for poachers. Atkins his name was, and
he *was* an Atkins. And my grandfather knew him
perfectly well, always been good friends, you know.
But he saw him with these other fine men, and he
shouted them to stop (of course they begun to run,
you know), said if they didn't stop he'd shoot at
them ; he had his gun. These two fine górgios were

N

much younger men than my grandfather, they could
get on much quicker, and they got over the gate ; it
was a good way on. And just as my grandfather
was getting over the gate, the fine rei come up, caught
him by the skirt of his coat. And he made himself
he didn't know my grandfather, said, if he didn't stop
and go with him, he'd shoot him there and then.
And he would have done it, such an unbominable
rascal. And my grandfather told him, said he
thought he never would have done such a trick as
that, and him knowing him so well, all for the greed
of a few mushrooms. My grandfather then said he'd
give him his name and where he was living and all, if
he wanted to summons him, you know. No, he said,
it wouldn't do ; he _would_ take him. My grandfather
said, Well, he'd see whether he could take him or no ;
and he got himself free, and started off, just two or
three yards from the gate, and dropped down dead.
And soon as ever the fine rei saw that, he shouted to
the two górgios to come back and help him to get
him round. They thought he was in a fit, you know ;
but he was quite stiff when they turned him over on
his back. Then they carried him on a hurdle to a
public, called the Blacky Boy, in the road ; and the
doctor was sent for, of course ; but it was no good, you
know. And the doctor said he'd died in a 'plectic
fit and heart-disease together. _Dórdi!_ it seems so
funny. Ay, and then the górgios took the news to
my granny, about nine o'clock in the morning. She'd
been waiting for him, with the breakfast ready ; and

when she heard that, I suppose she was in a most dreadful state, must have been.   She never lived very long after ; and that same pretty rei drove us out of the road once, wouldn't let us stop, and my mammy shouted to him, told him that he'd killed my grand-father.   He said, ' If he had done it, he didn't mean to do it ;' and then my mammy said, ' Die whenever you will, the devil is safe of you.'   And by all accounts he used to be in a frightful state ever after, got a sort of mad like, and always fancied he saw somebody coming to try and kill him.   Long and by last he shot himself."

Said Anselo, "He wanted shooting;" but the others sat hushed and awestruck by this tragedy of their great-great-grandfather, which will seem to my readers but an ancient vagabond's untragic exit. Presently, half crying, Ruth went on :—

"Last time we saw him, we'd been in the village, and that was our way back past their waggon ; and my mammy wanted to ask him for some money, and he gave her £15.   Then we stopped and had some tea with them ; and my grandfather had a pair of glasses on then, I mind, and breeches and leggings (he always wore breeches and leggings).   And he was looking very queer like ; and when we went away, he walked up a little bit with us, and talked about how he hadn't been feeling very well and that, and then he said to my mammy, ' Good-bye, my wench, you may never see me again,' just like that.

And he sat down with his back against the wall, and watched us as we went."

"Feyther, the Gipsies ha' got no souls," said a Staffordshire wench one day, at sight of a passing company of Gipsies. As a woman she married Polias Taylor; but that is neither here nor there, her remark serving merely to account for the quick-returning laughter of these children, who within two minutes were clamouring for "another story, reía."

"No, Leah, my stories are all done for to-night; but, if you will not follow Maggie's example, and go to your beds, 'like gude douce bairns,' you should ask old Roberts yonder for a tale."

'I'd *hing* [scorn] to be like your white-faced barns; but that old man, reía, him that was playing on that big thing, I shouldn't say as he knows many stories."

"Try him; he's fuller of them than an egg of meat, can spin them out for you by the yard together. Just go and ask him, 'Komós mé túki te péna bíta storíos?' and see what he will say."

"Hullo! that's funny Róm'nimus," said Christopher, "something like my daddy's in a shop at the Red Town [Reading] onest. He asked the fine shopman what some shirts were, and he told him two and threepence; and my daddy says to my mammy, 'Two-and-threepence'*us* cheap-*asar!*' thinking the górgio wouldn't understand him."

"All right, Christopher; only wait till you hear

this dear little *storlos*, and then you shall tell me what it's all about."

So Leah went off to proffer her request, and I followed her to see how it was taken. My motive in having thus left John to himself, was simply some knowledge of Gipsies' besetting weakness, a foolish jealousy, namely, which, had I seemed over-glad at his coming, or talked with him to the apparent neglect of my hosts, would have stopped their ears to his cunningest harping and most mellifluous discourse. To his face they would have treated him with decent courtesy, but, as soon as his back was turned, one would have carped at his looks, another at his manners, a third at his conversation; nay, they might even have called him górgio and no true Romani Chal, to such lengths can jealousy transport its subjects.

But, as it was, here sat John in his glory, lovingly hobnobbing with Silvanus, whose eyes were certainly twinkling, although he had not yet sneezed. They had plunged into endless genealogies, dear to your Gipsy as to any dowager, and had proved their cousin-ship in at least six different ways. Already John must have run over the four children, twenty grand-children, fifty-four great-grandchildren, and two hundred and odd great-great-grandchildren of Abraham Wood, the founder of the chief Welsh Romani clan, who "came up into Wales about one hundred and fifty years ago or thereabouts," and was "buried at a lonesome quiet little place by the seaside, on the road from Towyn to Dolgelly, in a church that's not been used for a church as long as I can remember." For when I strolled up, he was speaking of the Ingrams, who "with the Woods were the first as came to Wales. And the first place they took a liking to, on account of rivers and other things, was near Llanidloes, Llanbrynmair, and in the neighbourhood of Machynlleth; and near Aberystwith some of them bought little estates, and others took to travelling. The Ingrams lived near Llanidloes, and the Woods near Llanbrynmair. They were supposed to be in possession of abundance of gold, when taking these places; they were thought gentlefolks of in those days. But my great-grandfather Abraham, and Sarah his wife, still went about from one *granza* or building to another, for he liked the country so well that he would rather travel it than to stop in one place, after he came to find it out that the people were so kind, and that he liked the country food, rough as it was. They were getting plenty of fishing in those days, and the women would have no occasion to go only to a house or two, until they would be loaded with plenty of beef and bacon and flour and potatoes and—— From whence comest thou here, sweet child, like some dark angel as dropped down suddenly out of the blue skies?"

Leah was the object of this most bardic apostrophe, which so dumbfoundered her, that after all I had to act as spokesman, explaining that the children wanted a story, but hinting withal that the Cross

Foxes was, or would soon be, closed against him for the night.

"Bed, quotha, and inn!" said John, with huge disdain; "No, reía; which I am proud to reflect that I am addressing a gentleman of your superior talent, who has penetrated that deep into our mysteries as you have, but it is no Cross Foxes will ever see me tonight, nor yet the best-natured foxes going. *Romano Chall shom ma popalay*, that is to say, I am a Gipsy man once more; for by the leave of my respected kinswoman here (if I may take the pleasure of calling her so), it is my aim and intentions to sleep abroad this night in the luxuriant bed which her goodness allows me in her most elegant two-wheeled carriage."

"Bravo, John! Your name, in fact, is Macgregor, and your foot is again upon your native heath. I applaud your sentiments; only mind that your nightcap there keeps out the cold, and don't get choked by its strings like somebody (I forget his name) in the Commonwealth. But, such being your arrangement, you will probably have no objection to favour us with one of your dear little *storíoses*, to pass away the time and keep these clamourers quiet."

None in the world, provided it was agreeable to present company; and, the company unanimously assenting, a candle in a cleft stick (a veritable candlestick) was stuck in the ground where it would cast its light on the face of the story-teller, who without further prelude suddenly dashed off:—

"*Wel*, a conaw java te pena bita tatchanno *storee*os

temengay. Adoi ses trin meeray chavay yeck dives,
ta chingarenes kitaness ta potchenes boot colla vaver-
kengey. Yek kovva ses ta potchday any ses
mizzaben te mōrel chorey bitey chereklay. Ow
poradare pall pendas, Awa, ta basavo kova ses. Ta
ow vaver pal potchdas any ses mizzaben te maren
kanney. Ow tarnadare pall pendas, Nau, na ses kek,
te kindas la ta pesardas lakey. Chotchey yeck pall,
' So te veses apray ow borro doreyav undray bear-
estey, ta borro bavval te pordel tot na joneses kek
kai, so keses talla ? ' " &c., &c.

Pindar read by a modern Greek to an English
scholar, or Browning to a Yorkshireman by a
Devonshire ploughboy, may give some notion how
unintelligible was this story to the Lovells, though
hardly one word or form in it was strange to them.
Silvanus nodded and looked wise, but prudently said
nothing; and Anselo, who had listened open-eyed
and open-mouthed, answered my question what it was
all about with " How should I know, being I ain't no
scholard, but I'd swear there was something about a
fish and scolding. And talk of scolding, it was worser
than Rodi when she's on with Wisdom." Even Rodi
asked John to " Give us another, do, my uncle, something lively, not in that old-fashioned talk as none of
us young folks knows two words you're saying."

" Well, well ! " he said ; " I'll do my best not to ; but
I'm bound to put some of our talk in somewhere,
before it will come quite good. What do you say, refa,
to that story I sent you in the letter last October ? "

Yes, that would do famously; and here I give it from John's own MS., translating word for word the Romanes, in which all the dialogues and some part of the plot were written.

"JACK AND HIS GOLDEN SNUFFBOX.

"Once upon a time there was an old man and an old woman, and they had one son, and they lived in a great forest. And their son never saw any other people in his life, but he knew that there was some more in the world besides his own father and mother, because he had lots of books, and he used to read every day about them. And when he read about some pretty young women, he used to go mad to see some of them ; till one day, when his father was out cutting wood, he told his mother that he wished to go away to look for his living in some other country, and to see some other people besides them two. - And he said, ' I see nothing at all here but great trees around me ; and if I stay here, maybe I shall go mad before I see anything.' The young man's father was out all this time, when the conversation was going on between him and his poor old mother.

"The old woman begins by saying to her son before leaving, ' Well, well, my poor boy, if you want to go, it's better for you to go, and God be with you.' —(The old woman thought for the best when she said that.)—' But stop a bit before you go. Which would you like best for me to make you, a little cake and to bless you, or a big cake and to curse you ?' ' Dear,

dear!' said he, 'make me a big cake. Maybe I shall be hungry on the road.' The old woman made the big cake, and she went on top of the house, and she cursed him as far as she could see him.

"He presently meets with his father, and the old man says to him, 'Where are you going, my poor boy?' when the son told the father the same tale as he told his mother. 'Well,' says his father, 'I'm sorry to see you going away, but if you've made your mind to go, its better for you to go.'

"The poor lad had not gone far, till his father called him back; when the old man drawed out of his pocket a golden snuff-box, and said to him, 'Here take this little box, and put it in your pocket, and be sure not to open it till you are near your death.' And away went poor Jack upon his road, and walked till he was tired and hungry, for he had eaten all his cake upon the road; and by this time night was upon him, as he could hardly see his way before him. He could see some light a long way before him, and he made up to it, and found the back door and knocked at it, till one of the maidservants came and asked him what he wanted. He said that night was on him, and he wanted to get some place to sleep. The maidservant called him in to the fire, and gave him plenty to eat, good meat and bread and beer; and as he was eating his refreshments by the fire, there came the young lady to look at him, and she loved him well and he loved her. And the young lady ran to tell her father, and said there was a pretty young man in the back kitchen; and immediately the gentleman came to him, and questioned him, and asked what work he could do. He said, the silly fellow, that he could do any-thing. (Jack meant that he could do any foolish bit of work, what would be wanted about the house.)

"'Well,' says the gentleman to him, 'at eight o'clock in the morning I must have a great lake and some of the largest man-of-war vessels sailing before my mansion, and one of the largest vessels must fire a royal salute, and the last round break the leg of the bed where my young daughter is sleeping on. And if you don't do that, you will have to forfeit your life.'

"'All right,' said Jack; and away he went to his bed, and said his prayers quietly, and slept till it was near eight o'clock, and he had hardly any time to think what he was to do, till all of a sudden he remembered about the little golden box that his father gave him. And he said to himself, 'Well, well, I never was so near my death as I am now;' and then he felt in his pocket, and drew the little box out. And when he opened it, there hopped out three little red men, and asked Jack, 'What is your will with us?' 'Well,' said Jack, 'I want a great lake and some of the largest man-of-war vessels in the world before this mansion, and one of the largest vessels to fire a royal salute, and the last round to break one of the legs of the bed where this young lady is sleeping on.' 'All right,' said the little men; 'go to sleep.'

"Jack had hardly time to bring the words out of

his mouth, to tell the little men what to do, but what it struck eight o'clock, when Bang, bang went one of the largest man-of-war vessels ; and it made Jack jump out of bed to look through the window ; and I can assure you it was a wonderful sight for him to see, after being so long with his father and mother living in a wood.

"By this time Jack dressed himself, and said his prayers, and came down laughing ; because he was proud, he was, because the thing was done so well. The gentleman comes to him, and says to him, ' Well, my young man, I must say that you are very clever indeed. Come and have some breakfast.' And the gentleman tells him, ' Now there are two more things you have to do, and then you shall have my daughter in marriage.' Jack gets his breakfast, and has a good squint at the young lady, and also she at him.

(However, I must get on again with my dear little story.)

"The other thing that the gentleman told him to do was to fell all the great trees for miles around by eight o'clock in the morning ; and, to make my long story short, it was done, and it pleased the gentleman well. The gentleman said to him, ' The other thing you have to do'—(and it was the last thing),—' you must get me a great castle standing on twelve golden pillars ; and there must come regiments of soldiers and go through their drill. At eight o'clock the commanding officer must say, ' Shoulder up.' ' All right,' said Jack ; when the third and last

morning came and the three great feats were finished,
when he had the young daughter in marriage. But,
oh dear! there is worse to come yet.

 "The gentleman now makes a large hunting party,
and invites all the gentlemen around the country to
it, and to see the castle as well. And by this time
Jack has a beautiful horse and a scarlet dress to go
with them. On that morning his valet, when putting
Jack's clothes by, after changing them to go a hunting, put his hand in one of Jack's waistcoat pockets,
and pulled out the little golden snuffbox, as poor
Jack left behind in a mistake. And that man opened
the little box, and there hopped the three little red
men out, and asked him what he wanted with them.
'Well,' said the valet to them, 'I want this castle to
be moved from this place far and far across the sea.'
'All right,' said the little red men to him; 'do you
wish to go with it?' 'Yes,' said he. 'Well, get up,'
said they to him; and away they went far and far
over the great sea.

 "Now the grand hunting party comes back, and
the castle upon the twelve golden pillars disappeared,
to the great disappointment of those gentlemen as
did not see it before. That poor silly Jack is
threatened by taking his beautiful young wife from
him, for taking them in the way he did. But the
gentleman is going to make a 'greement with him,
and he is to have a twelvemonths and a day to look
for it; and off he goes with a good horse and money
in his pocket.

"Now poor Jack goes in search of his missing
castle, over hills, dales, valleys, and mountains,
through woolly woods and sheepwalks, further than
I can tell you to-night or ever intend to tell you.
Until at last he comes up to the place where lives
the King of all the little mice in the world. There
was one of the little mice on sentry at the front
gate going up to the palace, and did try to stop
Jack from going in. He asked the little mouse,
'Where does the King live? I should like to see
him.' This one sent another with him to show him
the place; and when the King saw him, he called
him in. And the King questioned him, and asked
him where he was going that way. Well, Jack told
him all the truth, that he had lost the great castle,
and was going to look for it, and he had a whole
twelvemonths and a day to find it out. And Jack
asked him whether he knew anything about it; and
the King said, 'No, but I am the King of all the
little mice in the world, and I will call them all up
in the morning, and maybe they have seen something
of it.'

"Then Jack got a good meal and bed, and in the
morning he and the King went on to the fields;
and the King called all the mice together, and asked
them whether they had seen the great beautiful castle
standing on golden pillars. And all the little mice
said, No, there was none of them had seen it. The
old King said to him that he had two other brothers:
'One is the King of all the frogs; and my other

brother, who is the oldest, he is the King of all the
birds in the world.   And if you go there, maybe
they know something about it' (the missing castle).
The King said to him, 'Leave your horse here with
me till you come back, and take one of my best
horses under you, and give this cake to my brother;
he will know then who you got it from.   Mind and
tell him I am well, and should like dearly to see
him.'   And then the King and Jack shook hands
together.

"And when Jack was going through the gates, the
little mouse asked him, should he go with him; and
Jack said to him, 'No, I shall get myself into trouble
with the King.'   And the little thing told him, 'It
will be better for you to leave me go with you;
maybe I shall do some good to you some time
without you knowing it.'   'Jump up, then.'   And
the little mouse run up the horse's leg, and made it
dance; and Jack put the mouse in his pocket.

"Now Jack, after wishing good morning to the
King, and pocketing the little mouse which was on
sentry, trudged on his way; and such a long way
he had to go, and this was his first day.   At last
he found the place; and there was one of the frogs
on sentry, and gun upon his shoulder, and did try
to hinder Jack not to go in; and when Jack said to
him that he wanted to see the King, he allowed him
to pass; and Jack made up to the door.   The King
came out, and asked him his business; and Jack told
him all from beginning to ending.   'Well, well, come

in.' He gets good entertainment that night; and in the morning the King made a curious sound, and collected all the frogs in the world. And he asked them, did they know or see anything of a castle that stood upon twelve golden pillars; and they all made a curious sound, *Kro-kro, kro-kro*, and said, No.

"Jack had to take another horse, and a cake to his brother, which is the King of all the fowls of the air; and as Jack was going through the gates, the little frog which was on sentry asked John should he go with him. Jack refused him for a bit; but at last he told him to jump up, and Jack put him in his other waistcoat pocket. And away he went again on his great long journey; it was three times as long this time as it was the first day; however, he found the place, and there was a fine bird on sentry. And Jack passed him, and he never said a word to him; and he talked with the King, and told him everything, all about the castle. 'Well,' said the King to him, 'you shall know in the morning from my birds, whether they know anything or not.' Jack put up his horse in the stable, and then went to bed, after having something to eat. And when he got up in the morning, the King and he went on to some fields, and there the King made some funny noise, and there came all the fowls that were in all the world. And the King asked them, Did they see the fine castle? and all the birds answered, No. 'Well,' said the King, 'where is the great bird?'

They had to wait then for a long time for eagle to make his appearance, when at last he came all in a perspiration, after sending two little birds high up in the sky to whistle on him to make all the haste he possibly could. The King asked the great bird, Did he see the great castle? and the bird said, 'Yes, I came from there where it now is.' 'Well,' says the King to him, 'this young gentleman has lost it, and you must go with him back to it; but stop till you get a bit of something to eat first.'

"They killed a thief, and sent the best part of it to feed the eagle on his journey over the seas, and had to carry Jack on his back. Now when they came in sight of the castle, they did not know what to do to get the little golden box. Well, the little mouse said to them, 'Leave me down, and I will get the little box for you.' So the mouse stole himself in the castle, and had a hold of the box; and when he was coming down the stairs, fell it down, and very near being caught. He came running out with it, laughing his best. 'Have you got it?' Jack said to him; he said, 'Yes;' and off they went back again, and left the castle behind.

"As they were all of them (Jack, mouse, frog, and eagle) passing over the great sea, they fell to quarrelling about which it was that got the little box, till down it slipped into the water. (It was by them looking at it and handing it from one hand to the other, that they dropped the little box in the bottom of the sea.) 'Well, well,' said the

frog, ' I knew as I would have to do something, so
you had better let me go down in the water.' And
they let him go, and he was down for three days and
three nights; and up he comes, and shows his nose
and little mouth out of the water; and all of them
asked him, Did he get it? and he told them, No.
' Well, what are you doing there then ?' ' Nothing at
all,' he said, ' only I want my full breath ;' and the
poor little frog went down the second time, and he
was down for a day and a night, and up he brings it.

"And away they did go, after being there four
days and nights; and after a long tug over seas and
mountains, arrives at the old King's palace, who is
the master of all the birds in the world. And the
King is very proud to see them, and has a hearty
welcome and a long conversation. Jack opens the
little box, and told the little men to go back and to
bring the castle here to them ; ' and all of you make
as much haste back again as you possibly can.'

"The three little men went off; and when they
came near the castle, they were afraid to go to it, till
the gentleman and lady and all the servants were
gone out to some dance. And there was no one left
behind there, only the cook and another maid with
her. And it happened to be that a poor Gipsy
woman, knowing that the family was going from
home, made her way to the castle to try to tell the
cook's fortune for a bit of victuals, was there at the
time ; and the little red men asked her, Which would
she rather, go, or stop behind ? and she said, ' I will

go with you;' and they told her to run upstairs quick.
She was no sooner up and in one of the drawing-
rooms, than here comes just in sight the gentleman
and lady and all the servants; but it was too late.
Off they went at full speed, and the Gipsy woman
laughing at them through the window, making motion
for them to stop, but all to no purpose.

"They were nine days on their journey, in which
they did try to keep the Sunday holy, by one of the
little men turned to be the priest, the other the clerk,
and third presided at the organ, and the three women
were the singers (cook, housemaid, and Gipsy woman),
as they had a grand chapel in the castle already.
Very remarkable, there was a discord made in the
music, and one of the little men run up one of the
organ pipes to see where the bad sound came from,
when he found out it only happened to be that the
three women were laughing at the little red man
stretching his little legs full length on the bass
pipes, also his two arms the same time, with his
little red night-cap, what he never forgot to ʾwear,
and what they never witnessed before, could not
help calling forth some good merriment while on
the face of the deep. And, poor things! through
them not going on with what they begun with, they
very near came to danger, as the castle was once
very near sinking in the middle of the sea.

"At length, after merry journey, they come again to
Jack and the King. The King was quite struck with
the sight of the castle; and going up the golden stairs,

wishing to see the inside, when the first one that
attracted his attention was the poor Gipsy woman.
And he said to her, 'How are you, sister?' She
said to him, 'I am very well; how are you?' 'Quite
well,' said he to her; 'come into my place, to have a
talk with you, and see who you are and who your
people are.' The old Gipsy woman told him that
some of her people were some of them from the
Lovells, Stanleys, Lees, and I don't know all their
names.

"The King and Jack was very much pleased with
the Gipsy woman's conversation, but poor Jack's time
was drawing to a close of a twelvemonths and a day;
and he, wishing to go home to his young wife, give
orders to the three little men to get ready by the
next morning at eight o'clock to be off to the next
brother, and to stop there for one night; also to pro-
ceed from there to the last or the youngest brother,
the master of all the mice in the world, in such place
where the castle shall be left under his care until it's
sent for. Jack takes a farewell of the King, and
thanks him very much for his hospitality, and tells
him not to be surprised when he shall meet again
in some other country.

"Away went Jack and his castle again, and stopped
one night in that place; and away they went again
to the third place, and there left the castle under his
care. As Jack had to leave the castle behind, he had
to take to his own horse, which he left there when he
first started. This King liked the Gipsy woman well,

and told her that he would like if she could stay there with him ; and the Gipsy woman did stay with him until she was sent for by Jack.

"Now poor Jack leaves his castle behind and faces towards home ; and after having so much merriment with the three brothers every night, Jack became sleepy on horseback, and would have lost the road if it was not for the little men a-guiding him. At last he arrived, weary and tired, and they did not seem to receive him with any kindness whatever, because he did not find the stolen castle ; and to make it worse, he was disappointed in not seeing his young and beautiful wife to come and meet him, through being hindered by her parents. But that did not stop long. Jack put full power on. Jack despatched the little men off to bring the castle from there, and they soon got there ; and the first one they seen outside gather sticks to put on the fire was the poor Gipsy woman. And they did whistle to her, when she turned around smartly and said to them, ' *Dordi !* *dordi !* how are you, comrades ? where did you come from, and where are you going ?' 'Well, to tell you the truth, we are sent to take this castle from here. Do you wish to stop here, or to come with us ?' ' I would like better to go with you than to stay here.' ' Well, come on, my poor sister.'

"Jack shook hands with the King, and returned many thanks for his kingly kindness ; when all of a sudden the King, seeing the Gipsy woman, which he fell in so much fancy with, and whom he so much

liked, was going to detain the castle until such time
he could get her out ; but Jack, perceiving his intentions, and wanting the Gipsy woman himself for a
nurse, instructed the little men to spur up and put
speed on. And off they went, and were not long
before they reached their journey's end, when out
comes the young wife to meet him with a fine lump
of a young SON.

"Now, to make my long story short, Jack, after com-
pleting what he did, and to make a finish for the poor
broken-hearted Gipsy woman, he has the loan of one
of his father-in-law's largest man-of-wars, which is
laying by anchor, and sends the three little men in
search of her kinsfolk, so as they may be found, and
to bring them to her. After long searching they are
found, and brought back, to the great joy of the
woman and delight of his wife's people-in-law, for after
a bit they became very fond of each other. When
they came on land, Jack's people allowed them to
camp on their ground, near a beautiful river; and the
gentleman and ladies used to go and see for them
every day. Jack and his wife had many children,
and had some of the Gipsy girls for nurses ; and the
little children were almost half Gipsies, for the girls
continually learning them our language ; and the
gentleman and the lady were delighted with them.
And the last time I was there, I played my harp for
them, and got to go again."

Story-telling is a rare and evanishing art, possessed

by John Roberts in a high degree. He suits both
voice and gesture to his words, which, however they
may read, proved, on this telling, a brilliant hit,
the children clearly " only half believing" them, and
Lementina observing admiringly, that sure he must
have a bag somewhere in which to carry all those
hideous lies.

"That's like my poor old mother," John made
answer; " and she was a real type of Romani women.
Often when my father would be telling us children
some funny bit of a story, she did say to him, ' Dere!
dere! what an old man it is to make people to
believe dem *hückabens!*' Oh dear! oh dear! how it
carries me back to my young days to find myself
sitting by a good Romani fire, with those beautiful
large tents, and everything else that is suitable. Just
how it was when I was a lump of a boy; and I did
use to like to go and see if the horses and donkeys
would be all right in the morning, and gather myself
a good armful of sticks before breakfast, and to hear
the birds whistling, and the smoke from the fire
curling up to the sky, and one of the girls singing
going for water, and the young men getting their
fishing-tackle ready, and the beautiful stream below
'bounding with some nice trout. And at night-time
we would have a good fire, singing and dancing
from the górgios; and, after they would go away,
we would burn down the stumps until it would
come to a red fire, and then the smokers would pull
out the pipes and tobacco, and begin to tell for the

best story. And then, when the old people would
get tired and go to bed, we would stop a little after
them, and begin to look at the moon and the stars
how beautiful they shone; and we would ask one
another, 'Who made the stars?' One said, 'The
same as made the moon, you silly.' 'Well, who
made the sun, then?' They all give it up. One said,
'It made itself.' One said, 'How can that be?' and
then that one would say it was too hot for any one
to go near it to make it. We would keep on that
way all night if we were left alone. And where are
they gone to now? Some to the churchyard, and
some of them beyond seas, and I, poor old Romani
man, *am* left alone, stoved up in four stone walls."

Again Silvanus nodded, more drowsily than wisely
now; the children had dropped off one by one to
bed; and John himself was to be up betimes, to play
for a wedding at Clywedog Mill. He would see us
again on Sunday, as he would be staying in Dolgelly,
where I promised to meet him after morning service.
Meanwhile I advised him to get to his "elegant
carriage," not sit up star-gazing, for moon and stars
were hidden by coming storm. Big drops were
falling as I crossed the meadows; and, passing the
dairy with its water-driven churn, I came to the farm,
there went to bed, and dreamed that I wandered with
the Scholar Gipsy, who asked me the Romanes for
frying-pan.

Chapter Eighth.

ATURDAY came, hueless with vapour of driving rain, that blotted out the hills. No chance of a bathe this morning, and I lay abed till after the postman's call, then, descending to breakfast, found a small pile of letters on the table. Among them was one from X., who, knowing my "craze for Gipsies," enclosed some newspaper cuttings, and hoped they might strike deep roots. X. is himself rather more than crazy about Rosicrucianism, so I let his taunt pass, and digested his cuttings slowly with my oatcake. Then I smoked a pipe over them, scribbled a few notes on them, and finally, with them in my pocket, started again for the tents. The Lovells had breakfasted two hours and more, for John's convenience, and Wisdom and Lancelot had joined him company; but the others were most of them in, and, whether it was their late downlying or early uprising, the weather, or all combined, seemed low and out of sorts, Silvanus only excepted. Lucretia was "on" again about the dog, "yowling and tootering all the blessed night;" even

Lementina grumbled at the "poverty, witching rain, come for a purpose," just when she meant to have called at Madam Morgan's.

"Stop, ma'am, I'll get a palace for you to live in, and a weather-glass in the best parlour; the lady shall always have it fine and delightful, not one spot of wet to spoil your 'plexion. For all the world, reía, like a drove of unsatisfied pigs;" and Silvanus winked at me with gay philosophy.

"Ah! you're too much like toad's breed, you are; thinks every one should be the same. You're"— but I dammed the waters of contention by offering to read them something from the papers, the promise of brighter days in store. And I read, mouthing the words that I have here italicised :—

"GIPSY CHILDREN.

"TO THE EDITOR OF THE 'STANDARD.'

"SIR,—Some years since my attention was drawn to the condition of these poor neglected children, of whom there are many families eking out an existence in the Leicestershire, Derbyshire, and Staffordshire lanes. Two years since a pitiful appeal was made in one of our local papers asking me to take up the cause of the poor gipsy children; but I have deferred doing so till now, hoping that some one with time and money at his disposal would come to the rescue. Sir, a few weeks since our legislators took proper steps to prevent the maiming of the little show children who are put through excruciating practices to please a British public; and they would have done well at the same time, if they had taken steps to prevent the warping influence of a vagrant's life having its full force upon the tribes of little gipsy children, dwelling in *calico* tents, within the sound of church bells—if *living under the body of an old cart, protected by patched coverlets*, can be called living in tents,—on the roadside, *in the midst of grass, sticks, stones, and mud;* and they would have done well if they also had put out their hand to rescue from idleness, ignorance, and heathenism, our roadside arabs, *i.e.*, the children living in vans, and who attend fairs, wakes, &c. Recently I came across some of these wandering tribes, and the following *facts*, gleaned from them, will show that missionaries and schoolmasters have not done much for them. Moses Holland, *who has been a gipsy nearly all his life*, says he knows about two hundred and fifty families of gipsies in ten of the Midland counties, and thinks that a similar proportion will be found in the rest of the United Kingdom. He has seen as many as ten tents of gipsies within a distance of five miles. He thinks there will be an average of five children in each tent. He has seen as many as ten or twelve children in some tents, and not many of them able to read or write. His child of six months old—with his wife ill at the same time in the tent—sickened, died, and was 'laid out' by him, and it was also buried out of one of those wretched abodes on the roadside, at Barrow-upon-Soar, last January. When the poor thing died he had not sixpence in his pocket. In shaking hands with him as we parted, his face beamed with gladness, and he said that I was the first who had held out the hand to him during the last twenty years. At another time, later on, I came across Bazena Clifton, who said that she had *sixteen* children, *fifteen of whom are alive*, several of them being born in a roadside tent. She says that she was married out of one of these tents; and her brother died and was buried out of a tent at Packington, near Ashby-de-la-Zouch. This poor woman knows about three hundred families of gipsies in eleven of the Midland and Eastern counties, and has herself, so she says, four lots of gipsies travelling in Lincolnshire at the present time. She said she could not read herself, and thinks that not one gipsy in twenty can. She has travelled all her life. Her mother, named Smith, of which there are not a few, is the mother of fifteen children, all of whom were born in a tent. A gipsy lives, but one can scarcely tell how ; *they generally locate for a time near hen-roosts, potato camps, turnip fields, and game preserves.* They sell a few clothes lines and clothes pegs, but *they seldom use such things themselves. Washing would destroy their beauty.* Telling fortunes to servant girls and old maids is a source of income to some of them. They sleep, but in many instances *lie crouched together, like so many dogs, regardless of either sex or age.* They have blood, bone, muscle, and brains, which are applied in many instances to wrong purposes. To have between three and four thousand men and women, and eight or ten thousand children, classed in the Census as vagrants and vagabonds, roaming all over the country, in ignorance and evil training, that carries peril with it, is not a pleasant look-out for the future ; and I claim, on the grounds of justice and equity, that if these poor children, living in vans and tents and under old carts, are to be allowed to live in these places, they shall be registered in a manner analogous to the Canal Boats Act of 1877, so that the children may be brought under the compulsory clauses of the Education Acts, and become Christianised and civilised as other children.

" I am, Sir, your obedient servant,

"GEORGE SMITH.

"COALVILLE, LEICESTER, *August 12, 1879.*"

" Hold hard, Silvanus ; that's only No. 1. Wait till you hear the next, which is as much more interesting as it is longer and more learned :—

" SIR,—The numerous correspondents who have taken upon themselves to reply to my letter that appeared in your issue of the 14th inst., and to show up gipsy life in some of its brightest aspects, have, unwittingly no doubt,

thoroughly substantiated and backed up the cause of my
young clients, *i.e.*, the poor gipsy children and our roadside
arabs, so far as they have gone, as a reperusal of the letters
will show the most casual observer of our *hedge-bottom
heathens* of Christendom. At the same time, I would say
the tendency of some of the remarks of your correspondents
has special reference to the adult gipsies, roamers and
ramblers; and, consequently, there is a fear that the attention of some of your readers may be drawn from the cause
of the poor uneducated children, *living in the midst of sticks,
stones, ditches, mud, and game,* and concentrated upon the
'guinea buttons,' 'black-hair'd Susans,' 'red cloaks,' 'scarlet
hoods,' the cunning craft of the old men, the fortune-telling
of the old women, the 'sparkling eyes' and 'clapping of
hands' and '*twopenny hops*' of the young women, who
certainly can take care of themselves, just as other un-
Christianised and uncivilised human beings can. I do not
profess—at any rate, not for the present—to take up the
cause of the men and women *ditch-dwelling* gipsies in this
matter, I must leave that part of the work to fiction-writers,
clergymen, and policemen, abler hands than mine. I may
not be able, nor do I profess, to understand, the singular
number of the masculine gender of *dad, chavo, tieno, morsh,
gongeo, racloo, raclay, pal palla;* the feminine gender *dai,
chai, tieny, jovel, gongell, raclee, racya, pen penya;* or the
plural of the masculine gender *dada, chava,* and the feminine gender *daia, chaia;* but, being a matter-of-fact kind of
man—out of the region of romance, fantastical notions,
enrapturing imagery, nicely-coloured imagination, clever
lying and cleverer deception, beautiful green fields, clear
running rivulets, the singing of the wood songster, bullfinch,
and wren, in the midst of woodbine, sweetbriar, and roses—
with an eye to observe, a heart to feel, and a hand ready to
help, I am led *to contemplate*, aye, and *to find out* if possible,
the remedy, though some of my friends say it is impossible
—just because it is impossible it becomes possible, as in the

canal movement—for the wretched condition of some eight
to ten thousand little gipsy children, whose home in the
winter is *camping half-naked in a hut*, so called, in the midst
of '*slush*' *and snow, on the borders of a picturesque ditch* and
roadside, winterly delights, Sunday and weekday alike. The
tendency of human nature is to look on the bright side of
things ; and it is much more pleasant to go to the edge of a
large swamp, lie down and bask in the summer's sun, making 'button-holes' of daisies, buttercups, and the like, and
return home and extol the fine scenery and praise the rich-
ness of the land, than to take the spade, in shirt-sleeves and
heavy boots, and drain the poisonous water from the roots
of vegetation.   Nevertheless, it has to be done, if the 'strong
active limbs' and 'bright sparkling eyes' are to be turned
to better account than they have been in the past.   It is
not creditable to us as a Christian nation, in size compared
with other nations not much larger than a garden, to have
had for centuries these *heathenish tribes* in our midst.   It
does not speak very much for the power of the Gospel, the
zeal of the ministers of Christ's Church, and the activity of
the schoolmaster, to have had these *plague spots* continually
flitting before our eyes, without anything being done to effect
a cure.   It is true something has been done.   One clergyman, who has 'had opportunities of observing them,' if not
brought in daily contact with them, tells us that some eight
or nine years since he publicly baptised two gipsy children.
Another tells us that some time since he baptised many
gipsy children ; as if baptism was the only thing required of
the poor children for the duties and responsibilities of life
and a future state.   Better a thousand times have told us
how many poor roadside arabs and gipsy children they have
taken by the hand to educate and train them, so as to be
able to earn an honest livelihood, instead of '*cadging*' *from
door to door*, and telling all sorts of silly stories and lies.
*How many poor children's lives have been sacrificed at the
hands of cruelty, starvation, and neglect, and buried under a*

clod without the shedding of a tear, it is fearful to contemplate.
The idlers, loafers, rodneys, mongrels, *georgies*, and gipsies
are increasing, and will increase, in our midst, unless we put
our hand upon the system, from the simple fact that by
packing up with wife and children and 'taking to the road,'
he thus escapes taxes, rent, and the School-board officer.
This they see, and a 'few kind words' and 'gentle touches'
will never cause them to see it in any other light. The
sooner we get the ideal, fanciful, and romantic side of a
vagrant's and vagabond's life removed from our vision, and
see things as they really are, the better it will be for us.
For the life of me, I cannot see anything romantic in *dirt,
squalor, ignorance, and misery*. Ministers and missionaries
have completely failed in the work, for the simple reason
they have never begun it in earnest; consequently, the
schoolmaster and School-board officer must begin to do
their part in reclaiming these wandering tribes; and this can
only be done in the manner stated by me in my previous
letter.

"I am, Sir, your obedient servant,

"GEORGE SMITH.

"COALVILLE, LEICESTER, *August 20, 1879.*"

I ceased, and looked around upon the dirt, squalor,
ignorance, and misery before me. Sticks—a small
stack of them stood outside the tent; stones—there
were walls, loose boulders, mountains, indeed, of
stone; grass—ay, a meadow-full of grass; and mud
—yon road assuredly was muddy. There was game
on the hills and fish in the river, so that only a
ditch was lacking in the picture; but ditches are
rare in Wales, and laziness sometimes hinders swine
from finding a wallowing-place exactly to their liking.
The squalor of the tents (odd that they were formed

of calico, and why not under the bodies of old carts?)
you know, dear reader; of the tent-dwellers' ignorance
you may have gained some notion. But how did
the hedge-bottom heathens, the plague-spots, look?
Conscience-stricken? Why, they looked much as you
or I might look on reading a libel upon ourselves
and families, written by no mere enemy, but by an
enemy we deeply scorned. This in itself was proof
of heathendom; yet after all it might be conscience
that kept them thus silent, fixed, and quivering. To
break which silence I asked Silvanus what he had
got to say.

Nothing apparently. He simply stooped and picked
up Lementina's teapot, an old-fashioned oddity, which
chinamaniacs might have fondled, but which here
stood poked among the glowing embers. He picked
it up and hurled it against the opposite stone wall,
remarking quietly, "There's your teapot all to atoms,
Lementina, and"—(with an outburst)—"I wish to
mi-Dúvel George Smith's head were into it." Then
the old man fell to a passion of sobbing; Lementina,
with a grim consenting smile, said, "*Mishto*, Israel!"
and the rest broke forth into tumultuous din. One
dominant wish seemed to possess them all, "to see
the man as had gone and made that letter," and pray
him doubtless not to neglect *their* cause. Their
words were earnest, heathenishly forcible; and I
think had I preached a crusade—pilgrimage, I should
say—to Coalville, the hills would have rung with their
Romani *Deus vult.*

But I, alas! was in no preaching humour. The gem-collector who learns that his big diamond is paste, the connoisseur who is shown " *Smudge pinxit* " on his priceless Turner, such were faint types of my discomfiture. I was like the changeling whose vision, opened by baptismal waters, sees Elfland stripped of all its faery glamour, dead leaves for garlands, cobwebs for cloth of gold. My Elfland from boyhood had been this Little Egypt, a region of lotos, mirage, and enchantments, whose crocodiles had seemed to me to weep, whose *júvas* for me had been no worse Third Plague than plaguey Cleopatras. Suddenly there had met me a Cook's excursionist, with telescope and *Highflying Dutchman's Guide ;* and I looked through his glass, and read in his book, and lo! my Nile became a ditch, the Pyramids mudheaps, dog Anubis a mongrel, the hieroglyphics cadgers' marks, the fleshpots—Faugh!

Others at least had been as blind as I ; and if one is to fall into a ditch, it is as well to have a leader on whom to fall. And kicking in this ditch lay Dr Bright (of " Bright's Disease " celebrity), the Rev. J. Crabb, " Lavengro,"[1] Samuel Roberts, " Hans Breitmann," and many another worthy man, but blind.

---

[1] I always supposed this word to be of Mr Borrow's coining, till I came in Grellmann on " *Latshila Wingro* [*i.e. látcho lavéngro*], falsch." *Nomen omen*, Mr George Smith might say. So I cite not Borrow; but whoso will may refer to the strong distinction drawn between tent-dwelling *Chorodies* (tramps) and Gipsies, in his *Romano Lavo-Lil*, pp. 266-75.

Take a few specimens of their blindness, they may
not be utterly uninstructive.

"For my own part," Bright sums up, "I have not
been able to discover all those marks of natural and
inherent depravity in the Gipsy character which have
been so obvious to others; and I am confident that
we are apt to appreciate much too lightly the actual
happiness enjoyed by this class of people, who,
beneath their ragged tents, in the pure air of the
heath, may well excite the envy of the majority of the
poor, though better provided with accommodation, in
the unwholesome haunts of the town. . . . What
renders this history [the Trial of Elizabeth Canning]
more valuable, is the great difficulty which, in general,
opposes itself to the gaining a correct insight into
their manners. No sooner does a stranger approach
their fire on the heath, than a certain reserve spreads
itself through the little family. The women talk to
him in mystic language,—they endeavour to amuse
him with secrets of futurity,—they suspect him to be
a spy upon their actions,—and he generally departs
as little acquainted with their true character as he
came. Let this, however, wear away; let him gain
their confidence, and he will then find them con-
versable, amusing, sensible, and shrewd; civil, but
without servility; proud of their independence; and
able to assign reasons for preferring their present
condition to any other in civilized society. He will
see them strongly attached to each other, and free
from many cares which too frequently render the

married state a source of discontent. At the approach of night, they draw around their humble but often abundant board, and then, retiring to their tent, leave a faithful dog to guard its entrance. With the first rays of morning they again meet the day, pursue their various occupations ; or, rolling up their tent, and packing all their property on an ass, set forward to seek the delights of some fresh heath, or the protection of some shaded copse. I leave it to those who have been accustomed to visit the habitations of the poor in the metropolis, in great cities, in country towns, or in any but those Arcadian cottages which exist only in the fancy of the poet, to draw a comparison between the activity, the free condition, and the pure air enjoyed by the Gipsy, and the idleness, the debauchery, and the filth in which a large part of the poorer classes are enveloped."—*Travels in Lower Hungary* (Edinb., 1818), pp. 528–30.

Crabb's *Gipsies' Advocate* (3d ed., Lond., 1832) is less extravagant, the following being among its wilder statements :—" Fifty years ago, from the paucity of carriers, the Gipsies were considered by the peasantry and by small farmers as very useful branches of the human family (p. 23). . . . Most of the Gipsies in this country are very punctual in paying their debts. All the shopkeepers with whom they deal in these parts, have declared that they are some of their best and most honest customers (p. 27). . . . They are not generally subject to the numerous disorders and fevers common in large towns ; but in some instances

they are visited with that dreadful scourge of the
British nation, the typhus fever, which spreads
through their little camp, and becomes fatal to some
of its families. The smallpox and measles are disorders they very much dread ; but they are not more
disposed to rheumatic affections than those who
live in houses. It is a fact, however, that ought not
to be passed over here, that when they leave their
tents to settle in towns, they are generally ill for a
time. The children of one family that wintered with
us in 1831 were nearly all attacked with fever that
threatened their lives (p. 31). . . . The mutual attach-
ment which subsists between the nominal husband
and wife is so truly sincere, that instances of infidelity
on either side occur but seldom ; and when otherwise,
the parties are deemed very wicked by the Gipsies.
They are known strictly to avoid all conversation of
an unchaste kind in their camps, except among the
most degraded of them ; and instances of young
females having children, before they pledge themselves to those they love, are rare. This purity of
morals, among a people living as they do, speaks
much in their favour. The anxiety of a Gipsy parent
to preserve the purity of the morals of a daughter is
strongly portrayed in the following fact. The author
wished to engage as a servant the daughter of a
Gipsy who was desirous of quitting her vagrant life ;
but her mother strongly objected for some time ; and
when pressed for the reason of such objection, she
named the danger she would be in in a town, far

from a mother's eye. It would be well if all others felt for their children as did this unlettered Gipsy (p. 33). . . . It is worthy of remark, that all the better sort of Gipsies teach their children the Lord's Prayer (p. 35). . . . Whoever has read Grellmann's Dissertation on the Continental Gipsies, and supposes that those of England are equally immoral and vicious, is greatly mistaken. The Gipsies of this country are altogether different, as monstrous crimes are seldom heard of among them. The author is not aware of any of them being convicted of housebreaking or highway robbery. Seldom are they guilty of sheep-stealing or robbing hen-roosts. In England they avoid poaching, knowing that the sporting gentlemen would be severe against them, and that they would not be permitted to remain in the lanes and commons near villages (p. 49). . . . There is not the least prospect of doing them good by forcing instruction on them. About the year 1748, the Empress Theresa attempted the improvement of the Gipsies in Germany, by taking away, by force, all their children of a certain age, in order to educate and protect them ; but such an unnatural and arbitrary mode of benevolence defeated its own object (p. 95). . . . A lady once said to one of my friends, ' My neighbours are always complaining that the Gipsies do them mischief, and rob them ; as for me, I cannot complain. I treat them kindly, and in return, when they are near my house, they guard it, and frighten away thieves. I never lost anything by having them near my house.' The author has had similar testimonials from farmers, gentlemen, and ladies of Sussex, Surrey, Hants, and Dorset, which prove that Gipsies can be honest and grateful" (p. 106).

What then shall one say of Samuel Roberts' *Gypsies* (4th ed., Lond., 1836), according to whose sketch of Romani character (pp. 75-82) the Gipsies are "a people more sinned against than sinning. Their better peculiarities have always been overlooked ; while those more objectionable ones, through the results of the peculiar circumstances in which they are placed, have ever been exaggerated, misrepresented, and multiplied, by prejudice and inhumanity. The crimes of which they have generally been accused, and for which they have been punished, have, for the most part, been such as could not be considered as crimes by them. They have been vilified, hunted from place to place, driven to banishment, prison, and death, for leading a life to which they were born—from which they had no inclination, no divine command, to depart. . . . What they have seen and experienced, of the effects of Christianity, unfortunately for the credit of that religion, has not been such as to cause them to think well either of it or of its professors :[1] that they have not been driven to hate and to shun them, seems the more

---

[1] Of the falsity of this remark one out of scores of proofs that might be brought is furnished by Woodcock's *Gipsies*, (Lond., 1865), p. 14, *note :*—"'On Tuesday morning seven Gipsies were charged before the Rev. Uriah Tonkin, at Hayle (Cornwall), with sleeping under tents,

surprising. This, however, has not been the case; to some of the rites of Christianity the Gipsies in this country conform, and with its professors they would, I believe, gladly live in peace. Generally speaking, there seems a peculiar steadiness and sedateness in the manners and the conduct of the Gipsies, which keeps them alike from cringing and presuming. . . . They are not drunkards, or even habitual drinkers; occasionally some of them are known to drink to excess, but not frequently; their character in that respect is that of sobriety. They are peculiarly abstemious in eating, and, indeed, in all their habits. . . . Let it be understood, that there are rogues and vagabonds of the worst description *personating Gipsies, and often passing for them,* and it is not improbable but the most of those who have been convicted of the greater crimes, have been of that description of vagrants. I have had, and heard of, the testimony of many respectable gentlemen, farmers, and others, near whose premises the Gipsies have long been in the habit of encamping, borne to their honesty, having never had reason to suppose that they robbed them of anything; while those who have treated them with kindness, by letting them encamp unmolested on their waste grounds, and giving them straw or any small matters,

---

and were each committed to twenty-one days' imprisonment in the county gaol, with hard labour. The party consisted of mother and six children, aged 20, 16, 15, 13, 10, and 8 years.'—*Manchester Examiner,* May 1864."

have found them rather protectors than destroyers of
their property. The Gipsies, I believe, rarely under
any circumstances apply for parochial relief; their
independence of spirit and abstemious habits incline
and enable them to do without it. This is an example worthy of being imitated by many of their
traducers. Another favourable peculiarity of theirs
is, that they are rarely, if ever, seen as common
beggars. On the late investigation throughout London and Westminster, one only instance occurred,
and even that a doubtful one. The females, I believe,
are rarely, if ever, found among those dreadful pests
to society in large towns, common prostitutes. Their
parental and filial affection is said to be exemplary:
their aged parents they tend to the last with a care
and attention not often witnessed in polished society;
and they are accused of being indulgent to their
children even to an injurious extent. . . . As to their
being fortune-tellers, it is much less disgraceful to
them, than to those whose ignorance (or wickedness)
encourages them to such practices. The Gipsies are
by far more intelligent and civilised than the depraved
part of the lower ranks in large towns. Let any one
who has opportunity look at such, and compare them
with the Gipsies; the comparison will little redound
to the credit of the former. See the mechanics at
their work, surly and dissatisfied with themselves,
their condition, their employers, their relievers, their
rulers, and with everything around them; dirty,
offensive, unhealthy, and miserable; unwillingly, and

with murmuring, performing that labour which God hath appointed as the needful task of all men on earth. Hear them, in almost every sentence that they utter, cursing and blaspheming, calling upon God to bear witness to the grossest falsehoods ; while, in language the most profane and indecent, they ridicule everything that is sacred and chaste. Follow them to the alehouse, and hear all this repeated amidst the roar of drunkenness ; follow them from thence, if you have sufficient courage and resolution, home to their wives and children,—but if you have, I must leave you to go without me ; I have seen them there too often ; my heart sickens at the recollection, and I cannot, without a stronger motive than curiosity, again pass their threshold. To turn from the view of such a scene as this which has been described to the contemplation of the family in the simple tent of the wandering Gipsy, is like exchanging the close and offensive lazar-house for the fresh and smiling fields and the glorious firmament of heaven." *Quid plura?* Enough that Mr Roberts comes on a family of Boswells washing, and is surprised to see the clothes, hung out on the hedges, " all equal in quality and colour to what one would expect to be worn by decent tradespeople." The tea-apparatus, too, is " quite of the better kind ; two feather-beds (with bedclothes good, and exceedingly clean), laid on dry straw, occupy the two ends of the tent," &c.

Take yet a few more specimens of blindness, gathered from scattered sources. From "My Friend's

Gipsy Journal" (*Good Words*, Nov.-Dec. 1868):—" I
wish I could give a vivid picture of the Gipsy tents
as they presented themselves to me—two or three in
succession.   There was an agreeable contrast between
the nomadic restlessness and comfortlessness without,
and the warmth, picturesqueness, almost luxury of
what has more the air of a Turkish divan than of
an Arab tent, within. . . . The cups and plates were
of china ; the silver was 'solid silver,' not electro-
plated, like that of most householders.   For that
matter, my friend told me that the most expensive
tea-service in the shop of one of the first Edinburgh
silversmiths was bought and paid for by a Gipsy
matron. . . . Dr Guthrie seemed pleased with his
visit, telling me that he did not think he had ever
addressed a more interested-looking audience.   So
he concluded by saying, ' I will never vex you by
calling your friends bad again ; indeed, I saw no
signs of wickedness amongst them, quite the reverse.
Such simple, guileless-looking people may be ignorant,
but they cannot be reprobate, for sin always leaves
its mark behind.' . . . The children were also very
diligent at school, and liked by their teachers, which
is a great comfort.   The fear about them contaminat-
ing the others seems likewise to have vanished. . . .
Old Mr R[eynolds] is dreadfully shocked with the
drunkenness amongst the Scottish lower orders; says
that if any of their women were seen in the state
that he sees some of the women in here in the
streets, they would be perfectly ashamed of their

GIPSIES TOMB
(Cathcart Churchyard)

Fr Col. Fergusson. del.

race. . . . The old and the young alike receive the tenderest care and treatment. . . . The Gipsies, more than any people I ever saw, have a reverence for the Bible, and when one of them takes an oath, and 'kisses the book,' as they term it, and afterwards breaks it, he is considered a great reprobate. Very much struck, too, by the frequent use of God's name, and yet it is not done in the same irreverent manner of our habitual swearers, though it often shocks me to hear them. . . . I was struck by little Logan's politeness,[1] which seems to be innate in the very children. . . . Those letters give me much insight into Gipsy character. This one was enclosing an order for a sovereign, which my friends were sending

---

[1] Poor little Logan, "beloved son of John and Lavithen Lee and brother of Nathan Lee and grandson of Elijah Smith," he was not long to practise his politeness, for he "departed out of this world on the 25th day of September 1873, aged 12 years. 'Suffer the little children to come unto Me, and forbid them not, for of such is the kingdom of God.'" He lies in Cathcart kirkyard, by the side of John Cooper, "beloved husband and son of Sarah and Phœbe Cooper, who departed this life 31st January 1872, aged 40 years." Lieut.-Colonel Fergusson describes, in *Notes and Queries*, December 19, 1874, the burial ground of this family as "very neatly laid out, ornamented with the traditional cypress and yew. The tombstones are executed in an excellent style, and the ground is enclosed with an exceedingly handsome cast-iron railing—the design vine-leaves and gilt clusters of grapes; the whole giving one the idea of a burial place of some very substantial and well-to-do citizen of the neighbouring town of Glasgow. To Colonel Fergusson I am indebted for the accompanying sketch of Logan's grave, and to Dr Smith, the minister of Cathcart, for this account of Logan's burial:—"A person of very gentlemanly manners and appearance called on me on the day of his cousin's death, to request that I would attend the funeral, and conduct it in the usual manner, with the addition of a prayer at the grave. . . . I met the party there, and took part in the

to a poor relation. As I knew it was the second to
the same person within a short time, I said, 'This
is hard upon you; has she no nearer relatives?'
'Why, bless you, yes, miss, she has a father and
brothers.' 'The burden seems to fall upon you.
Should they not help her?' I next asked. 'Well,
I don't know, miss, aught about that; we never
thinks of them ere things. She is our own flesh
and blood, poor thing, and has asked us to send her
a little, for her children are sick; then why shouldn't
we do it? Lack, miss, if you'll believe me, I could
scarce swallow no breakfast this morning for thinking
of them poor things; and as to father and brothers,
why they may help her if they like; I dare say they

---

service, for which they expressed much gratitude. Among the principal
mourners were four females completely enveloped in mantles of deep
crape, who seemed much affected. On the following Sunday they all
attended church in the same attire." Such, see you, is Gipsy "burial
under a clod, without the shedding of a tear."

One frightful instance of how Romani children's lives are "sacrificed
at the hands of cruelty, starvation, and neglect," is furnished by *The
Times*, 2d March 1862:—"'About six weeks since a party of Gipsies,
bearing with them a very beautiful girl, named Lepronia Lee,
evidently in the last stage of consumption, encamped on the grounds
adjacent to the Greyhound public-house, about eight miles from
Ipswich. No sooner had they taken up their quarters than the
intelligence of the illness of one who appeared to be a great favourite
with the tribe was sent to all parts, and in a few days Kirton was the
centre of an encampment numbering some fifty or sixty men, women,
and children, some arriving from Norwich and other distant places.
Medical aid was immediately called in, and Mr Taylor, surgeon, of
Bucklesham, was daily in attendance upon the poor girl. Dr Bartlett
was also consulted, but from the first all hope was gone. During the
illness of the girl at Kirton, which extended over six weeks, she was
frequently visited by the Rev. Mr Bartlett, his wife, and several other
ladies residing in that neighbourhood, who spent some hours with her

does.' . . . One day when telling a number of them about a Socinian, that he was one who did not believe that Christ was God, a sort of shudder passed through them, and one of them said, ' How can any one think that? for, ignorant as we be, we have always heard that our Saviour was the Son of God.' "

From an account in the *Birmingham Daily Post*, June 7, 1869, of how fifty Gipsies were "packed together" at Kidderminster in seven tents and seven sleeping-waggons :—" The tents are tolerably roomy affairs, the framework being constructed with long supple sticks, which are bowed towards each other, and covered with a warm flannelly material. The interiors are warm and snug ; and, more than this,

---

daily, reading portions of the Scripture. Indeed, so great was her desire for the consolations of religion, and her affection for those of her sex who so kindly visited her, that she never appeared satisfied but when they were present. On Sunday afternoon, the 2d inst., the poor girl breathed her last, having retained her consciousness until the last moment, and with her last breath expressed her hope in a glorious immortality. The greater portion of the tribe were at Kirton Church at the time her death took place, and when it became known, the moaning and lamentations of her people are described as dreadful in the extreme. The deceased was interred in Kirton churchyard on Friday, the 7th inst., the procession being headed by a hearse, after which followed the two sisters and cousins of the deceased, dressed in white muslin, corded with white silk, their heads covered with white veils, reaching almost to the ground. The men were dressed with black silk hatbands, tied with white riband, and also wore white gloves and neckties. The women of the tribe were in deep mourning. Many hundred persons came from all parts of the district to witness the procession. The greatest decorum was present throughout, and shortly after their return from Kesgrave, the members of the tribe started for their various destinations. The tribe appeared to be in affluent circumstances, and consisted of the families of the Lees, Youngs, Smiths, and Chilcotts.'—*Bury and Norwich Post*."

there is an air of comfort about them which house-dwellers would hardly believe could be had under Gipsy conditions of life. Chairs and tables are not a pre-requisite here as in ordinary dwellings, but the Gipsies appear to be abundantly supplied with such fabrics and appointments as give a somewhat Eastern air to their habitations. They are well dressed, not uncommunicative, and very easy and self-possessed in their manners."

From Mr C. G. Leland's *English Gipsies* (Lond., 1873):—" Everything in the Gipsy cottage was scrupulously neat,—there was even an approach to style. The furniture and ornaments were superior to those found in common peasant houses. There was a large and beautifully-bound photograph album. I found that the family could read and write,—the daughter received and read a note, and one of the sons knew who and what Mr Robert Browning was (p. 156). . . . In conclusion, I would remark, that if I have not, like many writers on the poor Gipsies, abused them for certain proverbial faults, it has been because they never troubled me with anything very serious of the kind, or brought it to my notice ; and I certainly never took the pains to hunt it up to the discredit of people who always behaved decently to me. I have found them more cheerful, polite, and grateful, than the lower orders of other races in Europe or America ; and I believe that where their respect and sympathy are secured, they are quite as upright. Like all people who are regarded as outcasts, they are very proud of being trusted, and under this influence will commit the most daring acts of honesty" (p. xi.).

From " Gipsy Life in Lancashire and Cheshire" (*Papers of the Manchester Literary Club*, 1877), by Mr H. T. Crofton :—" The older Gipsies can seldom read or write ; but most of them are anxious that their children should learn the three R's, and usually send them to school during the winter months. . . . It may be added that, with the police at least, Gipsies have earned a good character. . . . It seems to be a common superstition that Gipsies are great thieves, but this is wrong."

Romance, deception, imagery, lies, founded it may be, on twenty years of painful study ; but what is study without the "eye to observe," that piercing organ, which contemplates an unfound remedy? Without it, one reads in the last English Census, of " 8025 persons in caravans and tents and in the open air," and can as little guess how many of these may be Gipsies, as from the total of Irish M.P.'s infer the strength of the Home Rule party. But with it, one discerns " between three and four thousand men and women, and eight or ten thousand children, *classed in the Census* as vagrants and vagabonds ;" and straightway calculates that " there must be fully between fifteen and sixteen thousand Gipsies in England at the present time, four-fifths of whom are living in tents or vans." The calculation occurs in Mr Smith's latest publication, a letter to the *Graphic* (March 13, 1880), where

he announces some valuable discoveries,—that Firdusi
was an Arab writer of the year 1126 ; that Gipsies are
also called Lyuths ; that they arrived before Constantinople at the end of the fourteenth and early in the
fifteenth century ; and that they entered Scotland
about the year 1514.

Facts like these prepare us for the reception of Mr
Smith's solution of his paradox, propounded to the
Social Science Congress at Manchester in October
1879.[1] "Some few Gipsies" he said, *"who have
arrived at what they consider the highest state of
a respectable and civilised life,* reside in houses which
in ninety-nine cases out of a hundred, are in the
lowest and most degraded part of the towns, among
the scum and off-scouring of all nations, and, like
locusts, they leave a blight behind them wherever
they have been. . . . Lying, begging, thieving,
cheating, and every other abomination that low
cunning craft, backed by ignorance and idleness,
can devise, they practise. In some instances these
things are carried out to such a pitch as to render
them more like imbeciles than human beings en-
dowed with reason. Chair-mending, tinkering, and
hawking, are in many instances used only as a 'blind;'
while the women and children go about the country

---

[1] Pity that this Address was not illustrated by the fifty or so " ditch
heathens," then encamping at Cheetham Hill, in two meadows, for
which they paid £3 a week. One of their number, Mr Sylvester
Boswell, himself delivered an Address to the Manchester Literary
Club, 12th January 1880.

begging and fortune-telling, bringing to the heathenish
tents sufficient to keep the family. . . . Considerable
difficulty is experienced sometimes in finding them
out, as many of the women go by two names ; but
in vain do I look for any improvement among the
children. Owing to the Act relating to pedlars and
hawkers prohibiting the granting of licences for
hawking to the youths of both sexes under seventeen,
and the Education Acts not being sufficiently strong
to lay hold of their *dirty, idle, travelling tribes* to
educate them, except in rare cases, they are allowed
to skulk about in ignorance and evil training, without
being taught how to get an honest living. No ray
of hope enters their breast ; their highest ambition is
to live and to loll about so long as the food comes ; no
matter by whom or how it comes, so that they get it.
In many instances they live like pigs and die like dogs.
The real old-fashioned Gipsy has become lewd and
demoralised—if such a thing could be—by allowing
his sons and daughters to mix up with the scamps,
vagabonds, 'rodneys,' and jail-birds who now and
then settle among them as they are camping on
the *ditch* banks. The consequence is, our lanes are
being infested with a lot of dirty ignorant Gipsies,
who, with their tribes of squalid children, have been
encouraged by servant girls and farmers, by supplying
their wants with eggs, bacon, milk, and potatoes, the
men helping themselves to game, to locate in the
neighbourhood until they have received the tip from
the farmer to pass on to his neighbours. Children:

born under such circumstances, unless taken hold of by the State, will turn out to be a class of most dangerous characters. Very much, up to the present, the wants of the women and children have been supplied through gulling the large-hearted and liberal-minded they have been brought in contact with, and *the result has been that but few of the real Gipsies have found their way into gaols. Probably their offences may have been winked at by the farmers and others, who do not like the idea of having their stacks fired and property destroyed, and have given the Gipsies a wide berth.*"

Why, having "no heart to feel," I hitherto had foolishly contrasted the scores of English Gipsies murderously hanged, with the one English Gipsy ever hanged for murder; I had deemed it rather creditable to the *scum-blighting locusts*, that so few of them had ever been imprisoned for, heavier crimes than fortune-telling or stopping in the midst of sticks and grass. Bah! it takes philanthropy to know that this keeping out of gaol implies incendiarism,[1] and I can only hope that Silvanus's one imprisonment means that he has not often made the red cock crow.

But, as I write, a horrible suspicion rises unbidden

---

[1] Where are the records of this Gipsy villany to be found? Not in the *Gentleman's Magazine, Annual Register,* or in any other periodicals, newspapers, and such-like repositories of crime, that have fallen under my unobservant eye. Mr Smith's benevolence should really not allow him to slur over for one moment the wrongdoings of his miserable protegés.

in my mind. *Why are so few old Gipsies found in workhouses?* The fact is patent; and in all my dealings with the race I never knew of more than one, a venerable dame, who, having outlived all her near relations, found an asylum in the Bristol poorhouse. Some distant kinsfolk, hearing of the circumstance, at once removed her, "had her out of that" (to use their uncouth phrase); and three months later, by their account, she died. Now, what was their motive for thus removing her? Family affection, respect for age, honest independence? The notion were absurd. No, I turn for an answer to the article "Gipsies" in *Chambers's Encyclopædia* (ed. 1874), and read on p. 172 that "they were or are wont to eat their parents;" then call to mind how in 1782 forty-five Gipsies, men and women, were beheaded, broken on the wheel, quartered alive, or hanged, for cannibalism. Among them were their Bishop, a man of large appetite, and their "Harum-Pasha," the ornaments in whose cap were valued at £600. The mode of their detection, a lesson to our slothful police (with whom these monsters bear a good character!), was briefly thus. Arrested first by way of wise precaution, they were racked till they owned to theft and murder; then were brought to the spot where their victims should be buried, and, no victims forthcoming, were promptly racked again. It is tiresome work extracting truth from Gipsies, but the truth did at last come out, that in twenty-one years they had eaten eighty-three

persons,—Gipsies presumably, since natives missing
there were none; nay, sons confessed that they had
"dined off Father" (Von Heister, *Ethnographische
und geschichtliche Notizen über die Zigeuner*, Königsb.
1842, p. 47; and *cf.* Dyrlund, *Tatere og Natmandsfolk i Danmark*, Copenh. 1872, pp. 527-31).

But this, some devil's advocate may urge, took
place in Hungary, nearly a hundred years ago. An
idle plea; for I refer him to this extract from the
Times' report (10th March 1859) of the trial at
York of Guilliers Heron, who by-the-bye was un-
accountably acquitted:—"One of the prisoner's
brothers said they were all at tea with the prisoner
at five o'clock in their tent; and when asked what
they had to eat, he said they had a *hodgun* cooked.
His Lordship (Mr Justice Byles)—'What do you say
you had—cooked urchin?'   Gipsy—'Yes, cooked
hodgun. I'm very fond of cooked *hodgun*' (with a
grin). His Lordship's mind seemed to be filled with
horrible misgivings," &c. As well it might, to hear
the grinning young miscreant acknowledge his partiality for baby, for heathen baby let us only trust,
though our trust is not unmingled with darker
dread.

For Gipsies are notorious kidnappers. Did they
not steal the future Chief Justice Popham, and
brand him with a cabalistic mark, as graziers brand
the lamb that they fatten for slaughter? did they
not carry off young Adam Smith, who but for his
timely rescue might have been converted into *pottage*

à la Meg Merrilies de Derncleugh?[1]   There was
Elizabeth Kellen, too, who was " forcibly abducted
by a gang of Gipsies, stripped of her clothes and
dressed in some of their rags, treated as the most
abject in every respect, and threatened with death
if she attempted flight. Of the depredations of
these banditti, in milking cows in the night, stealing
poultry, &c., she gave a most probable account, and
said it was their intention to have coloured her when
the walnut season approached, to make her appear as
a real Gipsy" (*Annual Reg.*, 7th June 1802). That,
like her more famous namesake, Elizabeth Canning,
she was pronounced by the magistrates a gross im-
postor, and that the sixteen Gipsies were released
from prison with a handsome compensation, proves
chiefly the fallibility of magistrates, her probable
account being wholly substantiated by that other
Story of Elizabeth, the servant girl, namely, Elizabeth Collier, for robbing whom of pockets, money,
and clothes, Adam Lee, Thomas Lee, and Eleanor
his wife were condemned at Kingston and, most
likely, hanged (*ib.*, 1st April 1812). Here, again,
that the case for the prosecution rested solely upon
her evidence, that Adam twice had voluntarily sur-
rendered after having been let go free, and that the

---

[1] Was Mr Smith alluding to this incident when he wrote in the
Graphic:—" Other things, that an ordinary Englishman would throw
upon the dunghill, some of the Gipsies will carry home to make soup
of." As to the dunghill I hardly know, but a sucking political econo-
mist would probably be rather tough and dry.

prisoners' alibi was supported by a great number of
witnesses, proves chiefly the badness of Gipsies, since
who but bad persons could be thus condemned?
Lastly, in 1872, to make my long story short, forty-
seven Gipsies were imprisoned in Germany on suspicion of having kidnapped Anna Böckler, the only
child of a great Pomeranian farmer. A twelvemonth
later, as luck would have it, Anna's corpse was discovered in one of her father's barns, where the farm
boy, her murderer, had buried it; but the imprisonment of the Gipsies is at any rate satisfactory;
and a perusal, I doubt not, of *Der Neue Pitaval*
(new ser., vol. ix. pp. 113-224) will show the most
casual observer how plausible my theory is,—that
kids are the savoury meat which Gipsies love, and
that, failing kids, old mongrels are the next best
substitute.[1]

With diffidence I submit this theory to one who
has made the alarming and unlooked-for discovery,
that "*georgies* are increasing, and will increase, in
our midst, unless we put our hand upon the system."
Till now I always believed that *górgios* meant all
who were NOT of Gipsy birth, standing to *Romané*
as *Gentile* to *Jew*, *Barbarian* to *Greek*; I fancied
that philanthropists and school-board officers were
górgios, and of such there surely could hardly be too

---

[1] Gipsies have a well-known horror of wasting good victuals, even a
morsel of bread. Hence their seemingly fantastical averseness to selling
their dead to surgeons for dissection (*cf.* Crabb, p. 29).

many.[1] Even now this discovery dawns slowly on my mind; nor can I fully comprehend what sort of man this Moses Holland must be, to have been "a Gipsy nearly all his life." When *is* a Gipsy not a Gipsy? I never was good at riddles, and "When he's a górgio" seems the only answer; Moses Holland (I own it) having to my ears a thoroughly un-Gipsy ring. Yet who am I to judge of what is Gipsy, who have visited some few hundred caravans, and never in one single instance known that " besides a man and his wife and their own children there are several adult persons taken in as lodgers." As little was I aware that "Gipsies generally pitch their tents and form their encampments in swamps and low marshy places;" that "their tent furniture, cooking utensils, &c., consist of an old *chair*, a few old boxes, a large *saucepan*" —(query, fish-kettle, with *folding* handle),—"and one or two dishes;" or that "washing either themselves or their clothes is a luxury they seldom indulge in." True, their skins are not as white as snow, like the ploughboy's of Anselo's ditty; but then ploughboys and our lower orders generally have a standard of cleanliness that it were hard for ditch-heathens to attain to; and I have read besides, how in 1769 two gentlemen, riding over Hounslow Heath, came on "a

---

[1] *Rodney* is a title I gladly accept for Romani children, accepting also the definition thereof propounded by the Wolverhampton Factories Inspector—"To keep a boy from work till he is thirteen is to encourage idleness. In the expressive language of the district, it makes *Rodneys* of them."

gang of Gipsies, about twelve in number, who were
boiling and roasting in the modern taste, Al Fresco,
on account of a conversion as they called it, such
conversion consisting of rubbing or dyeing a fine
young girl with walnut-shell, it being the first day
of her entering into the society " (*Ann. Reg.*, xii. 128).
I pass over the corroboration that this affords, if
corroboration were needed, of Elizabeth Kellen's
probable account, and remark that those who have
antidotes need fear no poison, and that the frequent
ablutions of Silvanus and his family, indeed of all
Gipsies I have ever met, are certainly due to the
cheapness of walnuts in the parts they travel. Their
washing of clothes and bedding is still more easily
explained.   I have it from a superintendent of police
that Gipsies should never be suffered to camp on
roadsides, because they are everlastingly hanging out
washing on the hedges, where the white is certain to
frighten passing horses ; but he knew not that the
deep-dyed scoundrels contemplate this result, and
hope that the frightened horses may fling their riders,
whom they then rush forward to rifle, and probably
kill. That dirty Gipsies should themselves charge
górgios (as heretofore, I misapply this term) with
being filthy, is but fresh proof of Gipsy ignorance.
What filthiness can there be in washing a table-cloth
and smock together ("what you eat off with what
you wear"—Mrs Draper, Loughton, 4th July 1875)?
and why should Sinfi have scorned the good pudding

that the Scotchwoman boiled in a piece of her husband's shirt?

"If I go on writing with this red ink much longer, I shall begin to lose my subject," as John Roberts remarks on page 12 of his Tenth Epistle ; so contenting myself with remarking that nine-tenths of our philanthropist's statements have come to me as revelations, I will sketch my own pre-apocalyptic suggestions for bettering the Gipsies' lot.

First, then, a nominal census should be taken of Romani dwellers in tents and caravans. One to embrace our entire Gipsy population would doubtless be more interesting ethnologically, but it would be a work of infinite difficulty, and any external scheme for raising the condition of the race could hardly apply to Gipsy house-dwellers. Whereas by visiting the great race-meetings (Epsom, Doncaster, Chester, &c.), the chief fairs (Weyhill, Cirencester, Peterborough, &c.), and the metropolitan and country "Gipsyries," two men with a knowledge of the Romani tongue might easily in a twelvemonth draw up accurate tables, showing the name, age, calling, and acquirements of every nomade Gipsy, and distinguishing between full-bloods and half-bloods, between the few Gipsies who are constantly on the move and Gipsies who encamp in one spot for months at a time. The police force, I know, could furnish two such men ; or better, there are Gipsies qualified for the task,—John Roberts, for instance, and any of his sons.

They must possess a knowledge of the language,
the primary test of Gipsydom, Gipsy physique being
a secondary guide ; else they might class as " Gipsies"
the members of the London Lamb Lane encampment,
of whom the author of a long article in the *Weekly
Times* (8th Feb. 1880) writes :—" After spending
several hours with these people in their tents and
caravans, and passing from yard to yard, asking the
talkative ones questions, we came to the conclusion
that, in the whole bounds of this great metropolis, it
would have been impossible to have found any mis-
calling themselves Gipsies, whose mode of living more
urgently called for the remedial action of the law than
the tenants of Lamb Lane. In the first place, there
was not a true Gipsy amongst them ; nor one man,
woman, or child who could in any degree claim
relationship with a Gipsy." That tent-dwellers of
this stamp should ever be confounded with Gipsies
seems to anyone knowing anything of the latter as
absurd as would the confounding of quack-doctors
with regular practitioners, of Irvingites with Catholics.
There is a likeness, but likeness is sometimes the
deepest ground for difference.

Gipsies are a race as distinct as Jews from the
nations among whom they dwell, though like Jews
they have wedded with the sons and daughters of the
land,—with peasants, miners, shopkeepers, farmers
often, with native tramps and jail-birds hardly ever.
As I write, three Romani pedigrees lie before me,
extending respectively over four, four, and six genera-

tions.[1] The first, Sylvester Boswell's, printed in Smart and Crofton's *Dialect of the English Gipsies*, pp. 252–54, includes 68 members, all of them seemingly full-blood Gipsies. In the second, Silvanus Lovell's (114 members), three marriages occur, in the third and fourth generations, with a horse-dealer, a publican's daughter, and a farmer. The third comprehends 235 descendants of Abraham Wood; and in this the marriages with górgios outnumber those with Romané, such górgios being of all degrees, from a methodist preacher to an astronomer, but only one of

---

[1] These pedigrees afford some evidence of the rarity of Gipsies mating with jail-birds; but a more satisfactory, because much wider, proof exists in the entire absence of Cant words from Romanes, and the almost entire absence of Romani words from Cant. In Hotten's *Slang Dictionary* many of the words marked "Gipsy" are as little Romanes as they are Iroquois, *e.g.*, *bamboozle*, *bloke*, *cheese*, *gad*, *lunan*, *moke*, *mort*, *rig*, *slang*, and *snack*. Of terms of indubitable Romani origin, the following is the sum total:—*bosh*, fiddle (*bóshoméngri*); *cosh*, life-preserver (*kosht*, stick); *couter*, sovereign (*kótor*, piece, guinea); *dicking*, watching (*dikáva*, I see); *dookin*, fortune-telling (*dúkeráva*, I tell fortunes); *drum*, road (*drom*); *gorger*, swell (*górgio*, Gentile); *jibb*, tongue (*chib*); *lob*, word (*lav*); *lil*, pocketbook (*lil*, book); *loaver*, money (*lóvo*); *munging*, whining, begging (*mongáva*, I beg or pray); *nark*, to "nose" or suspect (*nok*, a nose); *pal*, friend (*pal*, brother); *parney*, rain (*páni*, water); *posh*, halfpenny (*posh-hórri*); *puckering*, talking privately (*púkeráva*, I tell; *raclan*, married woman (*rákli*, girl); *stir*, prison (*stáriben*); *vardo*, waggon (*várdo*); and *voker*, talk (*rókeráva*, I speak). A few more words of doubtful etymology might perhaps be added, *e.g.*, *dust*, money (? *dósta*, plenty); and *conk*, nose (possibly "Back Slang" from *knoc*, *i.e.*, *nok*); but, even with these, the Romani elements of Cant are greatly outnumbered by the Hebrew and the Italian. Several, too, of the above words are now disused by Gipsies, as having become intelligible to those by whom they would not wish to be understood. Thus *wóngar* (lit. coals) is now universally substituted by metropolitan Gipsies for *lóvo*, which had crept into Cant as early as 1567. This surely is a significant fact.

them (in the fourth generation) a *chóredo*, an Irish
tinker, like him above the pool.

The offspring of such mixed marriages are sometimes górgios, as in the case of the Ingram family,
and sometimes Gipsies, like the Robertses, John and
his wife being both great-grandchildren of Abraham
Wood, but both of pure descent only upon one
parent's side.   By górgios, I mean that they have not
the Romani look, language, habits, and modes of
thought ; by Gipsies, that they retain these distinguishing marks in a greater or less degree.   These
marks may co-exist in one and the same person, *e.g.*
in Silvanus, a full-blood Gipsy, whose face is of a
thoroughly un-English type, whole sentences of
whose Romanes would be quite intelligible to Turkish
Tchinghianés, who was born in a tent and hopes to
die in one, whose heart is as Romani as his face is
brown.   John, on the other hand, has for years been
a house-dweller, and bears few traces of the Romani
blood, yet speaks the language with far greater purity
than Silvanus, and is a storehouse of old Gipsy beliefs
that are lost to his English brethren.   Are we to pro-
nounce him a górgio, because he lives between four
walls, and is not so dark as several of his own sons ?
or the Crink down the lane a Gipsy on the score of
his tattered tent ?   Assuredly not ; one might as
fairly make an old-clo' bag and hooked nose the *sine
quâ non* of Jewish nationality.   Still, these three cases
illustrate the difficulty of drawing a hard and fast
line between Gipsies and non-Gipsies, and show the

one satisfactory test to be that of Language. Of
course every speaker of Romanes is not a Gipsy, any
more than a Hebrew scholar is necessarily a Jew; but
I would not admit the converse, that there are Gipsies
ignorant of Romanes. "Sar shan, bor?"—"So si tíro
nav?"—"Rómano shan tu?" these are easy shibboleths
by which the takers of our imaginary census would
determine the title of claimants to Romani birth.

Only by such a census could the question of Gipsy
criminality be satisfactorily decided for or against the
race, since who can at present say whether "Gipsy"
lawbreakers of newspaper reports really belong to it
or not?—J. Hodgkiss and S. Udall, for instance, who
were fined at Rugeley for "pitching their tents on the
highway at King's Bromley, 1st November 1879."
With only their names to go by, I incline to pro-
nounce them górgio besom-makers; but herein I may
be wrong, as one now and then comes on real Gipsies
with very un-Gipsy names. Still, the case is a typical
one, showing that Samuel Roberts had possibly some
grounds for writing, that "there are vagabonds personating Gipsies and often passing for them, and it is
not improbable but the most of those who have been
convicted of the greater crimes have been of that
description of vagrants." I find among my notes
upon "Gipsy" offenders, a Luke Castle, Samuel
Wheeler, Mary Jones,[1] Elizabeth Hamilton, Sam

---

[1] This lady, who got a month's hard labour in Carmarthen gaol for
vagrancy, seems to have been rather a remarkable character. "On
her person was found £6, 1s. 10d. in cash, and promissory notes to

Herbert, Mary Holt, John Davies, &c., names that are not suggestive of Romani origin.

As regards the wellbeing or poverty of Gipsies, my present knowledge leads me fully to endorse Mr Leland's assertion, in a long letter to the *Standard* (19th August 1879), that "a real Gipsy who cannot in an emergency find his ten, or even twenty pounds, is a very exceptional character." How many of our labouring or middle classes could expend from £20 to £130 upon a house? Yet the price of a Gipsy sleeping-waggon ranges between these sums, £40 being probably about the average. There are of course gradations of prosperity; but I suppose that the percentage of "Poor" is infinitely higher among our native population than in the Gipsy families of Lovell, Stanley, Boswell, Herne, Chilcott, Young, Lee, Reynolds, Buckland, Smith, Gray, Shaw, Cooper, Worton, Pinfold, Draper, Taylor, and Bunce. A census should prove or disprove my supposition.

Gipsy illiterates would assuredly outnumber Gipsy literates, though the proportion would vary greatly with the locality, most perhaps of the Welsh Gipsies, a fair number of the Lancashire Gipsies, very few of the East Anglian Gipsies, being able to read and write. It is also questionable whether this illiteracy does not arise as much from schoolmasters' aversion to Gipsies, as from Gipsies' aversion to schoolmasters.

---

the amount of upwards of £200; and she had besides, in six or seven bags, 11 shirts, 10 caps, 3 cotton gowns, 15 handkerchiefs, 3 pairs of stockings, and 20 other articles of clothing."

In how many of the places where Romané most do
congregate, where they stop for whole months at
a time, have any attempts been made to get the
children to school? and where such have been made,
what has been the attitude of Gipsy and of Gentile
thereunto? My own observation in this respect, at
Notting Hill and elsewhere, is too narrow for me to
come to a definite opinion, but possibly the remarks
in Boner's *Transylvania* (Lond. 1865) are partly
applicable to England. "Everywhere," he writes on
p. 348, " there is a degree of prejudice against Gipsies,
they being, as it were, the Pariahs of Europe. But
this is much stronger in the country than the town,
the peasant being far more conservative and aristo-
cratic in his notions than the citizen. And thus it
happens, that in the villages no Gipsies attend the
schools, as the peasants do not like to see their children sitting beside them. It is the same sort of feeling
that exists in America towards the black population.
Yet in the Saxon town of Bistritz several Gipsy children frequented the public school; their parents lived
in a good house at the end of the town; and I found
the boys could read and write and cipher well. At
first the townspeople wished to have their children
separated from those of Gipsy parents; but the
rector refused, saying, if they came to school cleanly
and neat, there was no reason why all should not
sit together; and they came in as orderly a condition
as the others." Just so the Edinburgh townsfolk
feared that their children would be " contaminated "

by the little Smiths; and verily, *if* those Smiths
were squalid, half-naked, hedge-bottom heathens, the
fear does not seem so altogether groundless.   If
they were not, but were so miscalled, the fear would
be groundless, but might still remain; the Smiths
might thereby be excluded from school; and the
fault of their exclusion would lie with the epithet-
coiners.

Let me mention a fact that fell within my own
experience.   A Gipsy widow, a Catholic, was killed
in a railway accident.   Her brother-in-law heard
from the people where he was stopping that two of
her boys might perhaps be got into a Catholic
orphanage, and I called by his request on a neighbouring priest to inquire about the matter.   He
was a pleasant, courteous man, this priest, and
seemed interested in the case, till I mentioned that
the mother was a Gipsy.   Then his whole manner
"we changed, and "You must be mistaken," he said;
have nothing whatever to do with that kind of
people.   Good morning."   He knew, be it observed,
absolutely nothing of Gipsies, except by hearsay;
by hearsay half our clergy and schoolmasters would
probably be led to make like answer.

In England, for my own part, I look for prejudice
against the Gipsies in cities rather than in rural
districts, less for the reason that town-bred Gipsies
are worse than their country cousins, than because
country folk know better than townspeople what
Gipsies really are.   A singular reason this, if Gipsies

were all that they are said to be! But take the
"Old Woman's" letter to the *Standard* (16th August
1879), one of those letters that "unwittingly substantiated and backed up the cause of our roadside
Arabs." The grand-daughter of a miller-farmer, she
speaks of the Boswells as "friends," between whom
and her family a "kindly feeling" subsisted, and
who on one occasion offered to discharge a considerable debt for her grandfather, a "kindness"
that was gratefully acknowledged. These were real,
old-fashioned Gipsies, who now, we are told, have
"become lewd and demoralised, *if such a thing
could be*." Perhaps it could not, for on 30th August
the Rev. J. Finch Smith, of Aldridge Rectory, near
Walsall, writes:—"During the thirty years that I
have been rector of this parish, members of the
Boswell family have been almost constantly resident
here. I buried the head of the family in 1874, who
died at the age of 87. He was a regular attendant
at the parish church, and failed not to bow his head
reverently when he entered within the house of God.
I never saw or heard any harm of the man. He was
a quiet and inoffensive man, and worked industriously
as a tinman within a short time of his death. If he
had rather a sharp eye for a little gift, that is a trait
of character by no means confined to Gipsies. One
of his daughters was married here to a member of the
Boswell tribe, and another, who rejoiced in the name
of Britannia, I buried in her father's grave two years
ago. After his death, she and her mother removed

R

to an adjoining parish, where she was confirmed by
Bishop Selwyn in 1876. Regular as was the old man
at church, I never could persuade his wife to come.
In 1859 I baptised, privately, an infant of the same
tribe, whose parents were travelling through the
parish, and whose mother was named Elvira. Great
was the admiration of my domestics at the sight of
the beautiful lace which ornamented the robe in
which the child was brought to my house. Clearly
there are Gipsies, and those of a well-known tribe,
glad to receive the ministrations of the church."

Clearly, too, at Aldridge, and in that miller's village (whose name unfortunately is not given), Gipsies
would hardly be looked upon as Pariahs; but it is
not in villages that Gipsies generally make long halts.
A night at B, two days at C, a week perhaps at D,
three days at E,—thus they perform their summer
circuits; whereas in the winter three-fourths at least
of the nomades cease to be migratory, assembling
on the outskirts of large towns. At Gorton, Clayton,
Bradford, Harpurhey, and Cheetham, near Manchester, over 200 Gipsies may be found encamped from
the end of October to the beginning of April
(Crofton's *Gipsy Life in Lancashire and Cheshire*,
pp. 38, 39); and equally large encampments are
regularly formed at several points round London, as
well as near Bristol, Wolverhampton, Birmingham,
&c.,—places where there are also Gipsies who have
not shifted their quarters for two, five, even sixteen
years. It is clear, then, that towns are the main

battle-field of Romani education; and this is the
more important, because in the conditions of a per-
manent encampment (for seven months or for seven
years) there is absolutely nothing to keep Gipsy
children from school. Let only their parents be
willing to send them, and schoolmasters be ready
to receive them, the battle at this point is won
without the striking of a single blow. ·

Now as regards the parents' willingness, we are
told by the *Christian Herald* (31st March 1880)
that "Mr Smith finds heartfelt sympathy *everywhere
among the Gipsies themselves;*" that they are sub-
scribing their halfpence and shillings to help him
in his work; that one of them, "with hands uplifted
and tears in her eyes, which left no doubt of her
meaning, said, 'I do hope from the bottom of my
heart that God will bless and prosper you in the
work, till a law is passed, and the poor Gipsy children are brought under the School Board, and their
parents compelled to send them to school as other
people are.'" Here, surely, must be some mistake, for
a law compelling willing parents to send their children
to school were like one forcing hungry folk to eat;
and I own I partly agree with the *School Guardian*
(13th August 1879), that "it is not easy to see what
special legislation is to do for the 30,000 (!) little
Bohemians of one kind and another who are
constantly on the move in England and Wales.
Authority to send them to an Industrial School
seems to be one obvious want, and this there ought

to be no difficulty in obtaining; but it would not meet the whole case." Decidedly it would not; not more, perhaps, than one-tenth of our Gipsy race,—the remaining nine-tenths having shipped for America on the very first hint that their children would be taken from them.

That were one way, the shortest maybe, out of the difficulty; but might not an ambulatory solution first be tried, viz., by clergymen and pedagogues trudging off to the Gipsy tents, and learning for themselves whether the children come to school or not, and if not why not, and whether there is no mode of bringing them thither other than by an Act of Parliament? Put your horse boldly at the fence, and see if he will not clear it, before you go to the trouble of having a crane erected to hoist him over; and for the life of me, I cannot see that at present there is anything (barring possible prejudice) to hinder the great majority of Gipsy children from getting as good schooling as Ned Boswell's got at their accustomed camping-place, Blackpool.

For the minority, the children of Gipsies who wander the whole year through, Gipsies themselves have furnished a suggestion. I lately received a letter from one of some Lees, nomade English Gipsies who travel in North Wales. Illiterate like most of their brethren, they are keeping with them Elijah Wood, a Welsh Gipsy lad, who can read and write well, so acts as their private secretary; and, more than that, is tutor to the entire family. My

letter was written by him, but at its foot stood a
huge and laborious "Manuel Lee,"—a hint, it struck
me, to Gipsy educationists.   My own experience is
that Romani children are delighted to spell, not
nose and *ear* and *eye*, but *nok* and *kan* and *yok ;*
and I propose that Gipsy schoolmasters should be
appointed for the children of our chief English
"Gipsyries."   But where could they be found ?   If
they were wanted, I would engage to find at least
a score.

Then there is the method of tent-instruction indi-
cated by "My Friend's Gipsy Journal," in *Good
Words.*   If during the next four winters fifty ladies
would imitate the work that is there described, a
work which I know has had abiding effects, there
might be hundreds of Romani children able to read
Mr George Smith's Bill for Gipsy Education by the
time that it passes into law.

Its scope is this :—"The plan I would adopt is
to apply the principles of the Canal Boats Act of
1877 to all movable habitations—*i.e.,* I would have
all tents, shows, caravans, auctioneers' vans, and like
places used as dwellings, registered and numbered,
and under proper sanitary arrangements and super-
vision of the sanitary inspectors and School Board
officers in every town and village.   With regard to
the education of the children, when once the tent
or van is registered and numbered, whether travelling
as gipsies, auctioneers, &c., their children are mostly
idle during the day ; consequently, with a book

similar to the half-time book, in which their names and attendance at school could be entered, it could be taken from place to place as they travel about, and be endorsed by the schoolmaster, showing that the child was attending school. The education obtained in this way would not be of the highest order; but through the kindness of the schoolmaster—for which extra trouble he should be compensated, as he ought to be under the Canal-Boats Act—and the vigilance of the School Board visitor, a plain, practical, and sound education could be imparted to and obtained by these poor little gipsy children and roadside arabs, who, if we do our duty, will be qualified to fill the places of those of our best artisans who are leaving the country to seek their fortunes abroad."

It is doubtless humiliating to begin by quarrelling with a counsellor and end by accepting his counsel; but to the scheme of education here proposed I have no objection to make. So far as I comprehend it, it seems to me *per se* a wise and good one, though to sedentary Gipsies it would apply not at all—to nomade Gipsies, as a rule, for barely half the year. To the terms of the proposal I have as strong an objection as I might have were I a regular auctioneer. Arabs and modern Egyptians make use of the very same alphabet, but the Red Sea severs Egypt from Arabia; Gipsies and roadside arabs may have the same lessons to learn, but their Isthmus of *Suez* is but a narrow link.

Nor, to have done with the unfamiliar subject of education, do I object to this proposed registration of

Gipsy tents and caravans, though I may doubt whether such registration is imperatively called for by sanitary considerations. This point could best be settled by statistics, showing the death-rate of Gipsy families. As a beginning, I offer the following :—Bazena Clifton (16 children, 15 living), Silvanus Lovell (13 children, 12 living), Sylvester Boswell (8 children, 7 living), Noah Boswell (14 children, 13 living), Edward Taylor (13 children, 10 living), Elijah Smith (9 children, 8 living), Ezekiel Boswell (5 children, 4 living), John Wood (7 children, all living), and Harry Organ, half-breed (6 children, all living). Dr Bath Smart should be able to furnish valuable information on this subject; but complete statistics could only be obtained by a Gipsy census. Meanwhile, I ask whether, for every unwholesome Gipsy tent and caravan[1] there are not a dozen such houses as that described in Weyland's *Round the Tower* (Lond. 1875), p. 36:—"There are eight rooms, one of which measures 18 feet by 10. Beds are arranged on each side of it, and are composed of bundles of straw, shavings, and rags. In this one room there slept last night twenty-seven male and female adults, thirty-one children, and

---

[1] Mr Smith must have felt inclined to say to the sketchers of "Gipsy Life" for the *Graphic* and *Illustrated* :—"I took thee to curse them, and, behold, thou hast blessed them altogether." In the one instance where the curse does fall, the "Tent upon Mitcham Common," it seems to have fallen on górgios, to judge at least from attitude and physiognomy. It was unlucky, too, that tent-dwelling Gipsy misery should have so often been confronted in those papers with house-dwelling Irish comfort—the "Interior of a Van near Latimer Road," with "A Bog-trotter's Cabin, Ballintober Bog."

three dogs; fifty-eight human beings were breathing the contaminated air of a close room, the window of which I never see open." A dozen to one! why, all the Gipsy tents in England, good, bad, and indifferent, must be far outnumbered by the dens of Spitalfields alone, if the Rector of Spitalfields tells aught of truth in his letter to the *Times* of 24th April 1880. "Working-Men's Lodgings" is its title; and it describes how, "in the lodging-houses, respectable artizans and working-men find their wives and children exposed to the vitiating influences of the society and companionship of the very dregs of the population, and for many there is no means of escape. The statistics afforded by a house-to-house visitation of any street in this parish, where large tenements are let out in lodgings, are appalling. The overcrowding is awful, and destructive of all sense of decency and propriety. Among a population of over 20,000, mostly poor, and many very poor, there are hundreds of large families occupying one room, and paying for this a very considerable weekly rent." I can well believe that work among slums like these is less interesting and less conspicuous than work among Gipsy tents; but query, is it not more required?

And yet I do advocate Gipsies' registration thus. The details of the system are unknown to me, but in Germany, Gipsies, on reaching a strange town or village, go straight to the police-station, exhibit their passes, and inquire where they have leave to stop. "Nowhere," an English policeman would answer;

but Gipsies, while Gipsies are, must needs stop somewhere ; so ours, in flat defiance of law, camp in green
lane, on common, or by roadside, and are fined on the
morrow for breaking a Highway Act. Or else they
get leave to "draw into" private ground, and heavily
they often have to pay for it. Those Reynoldses,
whom Willy Faa was speaking of, number six
adults and three children ; for permission to camp
upon Fisherrow Links, they paid the Musselburgh
Corporation a guinea a week (*i.e.*, at the rate of £54
a year), and had besides to hire a meadow in which
to "field" their horses. I propose, then, that some
such system as the German be adopted. All Gipsies,
entered in our imaginary census, should be at liberty
to take out travelling licences, tenable during good
conduct, and stipulating, it might be, for the education of their holders' children. The cost of such
licences might be fairly high (say £5), so long as
their privileges answered to their cost. Scattered
through England, there still are scores of places
where Gipsies formerly camped with no offence to
any one, and where they would camp to-day, if only
they durst. The re-opening of these to licence-hold-
ing Gipsies would be one obvious privilege. Among
minor boons, such as Gipsies themselves could best
suggest, might be renewed permission to "put up
cocoanuts" at the Epsom, Ascot, and other great
race-meetings. Why, unless in low betting men's
interest, the game was ever prohibited, is more than
I can say; but I know that a few years back it

brought in many an honest shilling to the younger members of the Gipsy families, often from £1 to £3 a day.

Heighho! while I thus sat and pondered these Utopian daydreams, with a little more perhaps and a great deal less, the day had cleared ; and in the brightening sky I read an augury of brighter things, —cocoanuts and industrial schools, licences and lanes, paced not by " hangmen," but by sanitary inspectors. By the end of my musings and sixth pipe I was almost alone, Lementina having started after all for Madam Morgan's, Silvanus gone down into the town for the condiments of some horrible cow-draught, and the rest dispersed on various missions of business and amusement.   Only Dimiti sat by me, with puckered forehead and solemn gaze ; and him I despatched to the farm to fetch me my fishing-rod.

" You won't catch much on the fly with this fresh on," he remarked ; and " No," I answered ; " but you shall find me some worms, and I'll try my luck with them."   So he brought me my tackle, and, walking with me to the bridge, got me some delicate grubs, with which I did catch two or three small trout, not much to boast of, still something towards a dish.

And as I angled, Dimiti told me how in the Snaky Lane he " lay awake onest, just when it was coming peep o' day ; and when I'd be looking up the trees, I could see little men and carriages sitting in the branches, as plain as could be.   Beautifully dressed they were, bor, all in green clothes like, and some in

white, and some in all sorts of colours. Oaktrees is
really the only trees I ever seen 'em on ; and they'd
sway themselves up and down every time as the
boughs would shake."

Anon he chattered of " canbottles," " peggies,"
" charts," and other birds with quaint provincial
names, unknown to scientific ornithology ; and while
he chattered, I thought of Kingsley's *Westward Ho!*
of Amyas Leigh, who " though he had never had a
single ' object lesson,' or been taught to ' use his
intellectual powers,' knew the names and ways of
every bird and fish and fly." I am not sure, Dimiti,
that I should take such pleasure in your company,
were you a reader of " Penny Dreadfuls," the current
literature of England's poor, or even were you
crammed with all the ologies that go to make up
liberal education. Like Amyas, you certainly are
grossly ignorant in science and religion, but also, it
may be, in some of the evil one learns at a public
school. You have picked up " fallen stars," have
you, " very cold, and like jelly, and just as big as
saucers ; " and you really believe that toothache may
be removed by a ceaseless cry of " O my dear blessed
Lord, do send me well ! " You think it good fun to
play *malade imaginaire*, when, camped on forbidden
ground, your daddy snifts a policeman in the air ;
policemen to you, as to all your backsliding race, are
natural enemies, emblems of progress, *i.e.* of " moving
on." You will always be thankful that you were not
born a górgio, and will strive to improve your talents,

especially in horse-dealing ; and two or three times a
year you will probably get drunk, at the cost of the
dancers to your fiddling.   For you with violin, and
the future Mrs Dimiti with tambourine, will " excite
the unholy dance, technically called the two-penny
hop ; " and that, say theologians, is an offence
unpardonable even to the most loving, generous,
trusting, pleasant nature in the world.   I don't mean,
Dimiti, that these are your good points ; for let whoso
will dissect the Romani heart, and fail, as everyone
has failed before him.   But somewhat like this you
will live, and will rear innumerable dusky children,
and spoil them shamefully ; and you will be known
to a good many friends, unknown to many more
detractors.   At last you will die and be buried, and
crowds of górgios will attend your funeral.   One of
them will suggest, perhaps, that Gipsies have got no
souls ; but more likely nobody will trouble himself
at all about the matter.   Well, I must be off now,
for I have a lot of writing to do this evening,—a
letter, namely, to the waste-paper basket of the
Standard editor.

Chapter Ninth.

N SUNDAY at noon, John Roberts joined
me on Dolgelly bridge. He looked more
than ever like a disguised divine, and the
wonder was that they had not asked him
to preach at the Welsh service, which he had just
attended. Seeing him coming, I hailed him from
afar, "Sor shan, míro párchano siménsa?" and
thought that at last I had caught the right intonation.

But no; he was hardly beside me before he began
that it was easy to see whom I had been studying
under; "which Mr Silvanus Lovell is a very agreeable
gentleman, as I am proud to own him for a cousin;
but, to tell the truth, I can assure you that when I did
speak with him the other evening, all he could answer
was, 'Yes, I jon, my brother;' instead of saying 'Na
jona ma kek so penesa.' Now, I should be shamed to
call myself Romano, and not know our mother's old
language no better nor that; and that, when I was
talking, górgios should understand the half of my
words, and so should make fun upon my head. Now,
Mr Groome, I want you to take particular notice to

this *ch* and the *ow* and *mw*, such as *chobben*, not
hobben, 'victuals.' *Ow* is an article, such as '*the* or *a*
sheep;' and *mw* can often be introduced instead of
mero. We often exempt the *r* in the word, as it
comes better after some other words, when placed
proper. Instead of saying, 'Mero pall is jalled to the
gav,' say 'Mw pall geyas kai ow gav;' and the *g* in
geyas sounds like the beginning of *gather*. Now with
regard to the word *parchannay*, the word means
'respected' (plural), *parchanno* (singular) for a gentleman, *parchannee* for a lady, *parchannay* for both;
tatchano for a gentleman, *tatchannee* for a lady,
tatchanay for both. Now, the *ch* when sounded in
the word *parchannay*, you got to make a curious
sound by letting the sides of your tongue touching
the grinders in the upper range of your teeth."

"Mercy on us, John, your phonetics are as formidable as a German professor's; and certainly, when a
Chair of Romanes is founded at either of our uni-
versities, you shall be its first occupant. But I should
like that better in a letter, for when you pour it forth
so fast, half of it gets spilt; with Silvanus I can only
say, 'I jon.' But how was it that you were away
from home when I ran over to Newtown ten days
since? You wrote me word that you probably would
not be going out at all this summer."

"And so I did; for, through one of my sons being
down at Welshpool, playing for the officers' mess, we
were very unsettled in our minds which way to take
for the best, for a summer's tour; and also through

all our singing, as we use to do in our concerts, being turned into a lot of barking dogs, which we all more or less were touched with a wilful cold. But now we have come to a conclusion to keep around the coast, through the following towns, that is, Machynlleth, Towyn, Dolgelly, Barmouth, Harlech, Portmadoc, and on to Carnarvon, and in the Isle of Anglesea, and out again. And from Bangor I did come over to Dolgelly, to play for this wedding, being as the miller Mr Thomas's mother was second cousin to my own father, John Robert Lewis of Pentre Foelas."

"Well I was quite disappointed at finding your house shut up, for I had been reckoning on our meeting, especially after my failure to visit you last Christmas."

"And was not I grieved and sorry then; for I do assure you I was so glad that you was coming to Newtown, so as you might have the chance to augment your knowledge, by hearing the true language spoken by my wife and myself and a cousin of mine which lives in the town. Had you have heard us three, you would hear it so purely spoken, which you would feel that proud that you would actually say, ' I will take you three up to London, and challenge all the Romany folk about there, around the town.' You must bear in mind, Mr Groome, that there are several instruction music-books for different instruments, but there is nothing like a master after all to get into the right way. I hope you will pardon me for being so plain."

"Surely, O Master. But what do you say, then, to all the plain truths contained in these letters to the *Standard?* You have seen or heard of them?"

"No; what letters?"

"Why, about the Romané, that they are mongrels and heathens, and wickedness knows what else. Gooseberries and Gipsies are filling up half the paper, and the ones are more monstrous than the others."

"No, I never seen no letters, lately leastwise. I remember I did read something in some paper two or three years ago, that a Mr Somebody wrote,[1] which I thought to answer it in real good style; and he well deserved it, for I never read such rubbish in my life. Such gentry like them ought to be downright shamed to attempt to do such things, and not knowing anything of the language. It would serve them right if I were to write a whole Romany letter in one of those papers, and to challenge e'er a one of them to answer it. Now, what do you think is best for me to do? When I see such things in the papers, I get very much vexed."

"I shouldn't wonder, but I have posted an answer myself to these letters, proving that Gipsies out-Angle the Angles in angelic qualities. When it appears, you shall write and back it up,—in English, though, not Romanes. Will you?"

"To the utmost of my ability I will, and glad of

---

[1] I rather think this letter was by myself. At least I know of none by any other to which John's words could refer.

it, being as it has often occurred to me how I should
like for you and me to bring a good book out, and
show before the world that there must be something
very far and unaccountable belonging to our race of
people, also to put some of those gentry in the shades,
if possible, whom has wrote such a lot of trash,
especially when it comes to the Romany language.
There they do make a awful havock of it. It grieves
me to think that my poor mother's language should
be so much messed about by such gentlemen as
knows but little about it, and wrongly informed in
many other things as well. They pretends to be
something what they cannot come to."

"Good, John. You and I will bring out a book;
and its title shall be *Romani Bards and Górgio
Revilers;* and there shall be a picture of you, robed
in your sable garb of woe, for frontispiece."

"Yes, a bookplate of me, playing my ancient prize
Welsh instrument, with all my exercitations for our
race."

"I don't quite follow you—exertions, how?"

"Why, how I have often had a great desire that I
should be permitted to go with my harp to visit some
English camps, and to play for them first of all, so as
they might not jeer me, and to try to say some little
to them about our Blessed Saviour. I feel a great
deal in that way; and if I could do them any good,
I would with all my heart, that is, if they would take
it in that light."

"So, I see; exertions you mean that you would

S

undertake, if only you saw your way. But up by London the Gipsies themselves are preachers to the Gentiles. There is Wester Lee's sister preaches; and by Shoreditch station I have read posters announcing Sermons by Converted Gipsies; and from Essex a friend once sent me a bill to the effect that Gipsies had hired a field (admission 3d.), and would hold a prayer-meeting (D. V.) on such and such a date. And yet the Gipsies are accounted heathens."

" Heathens!"—(with a small shriek)—"why, all our people were born, christened, and buried properly. I can almost tell the names of all the places, with the exception of my Uncle Valentine and my grandfather, William Wood. Of course I am also unable to say where my great-grandfather was born and christened. But there are hardly any now among our people, but what are turned either to the church or the chapel, and a good many to the Catholic chapel."

"Catholics, eh? That's curious in this land of Methodism; though I know that English Gipsies have retained a few rags of Papistry, such as crossing themselves to drive away the cramp, and keeping 'a kind of inverted Lent,' as Mr Crofton calls it, by abstaining from flesh for five Fridays following Good Friday. But there are very few real Catholics among them; and I remember with some of the Bucklands at Oxford there was a regular No Popery row, because one of the women had taken her baby to be christened at St Aloysius."

" Well, my old grandmother, you know, was one of

the Stanleys, and she used always to count her beads
that were around her neck every morning when she
rose up from her bed, and when she used to go upon
her knees to say her prayers. But didn't I never tell
you how Gipsy Mary got turned to be a Catholic ? "

" Never, that I remember. How was that ? "

" One of the Prices she was, kinsfolk of the
Ingrams, and she married my Aunt Silvína's second
son, Black Billy. And she was a very poor fortune-
teller, and none of our people would show her the
genuine way, because she had such an evil tongue.
So she had to do the best she could to come over the
górgios in her own way, and 'ticing them to do many
a foolish little thing, to get their money. And there
was one time that she found out a house to tell
fortunes at, and she got a five-pound note off the
woman, and told her to go to the shop and buy a
pound of soap, and to go to some running water and
wash, and was to say, ' I wash myself away from God
Almighty, I wash myself away from God Almighty.'
And after she did that, the górgie went mad, and she
was taken to the Denbigh Asylum, and died there.
But poor Gipsy Mary had three years illness for per-
suading the foolish woman to do such wickedness,
and she was quite unable to walk during the whole of
that time. When they used to be travelling, she used
to be carried upon a donkey ; and her husband used
to lift her up and down, and had a great deal of
trouble with her. Still and all she used to chatter
away like a magpie ; and neither her husband or her

never attended a place of worship at any time, but
still they were both of them very fond of hearing the
Scriptures read to them, on a Sunday particularly,
for I have read for them a many time.   But it
appears one time that they were in some part of
Flintshire, and near a Catholic chapel ; that she had
a great desire of going to one for the first time, that
she should say, ' Billy, don't you think that you could
carry me to the chapel door, as I may have a chance
to hear some little bit ?'   When my cousin William
said, ' I will, my dear, and glad of it.'   Her wishes
were complied with ; when she only attended a few
Sundays until she got quite well, and she is well and
hearty ever since.   And she sticks faithful and true
to her chapel.   I have seen her many times after she
came through that illness, and she told me many times
she thought that if she only once could have the
chance to go to a place of worship, that she would
get better.   And so she did ; and I am proud to say
that she has been the cause of many of our family to
do the same.   All of my wife's family are Catholics,
and I had some of my uncles and aunts, that are
dead, the same."

"But you yourself, John, belong to the Church of
England, do you not ? "

"Ay, sure.   Before I had my discharge from the
23d Fusileers, I used to keep myself in some curious
ways ; but after, and when I went to a place of worship on Sundays, I found myself beginning to be
more contented.   I did also turn my mother to her

church, and she had a very great turning, and I think
she died happy, poor old woman ; and I must say the
same for my poor old father.   Now my wife, James,
Albert, and Charley, belong to the Baptist chapel ;
Lloyd Wynne, Madoc, Johnny, Sarah, Anne, Reuben,
Ernest, Willie, and myself, belongs to the Church.   So
you see in one family there is a little difference between
us ; still it does not matter where we go so long as we
keep our mind with God."

" Well, that was a strange conversion, Gipsy Mary's.
Are she and her husband living now ? "

" She is ; but with regard to my poor cousin, William
Wood, he died one of these last days, and was buried
quite respectable in a town called Amlwch, in the
county of Anglesea.   They were both of them older
than me of some ten or twelve years, and for some
time they did keep a small shop back in this town
here, and he attended public and private parties
with his Welsh harp and violin when wanted.   She
is a very good little woman, Mary his wife ; and
him, poor fellow, he could not read nor write, but
between service times on Sundays he used to open
his Bible, and look at it for the space of a half an
hour without taking his eyes off it, thinking that
would be some good for him."

" And had they any children ? "

" Only two ; Caroline, which married Bena Wood,
William and Black Nell's son ; and the other was
a boy, and was drowned, poor thing, bathing at
Aberdovey.   And I could tell you something very

unaccountable about that, but I can only give you a little account. There used to be in the dining-room at Kinmel Park—a very large gentleman's house where I in generally play at—a very large picture with two or three different plates upon it of our Blessed Saviour, how he was served by the cruel Jews, just like some poor dear Romano Chal with a lot of nasty spiteful górgios round him. One of the forms was with his hand on his face, and his fingers extended, and his hair all over his forehead, looking very pitiful, and as much as to say, 'Look what I've come to.' And my poor Cousin Billy looked the very same, when sitting down on the grass, and his wife opposite him, and his poor drownded boy in some kind of an old building behind him, and did not know what to do. It struck me there and then how very much he looked like that picture. I am sorry that I can't explain it to you so well as I felt it."

"I think I know what you mean, for I have often been struck myself by the likeness that Romané find between themselves and *Mi-Dúvel*,[1] who was no house-dweller, and rode upon a donkey. But do you know, John, that down in Montenegro, close to

---

[1] "In the language of the Gipsies," writes Max Müller, "*devel*, meaning God, is connected with Sanskrit *deva;*" but the word's chance resemblance to our *devil* has led to one strange misunderstanding in "My Friend's Gipsy Journal":—"When my friend once read the psalm in which the expression 'King of Glory' occurs, and asked a Gipsy if he could say to whom it applied, she was horrified by his glib answer, 'Oh yes, Miss, to the devil!'"

Turkey, it is said that a Gipsy forged the nails for the Crucifixion, and that on that account his race has henceforth been accursed of Heaven?"

"Oh! that is a most wicked falsehood. Why, you know yourself (now don't you?), no Romané can't ever abear a Jew, because they were the people that murdered our Blessed Lord?"

"H'm. One of the Coopers has a Jewess for servant. Still, I fully agree with you that the legend was fabricated by górgios; and it seems to have been quite as unpalatable to foreign Gipsies as to you. For those of Alsace have a legend of their own, opposed to, and probably devised expressly to refute it. How there were two Jew brothers, Schmul and Rom-Schmul. The first of them exulted at the Crucifixion; the other would gladly have saved our Lord from death, and, finding that impossible, did what he could, pilfered one of the nails. So it came about that Christ's feet must be placed one over the other and fastened with a single nail. And Schmul remained a Jew, but Rom-Schmul turned Christian, and was the founder of the Romani race."

Those two legends are given, the one in Dr B. Bogisic's article on "Die slavisirten Zigeuner in Montenegro" (*Das Ausland*, 25th May 1874), the second in Dr G. Mühl's "Die Zigeuner in Elsass und in Deutschlothringen" (*Der Salon*, 1874). The first at least is of high antiquity, if, as I conceive, it is alluded to in "S. Joannis Theologi Commentarius Apocryphus MS. de J. C." (?No. 929 or 1021, Colbert

Coll. Paris Cat. MSS.). Whatever the date of that
Greek manuscript may be, it is certainly early; and
there, according to a citation in Meursius's *Glossarium
Græcobarbarum*, a *kōmodromos* is represented as helping to crucify Christ (καὶ ὅτε φθάσωσιν εἰς τὸν τόπον,
ἐλθὼν ὁ κωμοδρόμος ἂς σταυρώσει αὐτόν). Here to
endeavour fully to identify our modern Gipsies with
the *kōmodromoi* of Byzantine writers would take too
long, but the following are the main grounds of the
proposed identification. Firstly, Du Cange defines
kōmodromoi as "roamers (*circulatores*) and coppersmiths, who rove about the country, like those in
our midst to-day whom we call *Chaudronniers*;"
the modern Roumanian Gipsies are divided into
certain classes—*Calderari* (kettle-smiths), *Aurari*
(gold-workers), &c. Secondly, the five passages
quoted by Du Cange show that the *kōmodromos*
was variously a coppersmith (*chalkeus*) and a gold-
worker (*chrysochóos*), and that the coppersmith used
bellows made of skins, which at once recalls Harff's
admiration at the bellows of Naupliote Gipsies in
1497. Small points enough these, but they must
be viewed in relation to the metallurgical monopoly
enjoyed by Gipsies at the present day in South-East
Europe and in Asia Minor. So exclusively is the
smith's a Gipsy (and therefore a degrading) craft
in Montenegro, that when in 1872 the Government
established an arsenal at Rieka, no natives could be
found to fill its well-paid posts. And Mr Hyde
Clarke informs me, that "over more than one sanják

of the Aidin viceroyalty the Gipsies have still a like
monopoly of iron-working, the *naalband*, or shoeing-
smith, being no smith in our sense at all. He is
supplied with shoes of various sizes by the Gipsies,
and only hammers them on."

The Rom-Schmul legend is also curious, as offering
a possible explanation of the hitherto unexplained
transition from four nails to three in crucifixes during
the twelfth and thirteenth centuries. The fact of that
transition is treated in Dr R. Morris's Introduction to
the *Legends of the Holy Rood* (Early Eng. Text Soc.
1871). There it appears, that while St Gregory
Nazianzen, Nonnus, and the author of the *Ancren
Riwle* speak of three nails, SS. Cyprian, Augustine,
and Grègory of Tours, Pope Innocent III., Rufinus
and Theoderet, and Ælfric speak of four; and that
the earliest known crucifix with three nails only is
a copper one of (?) Byzantine workmanship, dating
from the end of the twelfth century. Now, supposing
Gipsies to have then possessed their present monopoly, this crucifix must have been fashioned by Gipsy
hands, when the three nails would be an easily intelligible protest against the belief that those nails were
forged by the founder of the Gipsy race.

I give the suggestion just for what it is worth, and
I take occasion to commend to the notice of English
archæologists M. Bataillàrd's theory,[1] that pre-historic

---

[1] Set forth in *Origines des Bohémiens* (1875), *Etat de la Question de
l'Ancienneté des Tsiganes en Europe* (1877), *Les Zlotars* (1878), and *La
Question du Bronze et du Fer Aryens* (1880); and supported in F.
Chantre's *Age du Bronze* (4 vols, 1877).

Europe gained from the Gipsies its knowledge of metallurgy. A startling theory, yet one that has won acceptance with several leading Continental *savans*. Against it history has nothing to object, our earliest *certain* knowledge of Gipsies in Europe showing them as slaves in Wallachia in 1372, and as obtaining a renewal of privileges at Nauplia in 1398. On the question whether the Romani language points to an early or to a late migration from India, philologists differ. Professor Ascoli, in his *Saggi indiani* (1876), vol. ii. pp. 312-17, is led by the "peculiar Sanskritic integrity" of Romanes to conclusions according with the pre-historic theory. Its ablest opponent, Dr F. Miklosich, fixes the first appearance of Gipsies in Europe at 810 A.D. (art. "Zigeuner," in Meyer's *Conv.-Lexikon*, 1878). And in Brockhaus's *Conv. - Lexikon* (1879) Professor Pott judiciously opines that the date of such appearance is unknown. In favour of the theory, we have the negative testimony of the Byzantine annalists, who are silent as to any Gipsy immigration ; and there is the positive fact that our modern Gipsies are the chief, often only, farriers, coppersmiths, bellfounders, and armourers in Hungary, and throughout the Balkan peninsula.

The paradox is certainly attractive, that cultured Europe should owe the best part of its civilisation to the uncultured Gipsies ;[1] to whom, too, our

---

[1] Certain it is that Montenegrin independence was saved by weapons of Gipsy workmanship ; and Dr Freeman's eulogies of the Black Mountaineers read strangely by the side of the Russian Bogisic's

weightiest authority on the subject ascribes the introduction of playing-cards. I do not vouch for the ascription, as neither do I exactly hold with that writer in the *Atlantic Monthly* (February 1866), who makes the Gipsies descendants of the Hussites, their name *Gipsy* being a "clumsy corruption" of *Tschischkta*. He should have gone a little further, and proved them propagators of primitive Protestantism, thus: Gipsies have been identified by learned scholars (Peucer, Goar, &c.) with the Athingani ; the Athingani were a branch of the Paulicians ; and the Paulicians, as every schoolboy knows, were the spiritual ancestors of the Albigenses, Wyclifites, Hussites, Lutherans, and Calvinists (Gibbon, ch. liv.). Q.E.D.

But I must submit for investigation my own pet guess, that the discoverers of the Stourbridge fire-clay were Romani Chals, the tradition of that discovery being thus given in Kelly's *Worcestershire* (ed. 1872):—"There are still in the vicinity of the town of Stourbridge descendants of a company (refugees from the kingdom of Hungary and pro-

---

account of how the forgers of those weapons fared. As strange is it to compare Dr Freeman's denunciation of him who "durst ask about the collar of Gurth at a time when," &c., with "Notes on the Gipsy Population of Moldavia," by S. Gardner (*Proc. Roy. Geog. Soc.*, 1857). For there one learns that the Gipsy slaves "have the lash continually applied to them, and are still subjected to the iron collar and a kind of spiked iron mask or helmet, which they are obliged to wear as a mark of punishment and degradation for every petty offence." But Mr Gardner was a Consul ; and after all the Moldavians are Christians, the Gipsies heathens.

vince of Lorraine in the year 1555 or 1556), headed
by a person of the name of Henzoil Henzey, who
trusting to their knowledge of, and practical skill
in, music as a means of existence, and not meeting
with that support in London which they anticipated,
left it and found their way into the Midland Counties,
and at length formed their encampment at the 'Lye
Waste.' Here the wanderers observed, with no small
degree of pleasure, the existence of the valuable
fireclay, out of which in their own country they had
formed the glass and melting pots. The precise spot
upon which the strangers took up their abode, and
where the first glass-house was erected, is still known
by the name of Hungary Hill." In Mr H. Sydney
Grazebrook's valuable *Collections for a Genealogy of
the Noble Families of Henzey, Tyttery, and Tyzack,
"Gentilshommes Verriers," from Lorraine* (Stourb.
1877) the tradition is briefly dismissed as "not
corroborated by any trustworthy evidence," but the
additional detail is furnished, that the discovery of the
fire-clay was made "in digging holes for their tent-
poles;" and further on we learn that the Hennezels
of Lorraine were a "noblesse originaire du Royaume
de Bohéme" (*cf.* Fr. *Bohémiens,* "Gipsies,"), that the
English Henzeys were dark-haired, and that a
favourite Christian name with them was Peregrine.

That is all the support which Mr Grazebrook's
work affords my guess; but neither does it disprove
it, since he merely states that his three families
settled in England "sometime in the sixteenth cen-

tury," without attempting to decide the exact when
or how or why. His genealogical collections begin
with the baptism of one Henzey near Stourbridge
in 1615, and the burial of another at Newcastle-on-
Tyne in 1617; and a passage in Camden's contem-
poraneous *Britannia* has seemingly escaped him,
where it is said that the Tyne glassmakers "are
foreigners, but know not well from whence they
came, only they have a tradition of their being
Normans, and that they came from Stourbridge,
and removed from thence hither in the reign of
Edward VI. or Queen Elizabeth."

With only the tradition, then, to go by, I assume
for the present its general credibility, and start by
remarking, that itinerant tent-dwelling musicians are
far more likely to have been Gipsies than Huguenot
refugees. And that Gipsies might have glassmakers
seems not impossible from these considerations :—
(1) Already in 1876 Mr Bataillard wrote, that "glass-
making, especially in its application to small objects,
such as cups, phials, &c., may well at certain epochs
have occupied a certain number of Gipsies ; and
one ought not to neglect the traces that tradition
may have preserved of such a fact" (*Origines des
Bohémiens*, p. 36). (2) Sir E. Hext's letter to the
Lord Treasurer in 1596 couples tinkers, pedlars,
glassmen, and proctors (Strype's *Annals*, vol. iv. p.
408); and in a Devonshire order regarding rogues,
we read of " petty chapmen, peddlers, glassmen,
tynckers, palmesters, fortune readers, Egiptians, and

the like" (A. Hamilton's "Quarter Sessions under
Charles I." in *Fraser's Mag.*, Jan. 1877). *Glarmestere*,
"glaziers," is the unexplained title of certain Danish
vagabonds, whom Dyrlund considers of Gipsy origin
(*Tatere og Natmandsfolk i Dammark*, p. 219). (3)
The wandering "Muggers" and "Potters" of our
Northern Counties are likewise probably of Gipsy
origin; some of them have certainly a smattering of
Romanes.   I believe that, as a rule, they buy their
earthenware; but from *Good Words for the Young*,
September 1870, it would appear that there are
Derbyshire potters who mould a large quantity of
pots and pans, bake them in their ovens, load eight
or nine donkeys with the ware, and leave their homes
for months.   Observe, too, that Gipsies nowadays
generally buy their baskets, which formerly they
always made themselves.   (4) "At the Birmingham
Police Court, Daniel Moulton was summoned for
selling earthenware measures, beer mugs, which were
false.   The mugs were made in The Potteries, and
were received by defendant as plain cups.   They
were then distributed among his workmen to be
tested, and to have the pattern mark placed on
them.   They were told not to drill any which differed
from the standard.   Instead of testing, they bored
and affixed the pattern plugs to any, and put false
marks on the cups to get increased wages, as they
were paid according to the number that passed the
Inspectors.   They were 'half-gipsies.'   He could
not get others to do the work" (*Local Government*

Chronicle, 30th August 1879). On which it is just worth noting, that "the husband of Sarah Henzey [born at Stourbridge in 1687] is stated to have been one Moulton or Moulson, who lived at Putney."

Such are my arguments; an obvious objection whereto is, that these "noble" families of "gentils-hommes" could hardly have belonged to the "rank that is meanest and most despised of all the families of the land." That is the question. On the one hand, Chatrian, of Erckmann-Chatrian fame, himself a *gentilhomme verrier*, himself blew glass in his youth, so that such *gentilesse* need not depend on immemorial do-nothingness. On the other, the Falls of Dunbar, who gave that burgh members, provosts, and bailies, and who intermarried with the Scottish baronetcy, were believed by others, and believed themselves, to be descended from the Yetholm Faas (Simson, *Hist. of Gipsies*, pp. 237-41). *Noble* and *gentilhomme*, quotha! what are these titles to those of our epitaphs on p. 124? And in 1505 did not James IV. of Scotland commend to the King of Denmark "Anthony Gawin, Earl of Little Egypt?" in 1540 did not his successor grant letters under the Great Seal to "oure louit Johnne Faw, Lord and Erle of Litill Egipt, . . . to assist to him in executioun of justice vpoun his cumpany and folkis conforme to the lawis of Egipt?"

No, this at least is no very formidable objection; Mr Grazebrook himself does not suggest it in his courteous response to some queries addressed him a

year and a half ago. " I do not *think*," he writes,
" that the three families of whom my book treats were
of Gipsy origin, and certainly they did not come from
Hungary but from Lorraine, in which province the
manufacture of glass was carried on at an early
period.   Here they were known as Henzey, Tyttery,
and Tyzack, but in their own country they were de
Hennezel, de Thiétry, and du Thisac ; and the genealogy of the first-named family, as set forth in M. de
la Chenaye-Desbois' *Dictionnaire de la Noblesse de
France* (2d ed. 1774), commences with Henri Hennezel, who flourished towards the close of the fourteenth century.   It is curious that the place where
they established their glass-work should be known as
Hungary Hill ; but were not all wanderers called
Hungarians or Bohemians at that period ?   I think
it is highly probable that the people among whom
these refugees settled supposed them to be Gipsies ;
and they kept themselves aloof from their neighbours,
and intermarried much with each other, especially
those who settled at Newcastle. . . . I commenced
my letter by stating that I did not *think* these people
were of Gipsy origin, but I really know nothing
about that remarkable race.   I observed that Desbois
states that the Hennezels came originally from
Bohemia.   Does this support your theory? . . . I
forgot to mention that the three families were
Huguenots.   Some of the Tyzacks were subsequently
Quakers."

For the present, O Gipsies, take credit to yourselves for having introduced metallurgy, playing-cards, saddlery,[1] Protestantism, folktales, Magyar music, glass-making, and fast-and-loose, for having produced Solario, John Bunyan, and the "Tinclarian Doctor," for having——

"Eh, what, John? what do you say to the Rom-Schmul legend, that it's 'something more like now,' more accordant with your sense of fitness? Very good; but answer me one thing more. Why are Gipsies' animals—Romani hobbies, so to speak—so often found where they have not the slightest business in the world to be? You give it up? Why *Rom* means 'man,' and man in Latin is *homo*, and *Humanum est errare*, is it not? Certainly; but let's push on, else we shall miss our victuals: five minutes more will bring us to the camp."

At the camp great preparations were making for dinner, six gooseberry dumplings on the boil, each mightier than the pudding of the Blameless King; and there was nettle-broth, with a ham and two

---

[1] That is almost self-evident, the Ital., Span., and Port. *basto* coming clearly from the Romani *béshto*, "saddle" (pass. part. of *beshdva*, "I sit"), while *zen*, also Romanes for "saddle," is as clearly the Persian *zin;* and in Persia, according to Beckmann, saddles were probably invented. More than that, the Pers. *zíngar*, "saddler," is not merely the title of saddle-making Persian Gipsies (*Journ. R. As. Soc.*, xvi. 310) and of most of their European brethren, but is the etymon of the Mod. Gk. τζαγγάρης, "shoemaker." Hence it is likely that leather-working generally was introduced to Europe by the Gipsies, who are found at Nauplia cobbling and shoemaking in 1497.

T

rabbits for substance, Romani cake, and I know not what besides. All the women seemed cooking, and none of the men even had been to church. Rather the church had come to them, in the shape of three Welshwomen, who had sung Welsh hymns,—"blessed words," said Lementina piously, though she knows, dear old body, never a word of Welsh. Still, they were keeping Sunday in their way, by abstaining from fishing and fiddling ; and, after all, the Lovells are rather more regular church-goers than Berlin Protestants, whose churches accommodate one-fifth per cent., and whose churches are always empty. For, five or six times a year, the Lovells do go to church, where the parson is a particular friend, or where there is good music, as at the College Chapel on Tenbury Broad Heath, or for a christening ; and when they go, they listen with such painful earnestness as might disturb the balance of an unaccustomed preacher.

Greetings over, John and Silvanus, in the interval before dinner, fell to talking on military topics, for Silvanus's grandfather was a soldier ; so was his youngest sister Sinaminti's boy.

"Poor dear Gad Taylor," he said : "oh! that was in the Isle of Man, and he'd been very bad, down with a sort of fever. And the monkey whom he 'listed with, they were always a kind of friends like, so he said he'd lend him some money, ten shillings I think it was, till such time as he got his pay, to buy him some few little things, victuals and anything nice

that he could fancy. Then as soon as ever Gad was
getting a little better, that he was able to walk about
again, this fine fellow asked him for the money he'd
lent him. And he told him he shouldn't have it till
the next day, and he hadn't a farthing. And then
this monkey quarrelled with him about something or
other, said if he'd have knowed, he wouldn't have
lent him sixpence. And then Gad told him, as soon
as ever he'd got well enough, he'd fight him. And
that same afternoon, while they were sitting at their
dinners, this prodigal monkey was sitting opposite
Gad ; and, before anyone noticed what he was up to,
he drawed a pistol out of his pocket, and shot poor
Gad right through the heart, beseems. Then they
made this monkey carry his own coffin (that's what
was said leastwise), and walk over the grave that was
dug for him, and ten soldiers shot him, so there was
two dead men in one day. Lord ! " he concluded, " I
wouldn't have none of my boys in none of your
armies, not if you'd make me Pope o' Rome for it.
And however did you come for to go and do such
foolishness ? "

"Well," John explained, " I was only a lump of a
boy, fourteen years of age ; and it was a very poor
time with us, that wilful cold winter of 1829 ; and we
were down in Breconshire, and all of us went to the
town. I strolled to the barracks, and stood seeing
the soldiers go through their drill, and thinking how
fine it was, till I said to my father if I should go with
them. So there and then I enlisted for a drummer in

the Royal Welsh Fusileers, on the 7th of February 1830, in Brecon Barracks. And from there I did go to Plymouth, and from there to Ireland, where we were quartered some few years, till we came back again to England, to Portsmouth, and from there to Winchester in 1835. The next place was Weedon, and from there to Blackburn, when I left them the first time on furlough. I stopped away from them for a twelvemonths, for I married my cousin Perpínia, but I had a many a chase to be taken as a deserter. The worst time was when I was going to be taken was in Swansea, when I was chased and had to run through the river four times, and when they missed to catch me. And one of the policemen, name of Tommy Low, was considered one of the best runners in that part of the country. But after all I was taken in two or three days' time, by being too free and showing myself too bold, and taken to Dublin, and was tried by a court-martial, but did not get one day's punishment. After about three months' time I asked for a pass, from two P.M. until eight in the morning, where I was then in Holyhead and my father too ; so we did all escape to South Wales, but in Cardiff and the Welsh Hay I was very near taken again. Last I resolved to make up my money, what I was getting with my harp in all those gentlemen's, to go and give myself up to my regiment and purchase my discharge.

"When I went back to the Isle of Wight, I did take my harp with me, and before giving myself up

one of the 42d officers did ask me to play a tune, when
all the depôt were on parade ; and him, not knowing
that I was a deserter, took me down in front of the
officers' quarters, and where the Colonel's lady was at
the time. And when I was playing, all the officers
and soldiers came around me, and not one did not
know me until I gave myself up to the captain that
belonged to my regiment ; after that a good many
came to shake hands with me. I was tried by
another court-martial, but had no punishment again.
The Colonel's lady did beg me off, through the harp ;
and I was not very long until I had my discharge
and got myself clear from them altogether ; and
returned home to my wife and father and mother
and sisters, in a place near Llanrhydd and Llansyllin,
and very pleasant it was.

"They were camping out near a beautiful river-
side, where some of my sisters were some of them
washing themselves, with their long black hair hanging over their shoulders, and singing a song with the
words in it, wishing for me to come home. When all
at onest some of them did spy me out, and out they
give the run for the best, and said, 'Oh! my dear
brother is come home.' And then my wife comes,
as well as she could, for she had not long been up
from her confinedment, with Lloyd, my oldest son.
I comes to the tents, when my mother said, 'Veyan,
mw chavo? sar shonesa tot? Jona ta kino shan. Jaw,
chai, ta ceday kosey khosht, ta prastay to alley panes-
key, te keras *some* choben leskey. Jona ta bockaloo

sillo.'[1] My father comes home from Oswestry, thinking he would meet me there, on horseback. 'Well,
boy, did you come?' 'Yes, father.' 'You soon had
your discharge, after I wrote to the Duke of Welling-
ton.' 'Yes I did.' Mother speaks: 'Did they do
anything to you, my daddy?' 'No, mammy; they
done nothing whatever to me.' One of my sisters
speaks now: 'Dere, dórdi! don't you remember my
brother sending home in the letter, that the lady did
beg him free?' 'Well, ay, ay, child, I am moider-
ing; now I 'member all about it.' The people of the
neighbourhood soon came to know that I came
home, and a great many visited our camp, some of
the highest; and I had to play my harp for them
to dance upon the green, and they made me a very
great welcome. And I had plenty of money from
them, and the people don't forget the time ever since.
After I had my discharge I was more bold and free
to go anywhere, and I played at almost all the
head gentlemen's houses in both North and South
Wales, and good many in England, also played in
a many a Eisteddfod."

This, with some breaks, was the story of John's
campaigns. Dinner succeeded, during which the
talk turned on the concerts of the Roberts family;
and John told us how they had lately been playing

---

[1] John's own orthography : *Anglice*—"Art come, my child? how art
thou? I know that thou are weary. Go, girl, and gather a little wood,
and run thou down for water, that we may do some food for him. I
know that he is hungry."

at the Aberystwith skating-rink, but how they generally either hired a public hall, or got the loan of a
schoolroom from the clergyman. Also, how two
years back some of his boys had been orchestra to
a travelling circus.

" Not Holloway's ? " Starlína asked.

" I can't rightly remember the name," said John ;
" but it wasn't that. For why ? "

" Because that was a canvas theatre that I went to
at Gloucester with a young gentlemen, and I was far
back up among the górgios, right behind, you know.
And this young rei could understand a bit of Róm'nimus, coming up to our place so often ; and then one
of the young women come on the stage dressed like a
Romani chei, with a lot of baskets. Then presently a
young man come in, like a young Gipsy chap (he was
rather a nice-looking fellow too) ; and they began
talking together. She wanted to tell his fortune,
then suddenly she found he was a Romano. Then
he asked her (all in Róm'nimus) if she would marry
him, and then they began talking about having a nice
tan and pretty *chavé*, and all sorts of things like that.
And I was struck. I nudge the young rei beside me,
as though he could understand one half they said ;
and had the hardest task with myself to keep from
shouting to them. And then, two or three nights
after that, we were all in a public, and the men from
this theatre were sitting there drinking. My daddy
was talking to some of the boys, never taking no
notice of them. Suddenly we heard them chattering

away like a lot of Romani magpies; and my daddy said, 'Come on, let's go; they know too much here.' And we walked off."

"What theatre did you say say it was, 'Liná?" I inquired.

" Holloway's; a sort of travelling thing, not much account, rubbish. *The Flowers of the Forest*, that was the play."

" I asked because there was once a famous theatre, Richardson's, the greatest ever travelled. Kean belonged to it for several years. And I know that when old Richardson died (more than thirty years ago that must have been), it was taken on by a Nelson Lee. Of course there are Gipsy Lees, and Nelson is a common Romani name (Matty Cooper has a son called Nelson); so I have often wondered whether this Nelson Lee was not a Romano."

"Can't say, brother, I'm sure; but the man at Brummagem as we often gets our baskets off, he knows a good bit of the talk. A regular górgio, but he gets it from so many travellers coming to his shop."

"So! I must look him up some day. But, 'Lina, your story put me in mind of something that happened once at Baldock fair. There were a lot of the Shaws and Drapers and Bunces there; and they made up a party, of which I was one, to go to a Pepper's Ghost entertainment. When they got in they faced the darkness pretty stoutly; but as soon as ever it came to spectres and skeletons, they were up in an instant, and out they scurried, hustling the children before them, and crying, 'Devil's doings! witches! run for mi-Dúvel's sake!'   Dórdi! how I laughed."

"'Twasn't no laughing for them," Silvanus observed, "they thought, dear ignorant people, Old Nick was coming to fetch 'em."

"Like Riley Smith, eh?"

"Ay," Pyramus chimed in, "that stopped at Battersea, you'll mean. I've often heard tell on that, brother, but never knew the exact rights of it. What was it all about?"

"I hardly know myself; but I first heard the story from two of the Lees at Gorleston. Lucretia must have met them—George and Horace, one with a wife named Angelina, and the other married to a little Welshwoman. We were speaking of one of the Pinfolds, a cousin, I take it, of Lucretia's; and George declared that Annabel Pinfold had 'sold her blood to the Beng, like Riley Smith.' Of course I got asking who Riley Smith might be, and the story ran thus, as well as I remember. Riley was the unluckiest Gipsy going. He never bought a horse for less, or sold one for more, than its proper value; his purchases, indeed, were always falling lame, or drowning themselves, or doing something foolish of the kind. He never made a bet that he did not lose, and Riley was rather a sporting character. And Mrs Riley could hardly ever tell a górgie her fortune, without the misfortune to herself

of a month's hard labour in the county gaol. It
was at Ascot on a summer evening, and Riley sat
very melancholy in the mouth of his tent. He had
lost that day eight golden sovereigns at pitch-and-
toss; and 'Oh!' he was thinking, 'if I could sell my
blood, wouldn't I snap at the chance?' 'So you
can,' said a voice; and dórdi! just before him stood
a wizzened ill-looking mannikin, dressed very old-
fashioned like, with a villainous brickdust-coloured
face, not comely black like yours, and with two long
curls, hanging one each side of that face. 'So you
can,' he said; and as he spoke he kept wriggling
like an eel; 'and you shall have the finest luck in
the world, Riley, and nothing to do for it but to
come to the quarry'—(I forget its exact name, but it
was somewhere on the Berkshire Downs)—'on the
last Monday of every month at midnight, and pay
me a silver shilling.' These were easy terms, thought
Riley, and closed with the bargain; and for a year
and a half no Romano Chal was ever so lucky as
he. A splendid new waggon he had built at Leeds,
and in that waggon were five grand silver teapots,
and in each of the teapots one hundred glittering
sovereigns. But, wait a bit; one evening Riley was
sitting in the best parlour of the head public-house
at Newbury, with his pockets so stuffed with money,
that he had to pin them up to keep it from
rolling on the floor; and first he called for a glass
of beer, and then for a pint of ale, then for a bottle
of wine, and then for a pail of brandy. How much

of the last he swallowed, I cannot say ; at any rate, he never left the house that night, and this was the last Monday in November. Under the table he tumbled, and there he lay till daybreak ; and, as he lay, the crafty landlord emptied his pockets ; when he came to himself, he had not one farthing left. And few were the farthings that ever thereafter came into Riley's hands, for that very night his waggon was burnt to ashes, and his former unluck was luck to what it was now. Wretchedly poor, he died at last up by London. That was George Lee's account ; and I was telling it once to Chris Taylor's wife at Battersea, when she pointed out an old tottering desolate building as the house in which Riley died. And while he lay dying, the windows kept slamming up and down, the doors banging to and fro ; and this, Mrs Taylor declared, was a sign that the Beng was come to fetch Riley home."

"That was most horrible," said Lementina ; and, to dispel the horror, I proposed that John should exercise his story-telling talent, which, nothing loth, he agreed to do, premising that this tale was taken from the *Arabian Nights*, and that its title was

"AN OLD KING AND HIS THREE SONS
IN ENGLAND.

" Once upon a time there was an old King, who had three sons ; and the old King fell very sick one time, and there was nothing at all could make him well but some golden apples from a far country. So the three

brothers went on horseback to look for some of those
apples to recover their father.   The three brothers set
off together, and when they come to some cross roads,
they halted and refreshed themselves a bit ; and there
they agreed to meet on a certain time, and not one
was to go home before the other.   So Valentine took
the right, and Oliver went on straight, and poor Jack
took the left.   And, so as to make my long story
short, I shall follow poor Jack, and leave the other
two take their chance, for I don't think they was
much good in them.   Well, now poor Jack rides off
over hills, dales, valleys, and mountains, through
woolly woods and sheepwalks, where the old chap
never sounded his hollow bugle-horn, further than I
can tell you to-night or ever I intend to tell you.
At last he came to some old house, near a great
forest, and there was some old man sitting out by
the door, and his look was enough to frighten the
Devil ; and the old man said to him, ' Good morning,
my king's son.'   ' Good morning to you, old gentleman,' was the answer by the young prince, and
frightened out of his wits, but he did not like to
give in.

   " The old gentleman told him to dismount, and to
go in to have some refreshments, and to put his
horse in the stable, such as it was.   After going in,
and Jack feeling much better after having something
to eat, and after his long ride, begun to ask the old
gentleman how did he know that he was a king's
son.   ' Oh dear ! ' said the old man, ' I knew that

you was a king's son, and I know what is your
business better than what you do yourself. So you
will have to stay here to-night; and when you are
in bed, you mustn't be frightened when you hear
something come to you. There will come all manner
of snakes and frogs, and some will try to get into
your eyes and into your mouth; and mind,' the old
man said, 'if you stir the least bit, then you will turn
into one of those things yourself.' Poor Jack did not
know what to make of this, but however he ventured
to go to bed; and just as he thought to have a bit o'
sleep, here they came around him, but he never stirred
one bit all night.

"'Well, my young son, how are you this morning?'
'Oh, I am very well, thank you; but I did not have
much rest.' 'Well, never mind that; you have got
on very well so far, but you have a great deal to go
through before you can have the golden apples to go
to your father. So now you better come to have
some breakfast before you start on your way to my
other brother's house. Now you will have to leave
your own horse here with me, until you come back
here again to me, and to tell me everything about
how you got on.'

"After that out comes a fresh horse for the young
prince, and the old man give him a ball of yarn, and
he flung it between the horse's two ears; and off he
goes as fast as the wind, which the wind behind could
not catch the wind before, until he came to his second
oldest brother's house. When he rode up to the door,

he had the same salute as he had from the first old
man, but this one was much uglier than the first one.
He had long grey hair, and his teeth was curling out
of his mouth, and his finger and toe nails were not
cut for many thousands of years. So I shall leave
you to guess what sort of a looking being he was, but
still his Romani speech was soft and nice, much different to his younger brother.   He puts his horse in a
much better stable, and calls him in, and gives him
plenty to eat and drink, and lots of tobacco and
brandy, and they have a bit of chat before they goes
to bed. When the old man asks him many questions.
'Well, my young son, I suppose that you are one of
the King's children, and come to look for the golden
apples to recover him, because he is sick.'

"*Jack.*—'Yes, I am the youngest of the three
brothers, and I should like well to get them to go
back with.'

"*Old Man.*—' Well, don't mind, my young son. I
will send before you to-night to my oldest brother,
when you go to bed, and I will say all to him what
you want, and then he will not have much trouble
to send you on to the place where you must go to
get them. But you must mind to-night not to stir
when you hear those things biting and stinging you,
or else you will work great mischief to yourself.'

" The young man went to bed, and beared all, as he
did the first night, and got up the next morning well
and hearty, and thought a good deal of the old man's
Romani way the night before. After a good break-

fast, and passing some few remarks, What a curious
place that was, when the old man should say 'Yes' to
him, 'you will come to a more curious place soon, and
I hope I shall see you back here all right;' when out
comes another fresh horse, and a ball of yarn to throw
between his ears.   The old man tells him to jump up,
and said to him that he has made it all right with his
oldest brother to give him a quick reception, and not
to delay any whatever, 'as you have a good deal to go
through in a very short and quick time.'

"He flung the ball, and off he goes as quick as
lightning, and comes to the oldest brother's house.
(I forgot to tell you that the last old man told him
not to be frightened at this one's looks.)   Well, to
make my long story short, the old man received him
very kindly, and told him that he long wished to see
him, and that he would go through his work like a
man, and return back here safe and sound.   'Now
to-night I shall give you rest; there shall nothing
come to disturb you, so as you may not feel sleepy
to-morrow.   And you must mind to get up middling
early, for you got to go and come all in the same
day; for there will be no place for you to rest within
thousands of miles of that place; and if there was,
you would stand in great danger never to come from
there in your own form.   Now, my young Prince,
mind what I tell you.   To-morrow, when you go in
sight of a very large castle, which will be surrounded
with black water, the first thing you will do you
will tie your horse to a tree, and you will see three

beautiful swans in sight, when you will say, 'Swan, swan, carry me over for the name of the Griffin of the Greenwood ;' and the swans will swim you over to the castle. There will be three great entrances, before you go in. The first will be guarded by four great giants, and drawn swords in their hands ; the second entrance lions and other things ; and the other with fiery serpents and other things too frightful to mention. You will have to be there exactly at one o'clock ; and mind and leave there precisely at two, and not a moment later. When the swans carry you over to the castle, you will pass all these things, when they will be all fast asleep, but you must not notice any of them. When you go in, you will turn up to the right, you will see some grand rooms, then you will go down stairs and through the cooking kitchen, and through a door on your left you go into a garden, where you will find the apples you want for your father to get him well. After you fill your wallet, you make all the speed you possibly can, and call out for the swans to carry you over the same as before. After you get on your horse, should you hear anything shouting or making any noise after you, be sure not to look back, as they will follow you for thousands of miles ; but when the time will be up and you near my place, it will be all over. Well now, my young man, I have told you all you have to do to-morrow ; and mind, whatever you do, don't look about you when you see all those frightful things asleep. Keep a good heart, and make

haste from there, and come back to me with all the
speed you can. I should like to know how my two
brothers were when you left them, and what they
said to you about me.'

"'Well, to tell the truth, before I left London,
my father was sick, and said I was to come here to
look for the golden apples, for they were the only
things would do him good ; and when I came to your
youngest brother, I could not understand him well :
his speech was like the English Gipsies' and not like
yours.[1] You speak the same as the Welsh Gipsies,
and so I understood your second brother well. He
told me many things what to do before I came here.
And I thought once that your youngest brother put
me in the wrong bed, when he put all those snakes to
bite me all night long, until he [*i.e.* the middle brother]
told me ' So it was to be,' and said, ' So it is the same
here,' but said you had none in your beds, but said
when I came to you, I should find you a fine dear
Romani old man.

"*The Old Man.*—'So 'tis, my daddy; my youngest
brother ran away, when he was young, with the
English Gipsies, and their speech is not the same as
our speech. Well, let's take a drop more brandy and
a little tobacco, and then let's go to bed. You need
not fear. There are no snakes here.'

---

[1] This point is lost, of course, in my translation. In the original
MS. the youngest brother uses the broken dialect, put by John Roberts
in the mouths of all English Gipsies, while the two others speak in the
very deepest Romanes.

U

"The young man went to bed, and had a good night's rest, and got up the next morning as fresh as newly-caught trout. Breakfast being over, when out come the other horse, and while saddling and fettling, the old man begun to laugh, and told the young gentleman that if he saw a pretty young lady, not to stay with her too long, because she may waken, and then he would have to stay with her or to be turned into one of those unearthly monsters, like those which he will have to pass by going into the castle.

"'Ha! ha! ha! you make me laugh that I can scarcely buckle the saddle straps. I think I shall make it all right, my uncle, if I sees a young lady there, you may depend.'

"'Well, my daddy, I shall see how you will get on.'

"So he mounts his Arab steed, and off he goes like a shot out of a gun. At last he comes in sight of the castle. He ties his horse safe to a tree, and pulls out his watch. It was then a quarter to one, when he called out, 'Swan, swan, carry me over, for the name of the old Griffin of the Greenwood.' No sooner said than done. A swan under each side, and one in front, took him over in a crack. He got on his legs, and walked quietly by all those giants, lions, fiery serpents, and all manner of other frightful things too numerous to mention, while they were all fast asleep, and that only for the space of one hour, when into the castle he goes neck or nothing. Turning to the right, up-stairs he runs, and enters into a very grand bedroom, and seen a beautiful Princess laying full stretch on a

beautiful gold bedstead, fast asleep. It will take me
too long to describe the other beautiful things which
was in the room at the time, so you will pardon me
for going on, for there was no time to lose. He
gazed on her beautiful form with admiration, and he
takes her garter off, and buckles it on his own leg,
and he buckles his on hers ; he also takes her gold
watch and pocket-handkerchief, and exchanges his
for hers ; after that ventures to give her a kiss, when
she very near opened her eyes. Seeing the time
short, off he runs downstairs, and passing through the
cooking kitchen, through which he had to pass to go
into the garden for the apples, he could see the cook
all-fours on her back on the middle of the floor, with
the knife in one hand and the fork in the other. He
found the apples out, and filled the wallet well ; and
by passing through the kitchen the cook did very
near waken, and she did wink on him with one eye ;
but he was obliged to make all the speed he possibly
could, as the time was nearly up. He called out for
the swans, and off they managed to take him over ;
but they found that he was a little heavier than when
he was going over before. No sooner than he had
mounted his horse, he could hear a tremendous noise,
and the enchantment was broke, and they tried to
follow him, but all to no purpose. He was not long
before he came to the oldest brother's house ; and
glad enough he was to see it, for the sight and the
noise of all those things that were after him very
near frightened him to death.

"'Welcome, my daddy; I am proud to see you. Dismount and put the horse in the stable, and come in and have some refreshments; I know you are hungry after all you have gone through in that castle. And tell me all what you did, and all what you saw there. There was other kings' sons went by here to go to that castle, but they never came back alive, and you are the only one that ever broke the spell (for me to go from here). And now you must come with me, and a sword in your hand, and must cut my head off, and must throw it in that well.'

"The young Prince dismounts, and puts his horse in the stable, and they goes in to have some refreshments, for I can assure you he wanted some; and after telling him everything that passed, which the old gentleman was very pleased to hear, they both went for a walk together, the young Prince looking around and seeing the place all round him looking dreadful, also the old man. He could scarcely walk from his toe-nails curling up like ram's horns that had not been cut for many hundred years, and big long hair; and although his teeth was curling out of his mouth, he could speak the Romani language better than any other. They come to a well, and he gives the Prince a sword, and tells him to cut the old man's head off, and to throw it in that well. The young man, through him being so kind to him, has to do it against his wish, but has to do it.

"No sooner he does it, and flings his head in the well, than up springs one of the finest young gentle-

men you would wish to see; and instead of the old
house and the frightful-looking place, it was changed
into a beautiful hall and grounds. And they went
back and enjoyed themselves well, and had a good
laugh about the castle, when he told him all about
what had passed, especially when he told him about
the cook winking on him and could not open the
other eye.

"The young Prince leaves this young gentleman
in all his glory, and he tells the young Prince before
leaving that he will see him again before long. They
have a jolly shake-hands, and off he goes to the next
oldest brother; and, to make my long story short, he
has to serve the other two brothers the same as the
first, and he has to take to his own horse to go home.

"Now the youngest brother there was a good deal
of the English Gipsy in him, and begun to ask him
how things went on, and making inquiries and asking,
'Did you see my two brothers?'

"'Yes.'

"'How did they look?'

"'Oh! they looked very well. I liked them much.
They told me many things what to do.'

"'Well, did you go to the castle?'

"'Yes, my uncle.'

"'And will you tell me what you see in there?
Did you see the young lady?'

"'Yes, I saw her, and plenty other frightful things.'

"'Did you hear any snake biting you in my oldest
brother's bed?'

" ' No, there were none there ; I slept well.'

" ' You won't have to sleep in the same bed to-night. You will have to cut my head off in the morning.'

" The young Prince had a good night's rest, and changed all the appearance of the place by cutting his head off before he started in the morning, having a good breakfast, and supplying himself with a little brandy and a good lot of tobacco for the road before starting, for he had a very long way to go, and his horse had not the same speed as theirs had. A jolly shake-hands, and tells him it's very probable that he shall see him again very soon when he will not be aware of it. This one's mansion was very pretty, and the country around it beautiful, after having his head cut off; and off he goes, over hills, dales, valleys, and mountains, and very near losing his apples again. (I forgot to tell you that he give some to each of those brothers before leaving.)

" At last he arrives at the cross roads, where he has to meet his brothers on the very day appointed. Coming up to the place, he sees no tracks of horses, and, being very tired, he lays himself down to sleep, by tying the horse to his leg, and putting the apples under his head. When presently up comes the other brothers the same time to the minute, and found him fast asleep; and they would not waken him, but said one to another, ' Let us see what sort of apples he has got under his head.' So they took and tasted them, and found they were different to theirs. They took and changed his apples for theirs, and hooked it off to London as fast as they could, and left the poor fellow sleeping.

"After a while he awoke, and, seeing the tracks of other horses, he mounted and off with him, not thinking anything about the apples being changed. He had still a long way to go by himself, and by the time he got near London, he could hear all the bells in the town ringing, but did not know what was the matter until he rode up to the palace, when he came to know that his father was recovered by his brothers' apples. When he got there, his two brothers went off to some sports for a while; and the King was very glad to see his youngest son, and was very anxious to taste his apples. And when he found out that they were not good, and thought that they were more for poisoning him, he sent immediately for the head butcher to behead his youngest son; and was taken away there and then in a carriage. But instead of the butcher taking his head off, he took him to some forest not far from the town, because he had pity on him, and there left him to take his chance, when presently up comes a big hairy bear, limping upon three legs; and the Prince, poor fellow, climbed up a tree, frightened of him, and the bear telling him to come down, that it's no use of him to stop there. With hard persuasion poor Jack comes down, and the bear speaks to him in Romanes, and bids him to 'Come here to me; I will not do you any harm.

It's better for you to come with me and have some refreshments; I know that you are hungry all this time.'

"The poor young Prince says, 'No, I am not very hungry; but I was very frightened when I saw you coming to me first, when I had no place to run away from you.'

"The bear said, 'I was also afraid of you when I saw that gentleman setting you down from that carriage. I thought you would have some guns with you, and that you would not mind killing me if you would see me; but when I saw the gentleman going away with the carriage, and leaving you behind by yourself, I made bold to come to you, to see who you was; and now I know who you are very well. Isn't you the King's youngest son? I seen you·and your brothers and lots of other gentlemen in this wood many times. Now before we go from here, I must tell you that I am a Romano Chal in disguise; and I shall take you where we are stopping at.'

"The young Prince up and tells him everything from first to last, how he started in search of the apples, and about the three old men, and about the castle, and how he was served at last by his father after he came home; and instead of the butcher to take his head off, he was kind enough to leave him to have his life, and to take his chance in the forest, live or die; 'and here I am now, under your protection.'

"The bear tells him, 'Come on, my Brother; there

shall be no harm come to you as long as you are
with me.'

"So he takes him up to the tents; and when they
sees 'em coming, the girls begin to laugh, and says,
'Here is our Jubal coming with a young gentleman.'
When he advanced nearer the tents, they all begun
to know that he was the young Prince that had
passed by that way many times before; and when
Jubal went to change himself, he called most of
them together in one tent, and tells them everything
all about him, and tells them to be kind to him.
And so they were, for there was nothing that he
desired but what he had, the same as if he was in
the palace with his father and mother. He was
allowed to romp and play with the girls, but no
further, through his princely manners and the chastity
of the girls hindered all bad thoughts. Him having
lessons on the Welsh harp when a boy by some
Welsh harper belonging to the Woods or Roberts
family, who were Welsh Gipsies of North Wales,
made a little difference to his way of speaking to
that of the London magpies, when they used to say,
'*Dorda!* this young *rye* talks as if he was two
hundred years old; we can't understand him.' They
used to have a deal of fun with him at night-time,
when telling his funny tales by the fire. Jubal, after
he pulled off his hairy coat, was one of the smartest
young men amongst them, and he stuck to be the
young Prince's closest companion. The young Prince
was always very sociable and merry, only when he

would think of his gold watch, the one as he had
from the young Princess in that castle. The butcher
allowed him to keep that for company, and did not
like to take it from him, as it might come useful
to him some time or another. And the poor fellow
did not know where he lost it, being so much excited
with everything.

"He passed off many happy days with the Stanleys
and Grays in Epping Forest; but one day him and
poor Jubal was strolling through the trees, when they
came to the very same spot where they first met,
and, accidentally looking up, he could see his watch
hanging up in the tree which he had to climb when
he first seen poor Jubal coming to him in the form
of a bear; and cries out, 'Jubal, Jubal, I can see
my watch up in that tree.' 'Well, I am sure, how
lucky!' exclaimed poor Jubal; 'shall I go and get
it down?' 'No, I'd rather go myself,' said the young
Prince.

"Now when all this was going on, the young
Princess whom he changed those things with in
that castle, seeing that one of the King of England's
sons had been there by the changing of the watch
and other things, got herself ready with a large
army, and sailed off for England. She left her
army a little out of the town, and she went with
her guards straight up to the palace to see the King,
and also demanded to see his sons, and brought a
fine young boy with her about nine or ten months
old. They had a long conversation together about

different things. At last she demands one of the
sons to come before her; and the oldest comes, when
she asks him, 'Have you ever been at the Castle of
Melvales?' and he answers, 'Yes.' She throws down
a pocket-handkerchief, bids him to walk over that
without stumbling. He goes to walk over it, and
no sooner he put his foot on it, he fell down and
broke his leg. He was taken off immediately and
made a prisoner of by her own guards. The other
was called upon, and was asked the same questions,
and had to go through the same performance, and
he also was made a prisoner of. Now she says,
'Have you not another son?' when the King began
to shiver and shake and knock his two knees
together that he could scarcely stand upon his legs,
and did not know what to say to her; he was so
much frightened. At last a thought came to him
to send for his head butcher, and inquired of him
particularly, Did he behead his son, or is he alive?

"'He is saved, O King.'

"'Then bring him here immediately, or else I shall
be done for.'

"Two of the fastest horses they had were put in
the carriage, to go and look for the poor Welsh-
harping Prince; and when they got to the very
same spot where they left him, that was the time
when the Prince was up the tree, getting his watch
down, and poor Jubal standing a distance off. They
cried out to him, Did he see another young man in
this wood. Jubal, seeing such a nice carriage, thought

something, and did not like to say No, and said
Yes, and pointed up the tree ; and they told him to
come down immediately, as there is a young lady in
search of him with a young child.

"'Ha! ha! ha! Jubal, did you ever hear such a
thing in all your life, my brother?'

"'Do you call him your brother?'

"'Well, he has been better to me than my
brothers.'

"'Well, for his kindness he shall come to accompany
you to the palace, and see how things will turn out.'

"After they go to the palace, he has a good wash,
and appears before the Princess, when she asks him,
or puts the question to him, Had he ever been at the
Castle of Melvales? when he with a smile upon his
face, and gives a graceful bow. And says my Lady,
'Walk over that handkerchief without stumbling.'
He walks over it many times, and dances upon it,
and nothing happened to him. She said, with a
proud and smiling air, 'That is the young man;'
and out comes the exchanged things by both of
them. Presently she orders a very large box to be
brought in and to be opened, and out come some
of the most costly uniform that was ever wore on
a emperor's back ; and when he dressed himself up,
the King could scarcely look upon him from the
dazzling of the gold and diamonds on his coat and
other things. He orders his two brothers to be
in confinement for a period of time ; and before the
Princess demands him to go with her to her own

country, she pays a visit to the Gipsies' camp, and she makes them some very handsome presents for being so kind to the young Prince. And she gives Jubal an invitation to go with them, which he accepts, also one of the girls for a nurse; wishes them a hearty farewell for a while, promising to see them again in some little time to come, by saying, 'Cheer up, comrades, I'm a Romani myself; I should like to see you in my country.'

"They go back to the King and bids farewell, and tells him not to be so hasty another time to order people to beheaded [*sic*] before having a proper cause for it. Off they go with all their army with them; but while the soldiers were striking their tents, he bethought himself of his Welsh harp, and had it sent for immediately to take with him in a beautiful wooden case. After they went over, they called to see each of those three brothers whom the Prince had to stay with when he was on his way to the Castle of Melvales; and I can assure you, when they all got together, they had a very merry time of it. The last time I seen him, I play upon the Prince's harp; and he told me he should like to see me again in North Wales in company with Mr Groome. Ha! ha! ha! I am glad that I have come to the finish. I ought to have a drop of Scotch ale for telling all those lies."

"So you ought, John," I remarked; "for that is the finest of all your stories. I doubt, though, if it

is to be found in the *Arabian Nights ;* certainly it
was wanting in my copy."

"But that was where I did get it," said John, a
trifle nettled at my incredulity ; "leastwise if it was
not from my poor old mother, or else from my
grandmother, and she was a wonderful woman for
telling stories."

"I fancy that that was a more likely source ; but
where, then, did you study the *Arabian Nights ?* "

"It was at Pentre Foelas, Denbighshire, my father's
native place, and his cousin did keep a small farm
there ; and sometimes, when he used to be very poor,
my father used to send me to his cousin, to provoke
them when they would not send him some money,
when he wanted some ; and then I used to work
upon the farm. And there was onest, I remember,
when I was quite a little one, my cousin told me
to go to some lonesome house near some high
mountain, and get myself new boots or clogs. I
got the new clogs, and proud I was of them, the
very first time that I put them on my feet. The
servant-girl used to call me by the name of *Shonin,*
instead of *John ;* and I used to carry turf to put on
the fire and to wash potatoes for dinner and supper,
—that the first day I put on my new clogs, she sent
me to wash some potatoes. Which I used to pick
them up from the upper end of the building where
they used to keep the turf, and she used to be in the
bottom end of the building, churning and making
butter ; and I had to pass her place to go down in

the little field, where there was a clear little running
brook. So I went with the basket on my head as
usual, and flung it down in the water where I used
to ; and, looking for the besom what I used to scrub
the potatoes with, I could see the basket going down
the river, and ne'er a 'tatoe in it. I forgot to pick
the potatoes up, because I was so vainglorious of
my clogs ; and when I went back, the servant-girl
was splitting her sides laughing, because she knew
very well that I had no time to pick them up. That
and a great many more little simple things I could
mention, to show what a poor silly boy had to go
through ; but that was where I read this book, for
my cousin bought it from Wrexham fair ; and it was
full of very curious book-plates. Oh dear ! oh dear !
that was a many a day ago. But come, Mr Groome,
you are a celebrated literary gentleman "—(a back-
thrust this, for my impugnment of his story's origin)
—"you should give us some of the advantages of
your superior knowledge, something that *you* have
learnt from books."

"All right ; but what is it to be ? Another letter
from the newspapers, Silvanus ? "

"Dear blessed heart, man, no," Lementina inter-
posed ; " I can't afford a teapot every day."

" True, that would come too expensive. There is
one of the Grays I know, who lives up two flights of
stairs in a county town ; and whenever he and his
wife have a quarrel (twice a month on an average),
they pitch everything out of the window—crockery,

pots, and furniture, with which last they fortunately
are not overstocked. Poor old 'Shach, 'the gentleman what does the knives and scissors,' as Horace
Lee described him to me once. But let's consider—
oh! I think I have it. Dimiti, do you run to the
farm, and ask Mrs Price to give you the very biggest
of all my books. She can't mistake it."

Dimiti bounded off, and presently reappeared,
staggering under a volume of the *Illustrated London
News.* Half way he rested; and resting, discovered
the nature of his burden, that there were pictures of
fighting and killing and what not else inside. This
must be seen into; so, propping the book against a
rock, he stretched himself before it on his stomach,
and entered on a leisurely investigation. His notes
of amazement came to us on the breeze, till with a
final and *crescendo* "Dórdi!" he sprang to his heels,
resumed his load, and speedily covered the remaining
course, vociferating—

"My blessed daddy, you never seen such things in
all the born days of your life—horses, and soldiers,
and tents, a tent with Aunt 'Lína and my granny's
Tiny, and another with pretty hangmen and handcuffs, took most beautiful."

Yes, that was something everyone must see: the
next half-hour was spent in looking at the "po'traits,"
and many were the quaint remarks thereon. "They
looks awful pale," said Ruth of the victims of the
coup-d'état, as well they might, seeing the picture was
uncoloured; but when John announced that the girl

of the tent was actually a Sinfi, their wonderment knew no bounds. "Ay," remarked Anselo, "I'd swear to her big nose anywheres." "But she's got no boots on," Leah objected. At length they would have this mystery revealed : so, with Christopher for lectern, I read ; and what I read deserves a fresh chapter to itself.

X

Chapter Tenth.

GIPSY EXPERIENCES.

By a Romani Rei.[1]

———◆——

PART I.—MY FIRST GIPSY LESSON.

TWO words of explanation before entering upon these experiences. I am not Mr Borrow. I have not the pleasure of knowing that remarkable agent of the Bible Society. It is perhaps unnecessary to say, that I once had pointed out to me at a club table, next to that at which I was dining, a gentleman in black, like a colossal clergyman, with a very white head, and two very black eyes (I do not mean blackened eyes), who I was told was Mr Borrow. This is all I ever saw of the redoubtable adversary of *Blazing Bosville*. My own experiences of Gipsy life are confined to this country. They profess to be, and are, real experiences. My Gipsies are genuine, My Gipsy women are not the Gipsy women of the

---

[1] Reprinted, by permission, from the *Illustrated London News*, Nov. 29, Dec. 13, and Dec. 27, 1851. *N.B.*—The following foot-notes are my hearers' comments on the story.

theatre; they do not wear short red petticoats, worked at the bottom with black cabalistic signs, still less silk stockings or antique sandals on their feet, or turbans on their heads; nor are they called "Zarah," or "Zillah." My Gipsy men never, by any accident, swathe their legs in linen bandages, cross-gartered with red worsted lace; the nearest approach they ever make to a brigand's jacket is a velveteen shooting-coat, much the worse for wear; and altogether their appearance suggests rather a cross between a debauched gamekeeper and a Staffordshire pot-hawker, than anything like Mr O. Smith, or Mr N. T. Hicks, as he appears in *Lo Zingaro*.

It is curious, indeed, considering how many Gipsies there are still in England, and how much the race has been worked by painters, dramatists, and novelists, to find how untruthfully they have, as a rule, been represented by all these artists. Among our painters there is scarcely one, except Oakley, who has painted these people as they are. In the pictures and drawings of them there is an entire lack of truth, which can be detected at a glance by the *aficionado*, the true lover and student of Romani life. I cannot remember a single genuine Gipsy in a novel, though both Bulwer and Disraeli have tried their hands at the class. And among stage plays, the only one in which I have ever seen the Gipsy introduced, with evidence of a real life-like knowledge of the race, is in a version of *Sir Roger de Coverly*, played at the Olympic Theatre during the present year.

Mr Borrow, no doubt, knows the Gipsies well, and
could describe them perfectly. But his love of effect
leads him away. In his wish to impress his reader
with a certain mysterious notion of himself, he
colours his Gipsy pictures (the *form* of which is
quite accurate) in a fantastic style, which robs them
altogether of the value they would have as studies
from life. His English Gipsy vocabulary, so far as
I have been able to compare it with the language
actually spoken by the Romani race, is accurate and
trustworthy.

In my native county the real Romani is unknown.
We have "potters," or "muggers," who camp in
green lanes, and live by making and repairing small
iron and tin wares, much in the Gipsy fashion, com-
bining this industry with the manufacture and sale
of coarse earthenware and birch brooms, at question-
ably low prices. But I had never seen the thorough-
bred "Romani" till I had arrived at man's estate—
at least till I called myself "a man," being really a
freshman at —— College, Cambridge.

I suppose I must have a vagabond drop in my
blood,[1] otherwise I cannot account for the strong
attraction this people have always had for me from
the first time I came across them. If there be a
Romani camp within a mile, I wind it. In the
country I find "the spirit in my feet" that Shelley
sings of, always leading me across commons, and

---

[1] *Richenda.*—"Ah ! that's it. All mumply górgios will say that."

along green lanes, and into wayside woods, and bringing me up within sight of the thin blue smoke, curling mysteriously among the green boughs, and within scent of the pleasant pungency of the open-air wood-fire. No wonder that I have a tolerably wide acquaintanceship among the race. They see my relish for their company and appreciate it. It is to this that I owe the name by which they have kindly adopted me, of the "Romani Rei," or "Gipsy gentleman." I remember, as if it was yesterday (though it is now some twelve years ago), not exactly my first sight of a Romani, but my first lesson in their tongue,—which I may tell you, *en passant*, is a genuine language, in that state of mutilation which a language must fall into when transmitted orally only, in the hands of an entirely illiterate people. It is closely connected with the Sanscrit, and proves incontestably to every philologist who has ever seen a vocabulary of it, that the Romani are a North Indian race,[1] whatever may have been their migrations since leaving their original seat, if ever they had one, and have not always been Pariahs and vagabonds. But I have no intention of going into the philology or ethnology of my Romani friends just now.

I had been sketching all that day, or rather I had

---

[1] *John Roberts.*—"Now, didn't I tell you? Where on earth should they come from, if it wasn't from India? Anyone with any sense might tell that." Yet I remember when John addressed an Egyptian mummy in the British Museum as "Ancient Romano brother!"

been wandering about with a sketch-book in my hand, and a water-colour box in my pocket, stopping now and then to make believe to draw; but really enjoying an aimless ramble,—away from lectures, and "cram," and private tutor,—over the unfenced flats, and by the willow-fringed streams, and through the hap-hazard copses and still green lanes and primitive villages, which make even fenny Cambridgeshire beautiful, if a man has legs for a good day's walk, and eyes and heart to recognise beauty wherever he finds it, even in its homeliest garb. My ramble had been on the Huntingdon side of Cambridge. It was a bright May-day, and the sun was westering; and though I had no watch, my appetite told me it was hard upon Hall-time. I had set my face Cambridge-wards, and was tumbling along over the tufts of sedge grass, and ploughing through the fallows, and over the young wheat, taking a line of my own across the country, when I saw a thin spiral of blue smoke creeping up the trunk and under the lower branches of a noble beech, one of an irregular avenue of the same trees, that seemed to begin abruptly in the flat I was crossing, and to end as abruptly some half-mile farther on. As much from curiosity about the trees as the smoke, I turned out of my direction, scrambled through a sort of natural hedge of elder and bramble, and found myself in a still green road, that begins in the fields and ends in the fields, skirting one farmstead in its way; and therefore, I presume, claiming to be connected with a country road that runs at right angles to it some fields off one of its ends.

It is an old. Roman road. You may still see the vestiges of pavement under the grass that covers it. The people about call it "The King's Hedges." If I have among my readers a Cambridge man, fond of cross-country "constitutionals," he will probably recognise the place from my description. But to do this, he must be a man of about my own standing, I fancy; for the Enclosure Commissioners have been busy since then, and in that neighbourhood, too. Even at that day, I remember, I had come now and then across raw-looking squares of newly-broken-up common, with their lank, unpainted rail-fences, looking more like American zig-zags than genuine English work, and I had sighed to think of common-rights put an end to, and "constitutionals" abridged, on that side of Cambridge.

I came that day upon "The King's Hedges" for the first time; and its strange seclusion riveted me. Under the two broken lines of feathery beech-trees, on whose thin spring-green foliage the slant rays of the afternoon May sun were dancing, ran a low and broken hedge of bramble and elder, close up to which grew the short greensward, the stones of the causeway showing through it here and there, with no wear and tear of traffic on their velvety and irregular faces.

Some twenty yards from the point where I struck the lane, were grouped the three tents of a Gipsy camp, the rounded end of one towards me, while from the space they encircled rose the thin blue column of wood smoke that had first attracted my attention. A rough but light cart was pitched near the tents, and a rusty, saddle-galled, wall-eyed pony, with a couple of unkempt donkeys, a black-brown and a dun, were hobbling about, as well as their foot-ropes would allow them, after the short sweet grass of the hedge-side. I stepped up towards the camp noiselessly, for the foot falls without a sound upon that old sward, and was close upon the tents before a long-backed bandy-legged, yellow terrier, sleeping with his nose in the wood-ashes, was sufficiently aroused to a sense of his duty to fly at me, with that extra activity of yelping zeal which all functionaries are apt to assume when caught napping.[1]

"*Besh-to-lai, chukel*"[2] (lie down, dog), said a shrill voice from the nearest tent, across the entrance of which hung a patch-work quilt.

I lifted it without ceremony, and looked in. Its only occupant was a girl, sitting with her legs doubled under her, Indian fashion, and busied in weaving a small net.

As my shadow darkened the entrance, she let her small hands, every finger bedecked with rude silver rings, fall, with their work, slowly on her knees, and looked up steadily and composedly.

---

[1] *Ruth.*—" It's rather nice."
[2] *Anselo.*—"Well ! ! ! Dádia, bor ! "

．She appeared to me then a woman, but her age, as she afterwards told me, was fifteen. I have seen many beautiful Gipsies since then, but I have never seen one so beautiful as Sinfi Curraple (*Anglicè* "Smith"), my acquaintance of "The King's Hedges."[1]

Her features were small, and more Arab than Indian, and with nothing of the Jewish cast that is often seen in Gipsy women. Her eye had the veiled fire peculiar to the race, a sort of filmy languor that blazes up with passion, but which, even while unexcited, exerts still a strange, serpent-like power of latent fascination.[2] Her teeth were small, and white, and sound, as Gipsy teeth always are. Her blue-black hair,[3] in two short shining plaits, came low across her narrow forehead, and close along her cheeks, sharply marking (if I may be allowed the bull) the triangular oval of the face, by its dark line relieved against the blood-red silk handkerchief, which she wore coiffed, hood-fashion, on her head. On each side of her little mouth, and in the centre of her soft round chin, was a small blue tattoo mark, which heightened the mellow and velvety smoothness of her skin—dusky, but not sallow, and glowing under the sun like the side of a brown Bergamot pear.

---

[1] *Sinfi Faa.*—"Ah-h! and is all this true? But I never heard a name like that. Why, 'Smith' is *Pátuléngro !*"

[2] *Anselo.*—"There, bor; sarpents, by gum!"

[3] *Starlina.*—"Blue-black! well I never heard talk of such a thing as that."

She sat so—the beautiful young vagabond![1]—and looked steadily and calmly at me, without speaking, as the dog, in obedience to her voice, ceased yelping, and nuzzled at her side.

I stooped under the tent, asking, "May I come in?"

"Come in, my rei, and welcome, if you're not afraid to sit by the poor Gipsy;" and, untwisting her legs from under her, she rose without aid of her hand; and reaching a piece of carpet from a bundle of bedding that lay rolled up at the back of the tent, spread it for me on the straw, gravely and courteously. "Let me tell your fortune, my pretty gentleman," she began, after a short pause, in the musical, cajoling, jaunty, sing-song of the race; but seeing, I suppose, from my impatient "No— no—nonsense!" that it was not for this purpose, at least, I had introduced myself into the tents, she stopped, and began to beg in the true Gipsy fashion. "Give the poor Gipsy a sixpence, my rei." I felt the romance oozing out of me at this cool, cut-and-dry, business-like sponging, and said, "Don't beg, there's a good girl; if you don't ask for anything, you may get something, but if you begin to beg again I shall go."[2]

She stopped short at this formidable threat, and

---

[1] *Sinfi Faa.*—"Vagabond! What nasty highgags! Now, that is a shame if you like. I've never been called that before. If any one had, I'd have give it them. Better people than themselves, I declare."

[2] *Starlina.*—"'Go, then, highgag,' I'd say in a minute."

looking at my sketch-book, said, " I know what that is—it's the book you draw things out in. There was a rei came and drew us out, when we were camped in the Gorsehole, near Newmarket, with the tents, and the cart, and the fire, and the *chukel* yonder, and me, and aunt, and uncle, and all of us—as natural as life."

" Will you let me draw you, I asked ?"

" Me !" she said, and laughed, and looked archly in my face for the compliment she saw growing there.

" Yes ; you are very pretty, and you know it."

" Don't laugh at the poor Gipsy, my rei," she said, nestling back into the shadow, and coquettishly drawing forward her red hood, till the arch little face glowed again under the warm light reflected from it, while she let the fire gather slowly under the film of her infernal eyes, till I felt uncomfortable. However, I looked into them as little as possible, and drew on as I best might without it.

" Oh the *cushgar poshnikes !*" she suddenly exclaimed, as I took, to wipe out a light, a flaming yellow and crimson silk handkerchief ; how the deuce I came ever to have bought such a blazing Bandana I can't think, unless it was the Gipsy drop in me that I have spoken of before. " Oh the *cushgar poshnikes !*" and she fairly clapped her hands.

" What is the meaning of ' *cushgar poshnikes ?*' "

" It is *Romani rokkerpen*—it's Romani talk, my rei, and it means ' pretty handkerchief.'"

"I should like to learn the Romani talk. Will you teach me?"

She shook her pretty head doubtfully. "I don't know what Aunt Athaliah would say."

"Never mind Aunt Athaliah. Come, '*cushgar poshnikes*' (I put the words down), and I suppose I must call you '*cushgar*' too? What is 'pretty girl' in your language?"

"*Rincne rakli.* And now will you give me the handkerchief, my rei?"[1]

"Yes, *rincne rakli;* if you will ask for it in your language."

"*Pal, del mande* the *diklo.*"

"That means?"

"Brother, give me the handkerchief."

"There! What will you do with it? Tell me in your language."

"*Chiv* it *adri* my *churro*"[2] (put it on my head); and, with a rapid movement of her round arms and little fingers, she translated the words by replacing her red hood with my flaunting present. Somehow the vivid orange and crimson made a harmony with the glowing complexion, ·shining hair, and bright-coloured gown, all mellowed in the warm half-light that filtered through the brown tent. She was a magnificent bit of colour, seen so; and, as a painter,

---

[1] *Starlína.*—"There, bor!"

[2] *Silvanus.*—"'Chiv it adré!' Well, I never did hear the likes of that. I expect she said, 'Chiv it opré,' and he mistook the word."

I had a right to admire her, but hardly a right to put my next question.

"What is 'kiss' in your language?"

She gave a quiet little chuckle as she answered, " *Tshuma*."

"Will you *del mande* a *tshuma* for the *cushgar diklo?*"[1] You see I was profiting by my lesson.

She put out her cheek, without the least discomposure.

" *Ourli*, my *pal*."

I am bound to confess that, encouraged by the action, I took for granted that "*ourli*" meant "yes."

" *Kek vafardes na tshuma*," she said very soberly, as I resumed my sketch; and, answering my look, added the interpretation, "No harm in a kiss; it's a Romani saying, my rei."

"And a very good saying too. What is your name?"

"Sinfi Smith; there's Romani for the name of Smith—*Curraple*."

"And have you always lived in a tent, Sinfi?"[2]

"Yes; I was born in one—in the great snow. We were snowed up—I've heard from my *dia* (mother)— for three weeks, under Haslingfield Wood."

"Would you like to live in a house?"

" *Kek! kek!* " (No, no!) she replied with a peremp-

---

[1] *Starlina*.—"I'd say, 'No, highflier.' Was he supposed to have been quite a young fellow then?"

[2] *Ruth*.—"Ah! that's what mumply kennicks have said to me often, 'Live in a tint.'"

tory shake of the head. "The *keir's cushgar* for the *keiringro.* (The house is good for the house-dweller.) I've been in a *keir* often, at Cambridge; the stairs make my head swim, and you can't breathe."

"But it must be very choky here in your tent; at night, now, how many of you sleep here?"

"There's me, and Cousin Florentia, and Morella."

Three of them in a space of six feet by four, and about four feet high!

"Why, you must be suffocated. How do you breathe?"

"It *is* hot, sometimes; but then we lift up the *koppa* (blanket) over the tent mouth, and let the sweet air take us."

So we went on, she interspersing her conversation with Romani words, and interpreting them for me at my request, while I took them down. I had already filled some four pages of my note-book with the fruits of this pleasant lesson; and I must admit that my sketch did not advance quite as fast as my glossary. I found on her part no reluctance to give me the Romani words for the objects about; and I may remark, by the way, that I have never found any difficulty of this kind among the younger Gipsies. The older ones are occasionally more suspicious, and will often pretend that they have no word in their language when they think the knowledge of it likely to be turned against them. Thus, an old Gipsy man once gravely assured me that they had no word in their tongue for "thief." The old rogue, I may remark, was convicted of sheep-stealing at the Bury assizes, after he had solemnly assured me that the name and the practice were alike unknown among the Romané.

So our lesson went on for an hour or so. Sinfi was the most patient of instructresses, pursing and torturing her charming mouth in a thousand ways to give me the accurate pronunciations, and racking her pretty head in the vain effort to comprehend my questions about nouns, and verbs, and preposi-tions. She had not the least notion of grammatical distinctions, and generally used her words (as the Romané all do) as roots, without inflection, inter-spersed with English. Occasionally I could detect an inflection in the concrete of a sentence, and I was careful to note these.

Though there was nothing either poetical or mys-terious in Sinfi's way of talking, there were turns of phrase, every now and then, which agreeably denoted the influence of a free, roving, open-air life; and, above all, there was an utter absence of vulgarity, both in the words and the manner of them. On the contrary, the thing that most struck me was the grace of her action in speaking and moving, and the gentle and quiet courtesy with which she brought me what I asked for—some water, a support for my sketch-book, and so forth. This gracefulness is to be found in all the Romané, and belongs to the East, like their small hands and lithe limbs. I ob-served now, too, in her, what since I find a universal

habit with the race, that she sat like an Oriental
woman, her legs folded under her. Indeed, I might
have fancied myself in Syria, looking on the slender
little body, with its Eastern head-gear, its bright-
coloured gown, loose upon the bosom, which was
covered by two or three layers of red and yellow
and green spotted handkerchiefs; the lower limbs
gathered under, and crossed, and the upper part of
the figure lying lazily back against the pile of bedding, which, under its covering of a gaudy carpet,
might have passed muster for a divan. There was
only the *narghileh* wanting; and I grieve, for the
effect of my picture, to say that, before our lesson
was interrupted, this was supplied in the form of a
short black cutty pipe, which Sinfi smoked with
great relish, declining the cigar I offered her. Cutty
pipe, however, and all included, I don't remember
that I ever spent a pleasanter hour in my life.

The sketch and the lesson were going on rather
irregularly, when a low whine of recognition from
the dog, and the sound of voices, announced a new
arrival. Looking up from my work, I saw a broad,
swarthy, black-browed woman's face staring into the
tent. Catching a sight of my drawing, the new
comer—whom I rightly guessed to be the Aunt
Athaliah of whom Sinfi had expressed some appre-
hension—burst out into a wild and incoherent gabble,
half English, half Romani, from which I could just
make out that she was consigning me, and my work,
and my poor little sitter to the most disagreeable

places. Then stooping under the tent before I was aware, she clutched my sketch-book with one hand, and sent it spinning along the road, while with the other she seized poor Sinfi by the shoulder, and lugged her up, and out, through the straw and wood-ashes in front of the tent, shaking her violently and cursing her—" I'll *maur* (kill) you, you *chikli Beng's chavi* (dirty devil's daughter). How dare you let a *gorja chiv* you *adra* his *lill* (how dare you let a man put you in his book), to *chore* the *raht* of your *mui* (to steal the blood from your face)?" All this was said with inconceivable rapidity and vehemence; and her assault had so astounded me, that, for an instant, I could neither avenge my outraged sketch-book, nor go to the rescue of Sinfi, who offered no resistance to the cuffs and shakings of the redoubtable Athaliah. At last, however, gathering my scattered senses, and seizing the old lady by the shoulders, I whirled her round. " Hands off, you old fagot ! By Jove! if you strike the girl again, I'll knock you down." She twisted in my hands, and foamed at the mouth, transferring her abuse from Sinfi to me.

" What's the matter, you old fool ? "

" I won't have her drawed out ; I told her I'd make her scrawl the earth before me, if ever she let herself be drawed out again."

" Why, what harm can there be ? "

" I know there's a *fiz* [1] (a charm) in it. There was

---

[1] *Plato.*—" A *fiz!* what's that ? "

my youngest, that the gorja drawed out on Newmarket Heath, she never held her head up after,
but wasted away, and died ; and she's buried in
March churchyard." [1]

"Nonsense, you old idiot! Anyhow, I won't let
you touch the girl while I'm here; so sit down
quietly, and I'll draw *you* if you like."

She ground her teeth at me, but sat down, sulkily
muttering, near the fireplace; while Sinfi, who did
not appear much the worse for the *bourrade*, gathered
sticks, and prepared to make a blaze.

"Take a cigar, old lady," I said, after a minute or
two, handing her my case.

She took one ungraciously, lighted it with a lucifer
match, of which she produced a box from her pocket,
and began to puff,—Sinfi looking up from her work
now and then, with a sly smile at me, and a sort of
wink in the direction of her aunt.

Tobacco is a great sedative, and before the first
cigar was half smoked, Athaliah and I were as good
friends as if our introduction had been the pleasantest
one in the world.

Athaliah Shaw was about the ugliest Romani I
ever saw, standing close on six feet high, with a
face like a vicious horse, and hair as coarse as his
tail. She wore a long bright tartan shawl, draped
awry, an old black straw bonnet on her head, with

---

[1] *Lementina.*—"Ay, nearly all the pretty Romané say that, that it's
bad luck."

a green and yellow handkerchief under it, a rusty black dress, and boots like a navigator's. Uncle Euri, who came lounging up a few hundred yards behind her, with a couple of terriers at his heels, was a thickset, sturdy fellow, of six-and-forty, brown as a hazel-nut, with small black eyes, a coloured handkerchief loosely twisted round his bronzed throat, a fur cap on his head, a long calf-skin sleeved waistcoat, loose drab breeches, and leggings half unbuttoned over his strong ankle-boots. He had looked on without interfering in the scuffle, and touched his hat civilly to me, as he sat down opposite to me on the other side of the fire-place.

"The women don't like it, sir," he said apologetically. "I don't care about it; you may draw me out as much as you like for a pint of beer and a pipe of tobacco;" and with this philosophic remark he applied himself to his cutty with perfect composure, and great lazy enjoyment.

Meanwhile, stirring Sinfi had gathered sticks, and turned the hooked fire-rod round, and slung upon it a big black kettle, which stood, ready filled, under the shade of the hedge. Aunt Athaliah, much appeased, but still grumbling inwardly, like a volcano in the intervals of eruption, was taking out, from a sort of huge wallet (formed by doubling her stout apron and securing the corners to her waistband), a most miscellaneous collection of town purchases,—lucifer matches, a quarter of a pound of tea in a paper, two quartern loaves, a lump of salt butter, a paper of moist sugar, some tobacco, a bunch of candles, and other things, which all reposed comfortably side by side in that capacious receptacle. Uncle Euri, meanwhile, had leisurely, and without rising, gathered a few handfuls of straw and small sticks into a hollow wisp, into which he thrust a lighted lucifer, and rapidly putting it down, disposed larger sticks about it, so as, in a few minutes, to have a good, well-piled fagot[1] crackling and blazing under the pot.

The old woman and he exchanged some words in Gipsy with Sinfi. "*Muk* us *pukhar* the rei to *holl* a *crumer* of *hawben*." (Let us ask the gentleman to eat a bit of victuals.)

Sinfi interpreted the invitation : "Uncle says, my rei, will you eat with the poor Romani ? "

"Won't I, Sinfi ? I'm desperately hungry, Aunt Athaliah ; and I was going to ask myself, if you hadn't invited me."

"Eh ! Why, you'll never *com* (like) the *moulo mass* (dead meat) that the Romané eat, my rei," said Uncle Euri, in their whining sing-song, full of *calinerie* and mock humility.

" I can eat anything," I answered.

"Can you eat *hotchiwitchy* and *bourri-zimmins ?* " asked Sinfi, laughing to her uncle over the potatoes she was peeling into a red earthenware dish.

" Talk English to the rei, Sinfi," said Uncle Euri.

---

[1] *Ruth.*—"A well-piled fagot ! Dádia, what a mumper's word ! Ah, indeed ! "

"He wants to learn Romani, uncle; look, he puts all the words you tell him down in his *ticknee lill* (little book) there—oh, so fast! and he learns them off directly."

"Ah!" said Euri, sententiously; "I've knowed reis as did that afore. There was young C——k, Athaliah; him that *jaed* to the *vellgouris* (went to the fairs) with us for three months, and *kerred* the *bosh* and the *tumbo*[1] (played the fiddle and tambourine) like a *tatcho* (true) Romani."

Athaliah shook her head. "He had *doster colas* in his *shurro* besides *juvlas* (he had many things in his head besides lice). He *jinned* the *mulo Beng's hoknapans* (he knew the devil's tricks)—*he* did. Yes, my rei, he could make himself as big or as little as he liked, and he could raise the *Beng*, he told us; and often when he was *kerring* the *bosh* with my *rom*, there, in the *kellapen* (when he was playing the fiddle with my husband at the dance), he would laugh till he almost fell off the table. It was awful to hear him! Eh, Euri?"

Euri nodded a reverential assent. It was clear that poor C——k had left an enviable reputation behind him, among his Romani friends. He was mad—poor fellow—but full of humour. Who is there of his standing at Cambridge that does not remember "Athanasius Gasker," and his museum,

---

[1] *Lancelot.*—"Lord bless us all, the *tumbo!* I should say *tom-tom.* Why, they were half mumpers, half highgags."

and the library of useless knowledge? And among
his other eccentricities, I now learned for the first
time that he was an *aficionado*, one of the Gipsy-
stricken.

"But what are we to have for dinner?" I asked;
for Sinfi had put on the kettle, which was already
simmering, and which, as she removed the lid to
stir it carefully, I saw was full of a sort of white
soup, with something in it that looked like oysters.
"Deuced odd!" I thought to myself; "oyster-soup
here!"

"It's *bourri-zimmins*," said Sinfi, importantly;
"but I won't tell you what that is till you've eaten
it."

"And where's the *hotchiwitchy* the *chukel* (dog)
caught this morning?" asked Euri, getting up lazily.

"*Adri* the *vado* (in the cart)," said Sinfi.

"What the deuce is a *hotchiwitchy*?" I thought
to myself, as Euri, arming himself with an old
clothes-brush, worn to the stump, lounged to the
cart. He came back, and in his hand I saw a
young fresh-killed hedgehog.

"So that's a *hotchiwitchy*?"

"*Ourli*," said Sinfi.

"And do you mean to say you eat hedgehog?"

"Eat it!" said Euri, with a stare of surprise.
"There ain't any game as runs or flies can beat
it, that is, afore the winter; they're thinnish now,
but a fat un's as rich as pig, and as delicate as
pheasant."

While he spoke, he commenced his culinary opera-
tions. As there is no receipt in Soyer, Ude, or
Carême, for cooking a hedgehog, I feel it my duty
to be minute in my description of the process.

Euri began by throwing his hedgehog on the
ground; then, pressing his foot on the back, the
body yielded, and from a ball grew a straight little
cylinder of bristles. Throwing this on the fire,
which had now burnt down to a clear red *braise*, he
snatched it off again at a certain point of singeing
—this point it is a very delicate matter to hit, mind
—and applying his old clothes-brush to the smoking
stubble, speedily stripped poor piggy of the best part
of his bristles, and ran a knife up the skin of the
belly. Then taking a mass of stiff clay, which lay
ready kneaded under the cart, he proceeded to invest
the unseemly little body in a clay coffin, of about a
quarter to half an inch thick; and depositing this in
the heat of the fire, gathered the red ashes about and
over it.[1] I watched with undisguised admiration,
till Sinfi laughed again, and let her soup boil over, in
her amusement at my interest in Euri's proceedings,
which brought upon her a sharp rebuke from Aunt
Athaliah, whose temper was not improved, as I now
found, by a touch of rheumatism.

Meanwhile, plates, dishes, and porringers had been
rummaged out, with an odd knife and fork or two,

---

[1] *Lementina.*—"Well, I never saw a hedgehog done in that way in
my life."

sundry battered iron spoons, some salt and pepper in a paper, and an elderly teapot (which Aunt Athaliah seemed to have under her special charge), flanked by a most miscellaneous array of cups and saucers. Sinfi was busy seasoning her soup, which really smelt uncommonly nice, though I was not at all easy about the ingredients.

"There, my rei," she said triumphantly, as she poured me out a basinful, and put it before me with a hunch of bread. "*Holl* that, and you can tell the *gorjas* you have eat *bourri-zimmins* with the poor Romani."

I was uncommonly hungry, and the soup smelt so appetising, and Sinfi offered it me with so much grace, and such a triumphant twinkle of her black eyes, that I threw my misgivings overboard, and fell to.

Bourri-zimmins, whatever it might be, was decidedly a hit; rather like *soupe à la reine*, with little lumps of something I took to be a mild kind of forcemeat—decidedly they were *not* oysters— swimming in it. Sinfi looked at me inquiringly.

I nodded, "Capital, Sinfi."

She clapped her hands with glee. "Ho! ho! *Dik, bibbe* (look, aunt); *dik, cokko* (look, uncle)— *Dik* at the rei *hollin* the *bourri-zimmins!*"

What the deuce could *bourri-zimmins* be?

But Euri having also despatched his basinful, was now extracting his dirt-pie from the ashes. Holding it with a pair of smith's pincers, he broke the red-hot clay with a hammer, and neatly took off the crust, with bristles and skin embedded in it. In fact, the hedgehog was beautifully skinned, and baked to a turn, with all his gravy in. Then, with his knife, Euri opened the body along the chine, and, with one sweep of the hand, brought out the entrails, in a lump, by the back slit, which mode is resorted to, as he told me, because the gall-bladder is less likely to be broken than when the "giblets" are taken out by the belly.[1] And now *hotchiwitchy* was ready for eating, and really looked so plump and nice as he lay on the dish, bathed in his own oozing juices, and sent up such a grateful odour, that I got over any qualms I might have had, and played a worthy knife and fork with my new friends.

I have often eaten hedgehog since, and have served it at my own table, when it has been tasted and praised in blessed ignorance—for it really is capital eating when in season—but I never enjoyed one so much as this my first. You want to know what it is like? Imagine a blending of sucking-pig and grouse, the bland unctuousness of the one mingling with the piquant game-flavour of the other, and you may form some notion of the taste of *hotchi-witchy*.[2]

---

[1] *Lementina.*—"Oh, my blessed dear goodness! roasted it as it was! Well, I never in all my born days heard tell of such a thing. That is most horrible. Dórdi!"

[2] *Richenda.*—"Sure, it must have been good, done like that. There was your Gipsy cooking. Dirty pigs enough."

"And now, Sinfi," I said, after I had put down my knife and fork, "what is *boùrri-zimmins* ?"

"What do you think ?" she said, swelling with the pleasant secret.

"I haven't a notion—but it's uncommonly good. Tell me what it is, there's a good girl. I'll give Hudson the receipt," I added to myself, "for the Trinity kitchen. Come, what is it, Sinfi?"

"Snail-soup !"

"Snail-soup !" and I jumped up. "Confound it! you don't mean to say I've been eating snails ! "

Ugh! At that moment I could have boxed her ears, pretty as they were. I leave you to imagine my sensations. However, imagination apart, snails are very good eating, stewed in milk as Sinfi stewed them, with pepper, salt, and herbs. And though I don't mean to say I ever repeated the experiment, I have no doubt, if one *could* get over the fancy of the thing, snails would be as popular among us as oysters.

Dinner over, we sat, and smoked, and I went on with my Romani lesson. I don't think I quite enjoyed it as much with the old people as with Sinfi, and I am certain I didn't get on half so fast. However, they seemed pleased at the interest I took in their language; and Euri promised to pay me a visit at my rooms in college, and to give me a course of lessons, for the sum of half-a-crown per lesson.

Aunt Athaliah was an inveterate old *monger* (beggar); and it was only my solemn assurance that she would not get a penny by asking for it,

that I managed to stop her infernal whining sup-
plications for *backsheesh*. In fact, the old woman
was a bore, and but for Sinfi, I don't know that
the acquaintance would have lasted beyond that
day at the King's Hedges. However, it was not
destined to close so soon; in fact, it still subsists.
I saw Sinfi only last summer near Margate, under
rather curious circumstances, as I may hereafter
have to tell.

I was not at all prepared for the interruption that
brought my lesson to an abrupt close on that day.

I have mentioned the names of Florentia and
Morella, Sinfi's cousins, who shared her tent.

After dinner, Euri and Athaliah fell into a talk,
carried on almost entirely in Romani; which I concluded, therefore, they did not wish me to understand.

I had no objection whatever to a *tête-à-tête* with
Sinfi. I have not known many of the Romani *chais*
(Gipsy girls) who were agreeable companions in a two-
handed talk. Either they are intolerably rapacious,
asking for everything that pleases them, or grossly
and tiresomely *soft-sawderish*, or pruriently coarse.
Sinfi had none of these faults, but was really frank,
innocent, and natural, in her questions and answers;
as limber and graceful as a lizard in her movement,
piquant in the little touches of savagery that crossed
her Oriental and lazy courtesy of manner. She was
certainly not only the prettiest, but the most attractive young Gipsy I have ever known.

I can quite conceive the mad passion that such a
creature may create in a man, and has created, in
our own times too. We need not go back to Spain,
and the days of Cervantes, to find a Preciosa. Not
a few Oxford men, of nine or ten years' standing,
could tell a. tale of frantic passion for a Gipsy girl
entertained by two young men at one time, one of
them with ducal blood in his veins, who ultimately
wooed and wedded his Gipsy love. So that it is no
way impossible (the heirs to the dukedom being all
unmarried, and unlikely to marry) that the ducal
coronet of —— may come to be worn by the son of
a Gipsy mother.

Our *tête-à-tête* might have lasted an hour, and the
sun was on the rim of the horizon, when Euri—who
had walked more than once to the end of the green
lane, and restlessly looked north and south, and east
and west, as if in expectation of an arrival—suddenly
jumped up, and touching Athaliah's arm, directed her
attention to two young women, whom I now saw
coming rapidly towards us across the common which
I had been traversing when the smoke of the camp
attracted my attention.

" It's Florentia and Morella," said Sinfi to me.

As they came nearer, I saw by their flushed faces
and rapid breathing that they had walked fast and
far. They were lusty lasses, of about Sinfi's age, but
coarser of feature and bigger-limbed than she was ;
dressed, *au reste*, much in the same fashion.

They waved their hands as they came near, and

called loudly some words in Romani. All I could distinguish was, "*Bori Hokani.*" When I asked Sinfi the meaning of these words, I observed Euri frown at her. She avoided answering. There was clearly some mystery that I was not to be initiated into.

The girls had now reached us. They did not address any words to me; but it was evident from the looks they threw in my direction, as they talked earnestly apart with Euri and Athaliah, that my presence was unwelcome. I observed, too, that one of them hurriedly transferred to Euri a small but heavy packet, which that worthy consigned straightway to his pocket.

It needed all Sinfi's control of herself to keep her from leaving her seat near me at the fire, and joining her cousins. Seeing this, I was just about to take my leave, when Euri anticipated me.

Holding out his hand, he gave me the Romani farewell. "*Cushgar bok,*" (good luck) my rei; we are going to strike the *ranyeh* (tent-sticks). Clap the *sallivandras* (saddle) on the *grei* (horse), Florentia."

"What! going to-night?" I said to Sinfi. Euri answered for her.

"Yes, we shall be a good many *stretch* (miles) away before this time to-morrow."

"And my Romani lessons?"

"Next time we come this way, sir; we take the King's Hedges in our beat;[1] it's one of the best

---

[1] *Ruth.*—"'In our beat!' Mercy on us, what highfliers!"

consas (camping corners) in the county. Now my *chais* (girls), *had, had* (lift, lift);" and while he spoke, he had already stripped the blankets off the tent-sticks, while Aunt Athaliah was busy in stowing away pots, pans, and tea-things in the large covered baskets, flat on the inside, and curved on the outside, for slinging on the asses, whose foot-ropes Morella was untying, while her sister saddled the horse, and Sinfi packed the straw into a bundle with the bedding.

"*Lel* the *tshar ari*" (take away the ashes), said Euri to her. At this order she extinguished the embers with water; then, collecting the ashes in her apron, she began strewing them thinly in the thickest part of the bushes and on the flat beyond, so that very soon, except the blackened circle on the sward, no trace of fire was visible. In the few minutes that I stood there, it was wonderful to see what a clean sweep of all vestiges of the camp had been made by the united efforts of the family.[1]

I lingered still, in the hope of a farewell from Sinfi. I was not disappointed. After she had shaken the last of the grey ashes from her apron, she came to where I stood, and gave me her hand.

"*Cushgar bok*, my rei. Wherever you go, you won't forget Sinfi?"

"And you won't forget me, Sinfi?"

---

[1] *Dimiti (contemplating the illustration with the air of a discoverer).*— "There they are, look at 'em. There's Euri. That must be my Uncle Pyramus."

"No! I shall always think of you when I wear your *diklo.*"

"But why are you off in such a hurry?"

She shook her head.

"Where shall I find you to-morrow?"

"*Ko jin?*" (who knows?) she said, with a shade of gravity upon her face; "but we shall see each other again, my rei; and mind, the next time, you must know how to *rokker* (speak) Romani like Uncle Euri yonder."

A whistle from the camp recalled her. I saw the horse was in the cart, the panniers and tent-sticks packed upon the asses.

"Good-bye, Sinfi." I still held her hand.

"*Cushgar divus* (good day), my rei." With these words she drew her fingers sharply through mine, and ran like a deer towards the camp. When I looked again the little caravan was in motion.

PART II.—MY FIRST AND LAST GIPSY HUNT.

I stood where Sinfi had taken leave of me, and watched the caravan till her bright shawl disappeared round a turn of the green lane. I flattered myself she looked round just before she vanished. And then, when the lane was still and lonely again, I turned my face towards Cambridge. "The King's Hedges," I have said, end abruptly in the fields, from which the road is divided by a low quickset fence.

I was making a gap in it large enough to let me
through, when I was pulled up by a gruff voice,
which exclaimed in the true nasal *twang* of Cambridgeshire—" Neow then, where are yeou a geowing
teow?" It was the farmer, who didn't relish my
unceremonious way of dealing with his young quickset. I explained, as satisfactorily as I could, that as
it was obvious I must get out of the lane, it was
perfectly clear I must trespass on his enclosures.
He tried to set me right on that point, by recom-
mending that I should go round by the Linton
road, an addition of some three miles to my walk,
which, as the sun had set, I had no inclination for.
However, by dint of discussion, we became better
friends, strange to say; and at last our reconciliation
was so complete that he showed me round to a gate
which led to his homestead, and thence guided me,
without interfering with his fences, or trampling down
his young wheat, to the high road. I told him of my
Gipsy encounter, and learned from him that the lane
was a regular camping place for these people; that
he had nothing to complain of from them, and that
if they stole fowls and ducks, and killed sheep,[1] it
certainly was not in the neighbourhood of the camps,
where suspicion was sure to fall upon them, and
where the discovery of a cock's feather or a duck's
foot would certainly be proof enough, in the eyes

---

[1] *Silvanus.*—"Kill sheep! Who ever knew a Romano to kill a
sheep?"

of a couple of county magistrates sitting in petty
sessions, to justify a summary committal of the gang
as rogues and vagabonds. We parted company at
the road. I proceeded quietly to college, supped,
slept, and dreamt I was making wonderful progress
in Romani under the tuition of Sinfi.

Two days after, however, I had ceased to think
much about Gipsies, being by that time deep in
preparation for our annual college examination,
which was close at hand, and with the importance
of which I was duly impressed, as a decent and
sober freshman ought to be. On the third day, I
was disturbed in a struggle with Müller's Dorians,
by a rap at my oak, which was sported as befitted
the time and my great resolves. "I won't open,"
thought I. The knock was repeated, peremptorily.
It was clearly some one determined to come in. I
had no duns then, and few "rowing" acquaintance,
so on the third summons I opened. The intruder
was a stranger, a mild though determined-looking
man, of middle age, quietly dressed, but with a
sporting "something" in his style and manner
which told me at once he was neither a town touter
for orders nor a Cambridge tradesman. He told
me in a few words that he was a superintendent
in the London detective police; that he had been
ordered down from town in consequence of a robbery
of sovereigns, to a large amount, from a farmer's wife
in Huntingdonshire.

The robbery had been perpetrated by two young

z

Gipsy women, and had not been discovered by the victim of it till the morning before my visitor's call upon me.[1]

"I've not lost any time, sir," he told me, with a sort of quiet pride. "We seldom do. I've been looking up all the camps in these parts, and I think I'm on the right lay at last. But you must allow me to ask you a few questions."

"Certainly," I said.

"I've been told by Mr —— (my farmer of 'The King's Hedges'), that you were in company with some Gipsies near his place on Wednesday, who decamped the same day."

"Yes."

"Do you know their names?"

"Smith,—Euri Smith, Athaliah Smith his wife, and Sinfi Smith, their niece."[2]

He nodded. "Exactly; and two girls, called Florentia and Morella—strappers. One with a red and green tartan shawl, and a yellow handkerchief on her head; the other with a cloak, striped brown and green, and a blue and crimson handkerchief under a black beaver bonnet?"

The description was exact.

Two such girls, I told him, had come up, just before I parted company with the family.

"And now, sir," he said, "try and tell me what

---

[1] *Starlina.*—"There, bor! that's why they had to go away."

[2] *Ruth.*—"Pretty fellow! there, that's what comes o' being kind to monkeys."

time it was, as near as you can, what direction
they came from, and what passed."

I told him, as exactly as I could, not forgetting
the mysterious *Bori Hokani,* which had stuck in
my memory.

He struck his hand on his knee as I repeated
the words. . "I thought so," he said, after a moment;
"that's my lot, as sure as skittles. And there were
no other men there but this Euri?" he continued,
after another short pause.

"None; nor did I hear them talk of any."

"In course not, sir," he said, with a half smile;
"in course not. And now, sir," he added, with an
apologetic look at my open books, "if you could
give me an hour, sir, I should like you to go with
me as far as that camping place."

I hesitated at this proposal, I confess; for it
seemed a sort of treason to my Gipsy acquaintances.

As if he had read the motives of my hesitation,
he went on, "The fact is, sir, I only want to be
taken to the exact spot; or we shall have some
work to find the *pattran.*"[1]

"The *pattran?*" I said, interrogatively.

"Ah, I forget you ain't up to their games, sir.
The *pattran,* sir, is the Gipsies' way of letting their
friends know which road they've taken. There were

---

[1] *Anselo.*—"There, bor! He was a man as could speak Romanes
sceming-ly."

two men belonging to that camp, sir, who hadn't come in when they started, and they are safe to have left 'em the *pattran*. So if you *could* take a lift with us, sir——"

I confess I felt some curiosity to see how it would all end; and the prospect of a Gipsy-hunt was exciting. Besides, I had no intention of being in any way accessory to its *dénouement*, beyond honestly telling all I had seen; and I fancied it might be better for Sinfi that I should be on the spot, if the chase should end in a capture.[1]

Accordingly I intimated to Mr Keane my readiness to accompany him not only to " The King's Hedges," but as far as he liked to take me, filled my cigar case and a pocket flask of cognac, and proceeded in his company to the Bishop's Hostel gate, where his " trap," as he called it, was in waiting. This was a light but strong spring-cart, with a wiry little mare between the shafts; and which, I found, was to carry, besides ourselves, two sergeants of the Cambridge police, who had been placed by the magistrates at Mr Keane's orders, and who evidently looked up to their London brother with the greatest respect. We rattled off briskly for " The King's Hedges," and on the way Mr Keane explained to me the mysteries of the " *Bori Hokani*," and the " *pattran*," as follows :—

" You see, sir, these here Gipsies are a rum set,

---

[1] *Starlina.*—" Ah-h-h ! he'd do it for her."

and have their own dodges and lurks, quite different
from our London cracksmen, or the yokels either.
The men don't do much harm beyond making bad
money, and a little sheep-slaughtering, and a deal of
horse-jockeying, and such like—nothing to speak of.
It's the women that does the great stroke of business. They're uncommon knowin' at it, to be sure,
and gets in with ignorant servant girls, and such like,
and works the area-sneak, under the stall (cover) of
fortune-telling, and love-charms, and such like. But
of all their dodges, there's none they swag as much
by as the *Bori Hokani*, as they call it in their patter
—'the great trick,' that means, as I'm told, sir ;
leastways it *is* a great trick, and this is the way
they works it. They'll get round some old farmer's
wife, sir, in an out-of-the-way place, when they knows
there's money kept in the house,—for there's many of
them farmers as wouldn't trust the Bank of England
with a sovereign,—and when the husband's out of the
way, they sticks it into the poor ignorant woman, as
how they can make money breed money, all along of
a charm they've got. So they indooces the ignorant
woman to let 'em put up her husband's sovereigns
for her, which they does safe enough in a parcel,
and gives it her, and makes her lock it up in a
drawer, or a chest, or such like, and says some
gibberish, and acts some games over it, and tells her
that in such and such a time if she opens the parcel
she'll find two sovereigns for one. But don't you
see, sir, they had another parcel with 'em, made up

just like the one they've packed the sovereigns in
(and that's why they always puts it up themselves),
filled with lead dumps, or such like, and by a fake-
ment—I beg your pardon, sir; a sleight-of-hand like,
you know—they change the packet of sovereigns
for the packet of lead fardens, in giving on 'em up
to put into the box, and they walks their chalks with
the tin; and when the old lady opens her box, and
unfastens her parcel to look for her young canaries,
you know, sir, she finds the blessed dumps; and precious aggrawated she is, in course, and her husband
too—for he's safe to find it out. And that's the *Bori
Hokani*, sir; and those two limbs of girls as came
up when you was at the camp, sir, they'd been all
that identical day down near Alconbury Hill, and
they'd nailed nigh upon eighty pound at that game
I've told you; and that's what I'm arter, as I said
in your room, sir."

I anxiously inquired how far he supposed the
rest of the tribe were implicated.

"The old 'uns is safe to be afore the facts in it,"
he said; "as for the others, we'll see when we nails
'em. Leastways, I shall grab the lot, I know," he
concluded, with a pleasant look to his provincial
associates, who agreed with him in this, as in everything.

By this time we had reached the scene of my first
Gipsy lesson, which had not promised so exciting a
catastrophe. I pointed out every locality as exactly
as I could. The detective listened as if he was

riveting every word in his memory with a thump of his determined will, and when I had concluded, thanked me, and said quietly, "Now for the *pattran;*" and he looked at his provincial assistants with a calm consciousness of superiority. It was evident they hadn't the remotest notion what the *pattran* might be.

"Ah, I forgot; you ain't up to that. Look here, —and you, too, sir, if you like, for every pair of eyes is useful sometimes,—the *pattran* is the Gipsies' road-mark. They can track each other over all England by it. This is it: when they takes a turn right or left (and they goes uncommon queer roads, to be sure), either they make a cross in the road-way, if it's a place where there ain't much traffic, and the ground suits, with their nailed shoes; not planting the marks, mind, close together, so that you'd see 'em with half an eye, but careless like, here and there: if it's a cross, with the long end pointing the way they've took. But it ain't always that, by no means. Sometimes it's a branch broken down to an angle, and pointing to their road; sometimes it's a rag stuck on a bush at the corner they turn; sometimes a wisp of straw as you'd think had been caught up out of a farmer's cart passing with a load; but there's a knot in it that *they* know, and that *I* know (*he said this with a chuckle*), for I was put up to the game by an old chap as had been a Gipsy himself, leastways he *is* one still, but don't travel; for he's turned respectable, and does a putting-up

job for us now and then. And now that you know
what the *pattran* is,"—he said to the provincials, with
the same careless consciousness of mastery which
marked all his communications with them,—"perhaps
you'll just open both your eyes uncommonly wide,
and help me to pick it out hereabouts."

"But," I suggested, "how do you know they have
left one?"

"Ah! there was them girls' two brothers as hadn't
come up when they started: they were safe to leave
them 'the Romani card;' that's what we calls it, you
see, sir."

While he spoke he had guided us to the lane end;
and now began a very exciting bit of *backwoodsman-
ship*. Keane quested and cast about like a hound,
now with his nose close to the ground, anon peering
with all his eyes into the hedge, carefully avoiding
any touch that could displace a twig or scatter a
pendent straw. His companions, at a long distance,
of course, followed his example as they best might.
I was absorbed by the London detective, who worked
like a bloodhound, while the provincials might have
been turnspits. At last Keane "pointed." I can
give no other name to the dead set with which he
suddenly stood transfixed. I hastened up, and found
him gazing intently at an insignificant bunch of grass
that hung on a low bush of elder, some ten yards
from the end of the lane, and which I should have
certainly passed twenty times without noticing it,
even after his description of the marks to be looked

for. "That's it," sir, he said, pointing to the bit of weed, with the same noiseless chuckle which I had before observed was his expression of self-content. "Look here, my lads," he added, to the admiring "yokels," who had now come up. "Now you'd say that was a bit of nat'ral grass, that had been flung up there in hedging-work; but look here," and carefully removing the bunch from its twig, he showed us three knots in it, the largest in the middle. "That's a Romani mark, that is; and they have taken this road; so on we goes again," he said merrily, as we remounted the spring-cart, and rattled along the road, which, luckily for us, was straight for nearly a mile, with no turn that did not end in a farm-steading or a dung-heap.

"But how the deuce are you ever to come up with them," I asked, after we had trotted along for some minutes, "if it is to take you as long at every turn as at that?"

"Ah! if they was continually a-running away from us that would be all werry true; but don't you see, sir, when they've put forty mile or so between them and these parts, they'll take it easy; for they're a lazy sort, and don't like fast travelling, when they can help it anyhow. It ain't often as they have one of *us* arter 'em, or they'd maybe not be so easy about distances."

"Will they travel at night?"

"Not arter the first night, sir. It don't suit 'em; and the *mokes* (donkies) ain't equal to more than thirty mile a-day, good going. I don't fancy, some-how, they're more nor sixty mile ahead of us, sir ; and the mare has covered more nor that between light and dark many a time. To be sure, that *pattran* is 'ockerd."

And so we jogged along, at a swinging trot of some eight miles an hour, Mr Keane enlightening us as to the detective dodges, of which he had an apparently inexhaustible repository, which the pro-vincial policemen drank in with a strong professional as well as personal relish.

We had by this time left the highway, and were on abominable cross-country roads. Every now and then we pulled up at a divergence of tracks, some-times coming to a puzzling place where three roads met. At every such point we made a cast for the *pattran*, with more or less success as to time, but always recovering our clue before we left the spot. I had by this time got so interested in this novel kind of hunting, that I had quite forgotten my qualms of conscience, and picked out the *pattran* more than once, eliciting a tempered commendation from Mr Keane, which was enough to give me great value in the eyes of the provincial functionaries.

We had now been about six hours on the road ; and as we had started at twelve, we could not look for more than two hours and a half, at most, of such light as we wanted.

The provincials had already turned the conversa-tion, more than once, on the subject of supper and

quarters for the night. But Mr Keane did not con-
descend to notice these low material wants while
there was business to be done and daylight to do
it by.

It might have been between seven and eight
o'clock, and we had made, stoppages included, some
four-and-twenty miles—for our little mare's frequent
rests enabled us to put the steam on, when we did
get a bit of unbroken road that permitted it—when
we pulled up at a place where not three, but five
roads converged. Keane looked annoyed.

"Not an hour's light afore us," I heard him mutter;
"and five of these blessed *droms* (roads) to choose
from—'owsomever;" and he swung out of the cart,
and made his cast without more grumbling, assigning
to each of us a road, and taking two to his own share.

We had worked for a quarter of an hour without
success, when a shout from one of the "locals," as
Mr Keane called them, drew us in his direction. We
found him on all fours, with his nose almost flattened
among the ruts.

"There, Mr Keane, sir," he said in an excited
manner. "'Ere's the cross, sir."

There *was* the cross, sure enough, marked in the
dust; and now the only point to determine was
along which road pointed the long arm.

"D——n the fellow!" Keane blurted out, after
a few minutes' careful observation. "If he hasn't
been down among the tracks, and a rubbin' on 'em
out all round, with his confounded 'ands and knees;

and now, for all I can see, both arms is the same
length!"

The unhappy local looked as if he would have
fainted on the spot. Here was a dilemma; two
tracks to choose from, and night coming on.

Keane was down in the dust again, at a wary
distance from the foot-prints, however, evidently
working out the most complicated sums in mental
arithmetic and mensuration. We watched him
intently.

"By George, it is!" he cried out at last, after an
anxious ten minutes, springing to his feet and slap-
ping his thigh. Then, seizing me by the arm, he
forced me down, almost on to my nose, exclaiming
—"Look 'ere, sir; there's nails, eh?" He clearly
disdained any appeal to the locals after this performance of one of them.

I ventured the opinion that they certainly were
nails, but that I could not say they belonged to
Gipsy shoes.

He chuckled, after his fashion. "You'll excuse
me, sir; but don't you see they've square 'eads, and
are only four of a row."

I looked closely, and verified the fact.

"That's a Gipsy shoe, sir. They have their own
makers, and their own ways of planting their nails.
Bless you, it's another of their dodges. There's never
a clod would think he was 'alf sprigged with four nails
in a row. But the Gipsies wants a light shoe, as well
as a strong shoe, and never carries more, and always

square 'eads. That there's a Gipsy shoe-sole, sir, and this here's our road."

Although I felt his argument might be contested, there was that quiet conviction in his tone which always carries the day; and there was not a doubt or dissenting murmur among us—none audible at least—as we remounted the cart, and "sprung" the lively little mare down the rough road in a style that did equal credit to her and the cart-springs.

By this time the night was gathering in, and it was evident to me that our tracking could not be carried on perfectly any longer. We clearly ought to be drawing near our quarters for the night. Yet I saw no public, nor indeed any signs of habitations. I was quite out of my latitude, and hadn't the least idea where we were. I ventured to ask Mr Keane his opinion on this point, as we pitched along.

"Well, sir, we are in Huntingdonshire, that's certain; and, so far as I knows, somewheres between Old Hurst and Warboys."

"You know this country, then?"

"Well, sir, not to say know it, as I does Essex, and Middlesex, and that way; but I was down hereabout after them Mepal burglars, you know, sir"—(I hadn't any notion of what he alluded to, of course)—"and I've a good eye for a country; and if we *are* where I fancies we are, you may make up your mind to camp out to-night, sir."

"Oh, I'm quite game for that," I said, rather rejoicing in the prospect, for the fun of the thing.

"But holloa! what's this?" said my companion, as the mare, turning a sharp corner, came to a dead stop before a stout gate.

Keane jumped down, flinging me the reins, and ran to the gate.

"Well, I am blessed!" he ejaculated, in a tone of deep disgust, after taking his observation. "Here's the road pulls up short—nowhere, like; it don't carry into that field."

"Then this wasn't the right line after all," exclaimed, with considerable satisfaction, the unhappy "local," who had made, and marred, our last *pattran* discovery.

Keane turned sharp round and looked about him, as if about to speak, but checked himself, and proceeded again to the gate.

An old and ragged black-thorn grew out of the hedge close to it.

Suddenly, and before I was aware of his intention, I saw Keane on the gate, plucking something from one of the lower branches of the thorn—it was now too dark to discern what. In a moment he was at my side.

"Look here, sir," he said, holding up a little fragment of stuff; "what d'ye make of that?" Looking more closely, I saw it was a bit of silk of a yellow and crimson pattern. A light flashed upon me! it was a tatter of my own *cushgar poshnikes*—of the blazing bandanna I had presented three days before to Sinfi!

And now arose a struggle of conscience: ought I to tell Keane what I knew of it, or not?

The doubt was momentary; I told him.

He gave his quiet chuckle, and said, "Well, now, I was a thinking something of the sort, sir."

Then turning to the luckless "local," he added, "So you see, mister, I was right after all." He then opened the gate, and led the way through.

Beyond the gate lay, not a field, as we thought, but a common.

Keane did not remount, but stood with his elbow on the mare's reeking flanks, "ciphering," as a Yankee would say.

After a few minutes he came up to me and said, "It ain't no use going on in the dark, sir, with our work; so we may as well look out for a sheltered spot. Tilt the cart, let the mare graze, and make ourselves comfortable."

There was nothing very formidable in a night out in the merry-month of May, though the common *was* rather a bleak bed-room.

"We'll find shelter from the wind to the lee of some of them there bushes," said Keane, as he walked forward a few steps to reconnoitre the ground. He ascended, for this purpose, a small eminence a few yards in front of the cart. All of a sudden I saw him stop short, and gaze long and steadily into the waste. He then came back to the cart, and said in a voice that, for the first time that day, betrayed excitement, "By God, sir, I believe we're close upon 'em!"

I jumped up in the cart, and so did the "locals."

"Be quiet," he said, peremptorily. "I don't know but there's a fire down yonder," pointing towards a straggling thicket of thorn that fringed a broken hedge, about two hundred yards in front of us. "I smell wood-smoke."

The wind set from that quarter, and I thought I smelt it too.

"What do you propose?" I asked.

"Why, first we'll stalk 'em, sir," he said, renewing his old tone; "and if they're our lot, we've got 'em as safe as darbies can make it."

"Shall I go with you?"

"No. Here, back the cart into the lane again, and keep close, all of you, till I come back."

We obeyed his orders; and then I saw him, bent double, creep forward till the gathering dark swallowed him up.

The ten minutes he was absent seemed an hour.

"It's them. By George, it's them!" he whispered, almost hoarsely, as he came back to us, in the same cautious fashion in which he had left us. "And the two lads are with them, and they're playing cards over their fire."

"Let's go in on 'em at once," said one of the "locals."

Keane winked quietly.

"Not if I knows it, mister; weazels and Gipsies always are best catched asleep. Let them get under the blankets first. And now, as we know where we are, let's make ourselves snug, sir."

As he spoke, he lugged some horse-cloths and rugs from under the cart-seats, and distributed them to us, while he set about carefully rubbing down the gallant little mare, and gave her her supper out of a nose-bag.

This operation over, he addressed himself to our comforts. Bread and cheese were not wanting, nor a gallon stone bottle of beer. One luxury he positively prohibited—a cigar; for, as he jocosely observed, "The wind *may* change in a jiffey, and blow the smoke and us both to them gents," and he jerked his chin in the direction of the Gipsy camp.

It was useless trying to sleep. I had no intention of taking part in the actual capture, but I listened with interest as Keane detailed his plan of attack to his local coadjutors. They were all three armed with pistols, besides their staves; but Keane was most positive in his injunctions to the provincials not to use anything more deadly than oak, unless they found it absolutely necessary in self-defence.

The night wore on slowly. Keane crept away from time to time to reconnoitre, but my Romani friends kept it up unusually late that night, secure in their escape, and exulting in their booty.

At last, just as grey dawn began to glimmer in the east, and I was beginning to dose (the locals had been snoring for two hours), Keane came up. I sat up as he approached.

"All quiet now, sir," he said. "Their fire's black out, and in half an hour I mean to go in on 'em.

2 A

I wish, though, they hadn't them d——d dogs ; not that I cares for a tussle, sir, but it may set those Gipsy chaps a resisting of us, and then mischief may come, yur know, sir."

At the end of the time he had mentioned, he woke the heavy-headed "locals," and I watched them with intense interest as they looked to the thongs of their staves, and put fresh caps on their pistols.

As they started, I felt a sort of shame at sitting out, reluctant as I was to appear to my late entertainers in a light which must give them suspicions of my fair faith.

Keane interpreted the expression of my face, and said firmly and quietly, " You'll be good enough to leave this business to us, sir. We understand it, and we're more than a match for them, women and all."

So I accepted the ignominious part of a watcher, instead of the more exciting one of an actor ; and with intense excitement watched them steal quietly forward, under cover of the bushes and broken ground, till the hedge of which I have spoken hid them from my view; and when I could not see, I listened. For a few minutes all was silence, made tenfold deeper by the hush of the early May morning.

And then came a quick sharp yelp of a terrier, and then a furious barking ; and then a wild hubbub —a confused shrieking of women, and cursing and trampling of men in fierce struggle, and then—one shot !—and then again silence !

I could stand it no longer—I ran to the scene

of conflict.   All was over: Keane and his brave
army had achieved a complete victory, if not quite
a bloodless one.

Panting, gory, dishevelled, half-dressed, as disturbed
suddenly from sleep, Euri and the two Gipsy lads were
sitting on the ground, handcuffed ; and in the same
ignominious plight, minus the blood, Athaliah, her
two daughters, and—alas the day !—my pretty Sinfi.

Keane was wiping his forehead with a cotton
handkerchief, while one of the locals was binding
up a broken head, which his comrade had received
in the *melée*.   The faithful bandy-legged yellow
terrier had perished.

"There, Starlína," I said, when I had ended, "what
have you got to say to that?   I could hear you
galdering from time to time."

"Oh! there's some things in it rather pretty; but
he *was* a híndo (caitiff) to go and tell.   Well, I never
did hear such things in all my life.   There, bor !"

"There, bor !" indeed expressed the feelings of my
entire audience, which certainly were not of unmixed
admiration.   They, one and all, had been most deeply
interested, their interest growing as the tale went on,
and showing itself in a hundred odd gestures, grimaces,
and ejaculations.   Still there was hardly a line that
they were not prepared to criticise, for none are so
hard to please upon Romani topics as Romani Chals
themselves.   The rarest instance of this fastidiousness
is the copy of Smart and Crofton's *English Gipsies*

owned by Sylvester Boswell, who has carefully erased
every word and sentence therein that did not emanate
from his own "great knowledge of grammaring," no
matter how genuine those words and sentences may
be. So, too, any Gipsy who pronounces the Romani
word for "blanket" *káppa*, will brand as a mumper
him who pronounces it *kóppa*, and *vice versâ;* still,
in this case, John started what seemed a tolerably
valid criticism.

"You'll pardon what I'm going to say," he began ;
"but I don't think, Mr Groome, you were quite
correct in one thing in that story of yours"—

"Mine, John! *I* never wrote that story; I wish
I had."

"Oh, very good; then I can speak out plainer
what I was purposing to say; but who ever heard
of two young girls like that (fifteen it said they
were, didn't it?) going and getting eighty pounds by
drokraben (fortune-telling)? Górgios *are* fools, as
no one is more aware nor you"—a doubtful compliment—"but I never will credit that any farmer's
wife would be so foolish as put belief in two poor
silly girls. And Romani Chals are sometimes foolish
too, but they'd never go leaving marks like that what
way they took, and not giving satisfaction, or else
getting clearer from where they done the drokraben."

"That's rather a dangerous line of argument, it
strikes me. What does it lead to?"

"Well, I don't quite know myself, rightly; but I
wouldn't like for it to face the world, not just as

you did read it. Of course, I am not for saying
that drokraben has never been committed, else why
were górgios made so foolish, and for what were our
poor Romani signs given to us?"

"Signs, as how?"

"Why, when my poor mother used to hear a very
small sound of a small bee, making a noise in the
middle of the night, when she used to be sleeping in
some building, when all of us used to be fast asleep,
that would be one great sign that hundreds of pounds
would be coming to her soon."

"Hundreds! I say, John, you are kúrin' (beating)
the very Curraples."

"Ay, or when she used to see a pig or a cow rub
themselves against a cartwheel, a post, or a gate, or
something else of the kind, she would be sure to
have gold that day. But the greatest of all her signs
would be some of us finding Broad[1] Gorse, Broad
Thistle, Broad Ash, and especially Holly, and different
other things. And onest, when I was a little young
boy along with my father and my mother, I remember
that we were very poorly off in Anglesea, in the town
by name of Beaumaris. We had no horse nor donkey,
but just a great wallet on my back; and away we
started from that town, quite early in the morning;
and there was nothing at all for us to take a little

---

[1] *Broad*, thus employed, denotes the fasciated growth, somewhat
resembling a bishop's pastoral staff. *Broddo-kóro* (broad-thorn), the
generic term for this growth, sufficiently indicates the phallic origin
of the beliefs connected with it.

refreshment, before we went upon our road. But never fear, my daddy; we were not long before I cut a fine Broad Holly, with a most beautiful plume, and gave it to my mother; and soon as she saw it, she did break it up in three, and did say some words to herself when she broke it up, and putting it into her pocket. I do not know what she used to say, but I think she used to say something about 'mw deary Devél,' and something else very curious; and she used to look up to the sky, and make funny eyes, and they were turning more black. But, however, we were not long after finding it, the very next house that my mother went to call, she made a great drokraben, and drew from four to five hundred pound-notes. And I can assure you that we were up and were not long before we got plenty victuals; and there we stopped a whole week near that house. After that we went up to Holyhead, and from there we did take the ship, and went all of us over to the Potato Country, Ireland, and came in the great town Dublin. We liked that town well, and there we stopped a long while, and then crossed from there to Liverpool. And there my father and my mother bought fine clothes for my sisters and for me and for themselves, and a good horse and cart; and then away we came from there up to the country of Wales."

"But, mercy on us!" Silvanus asked, a trifle incredulously, "weren't you feared, then, stopping so long by that house before you made your start?"

"That was according as my poor mother would

give the górgios sufficient satisfaction before she did
take the money, before we would go upon the road.
But sometimes we used to run by night; and there
is more fun in that than what you might imagine,
Mr Groome. How we used to go by night, and
rest in the daytimes, and have plenty tobacco and
brandy. Ha! ha! ha! we used to be as merry as the
impses themselves, when we did keep their company
by travelling by night, and never no fear upon us."

"She must have been a wonderful fortune-teller,
your mother," said Lementina. "Why, dear me,
then, if she got so much in a short time, she'd be
able to buy a grand estate; never want to be going
about, if she could get such maánzins as them. Why,
the most as ever I got was twenty pounds in two
five-pound notes, off a pretty schoolmistress, and a
little gold watch besides; and then I was that afraid,
I never went back for a long while after, though I
was to have gone for more, and we were stopping
at the time close to the woman's house. I was to
have given her the watch back again, for I said I
wanted it just to make out the time to work the spell.
And I got it in a beautiful little box, all covered
with shells; and next day I gave the box away to
a woman about a mile from there for a great big
piece of bacon. And Old Chicken [Silvanus] had
the watch, and he couldn't tell the time by it, didn't
know how to wind it up. Ah! I don't see górgios so
free in giving money away these days. What fools
they must be, when it's all for their own happiness."

"You really think so, Lementina?" but Lementina merely blinked at me, while John inquired if I had got such a thing as a lead pencil and a scrap of paper.

"I want," he said, "to show you, Mr Groome, how my poor mother used to work her manezins; for she always would rather have me for company for her, when she would have to turn out to call the houses, than any of my sisters. She used to say that I was more lucky to her than any of them, and that is how I came to know how she used to do."

John scribbled away, the Lovells all looking on; presently he gave me my paper back, and on it was the following charm :—

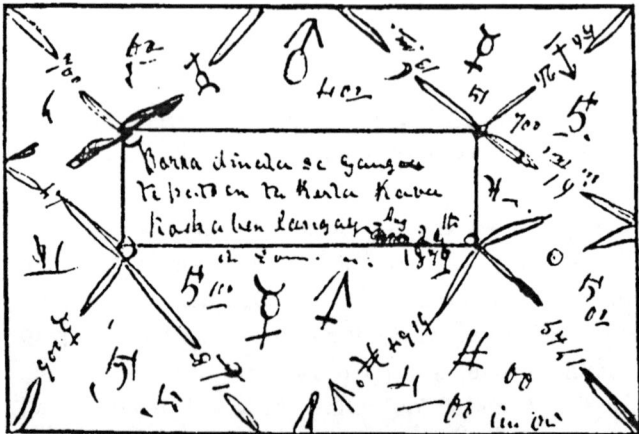

"I see," said I; "'Borra dinala se gaugea te patsen ta kerla kava koskaben langay,'—'Great fools are women to believe that this does them good.' Exactly."

"Ay, she never used to put no harm in it; only something to frighten the silly women, to draw their money."

"Oh, never no harm in it! But, John, you are a moral man; you were at church this morning, and there, I suppose, you heard the Commandments read. The Eighth, if I remember rightly, runs"—

"Thou shalt not steal," John answered patly enough.

"Steal!" exclaimed Lementina; "why, I never heard talk of such a mumper's word. What d'ye mean by *steal?* Why, that's a regular low-bred, padding-ken's word. As though anything could be wrong that you could sarve nasty górgios. Isn't dúkeriben just what has been for generations, and always will be? It's Romanis' livelihood, their trade; though goodness knows it's a poor trade nowadays. Without at Epsom or Ascot, and a few great gentlemen's houses, where a pusson's known and respected, I wouldn't tell a fortune, not if it was ever so. Everyone can tell fortunes these times. It isn't at all what it used to be. Even the lowest Irish tell fortunes now—for sixpence! and that's a thing ought to be put a stop to; it shouldn't ought to never be allowed."

"Then you see no great harm in Romani dúkeriben, for a pound, let us say, or even perhaps five shillings?"

"Harm, no; all the good in the world. They like to hear the notion of getting married. It is but natural, poor things; for goodness knows they some

on 'em has work enough. Now, if you will believe
me, almost the last young lady as ever I got much
off was a parson's sister; and she *was* a young lady,
something like—going for forty, and hardly a tooth
in her head. 'Toothless Betty,' I calls her. 'Oh,
Mrs Lovell,' she said, 'I wish you'd tell me about'—
such-and-such a young gentleman, you know (perhaps he'd be about nineteen)—'but do you think
there'll ever be any chance for me?' Of course I
tells her, 'Why, my dear young lady, there's all the
chance in the world, if you'll only be venturesome,
and let me try.' Then I asks her for one of her
rings, and a bit of her hair (bright red it was); and
she was as pleased as ever anything. And five
months after she did get married to quite another
gentleman; so, you see, I wasn't so far out after all.
And she was a parson's sister."

Clearly Lementina thought that this parsonic ele-
ment had a kind of sanctifying influence; but John
had been pondering the Eighth Commandment.

"You mustn't imagine," he observed, "that I'm
for upholding any such curious ways, for it was all
through me my people got turned from them, by
reason of things being very much stricter now, and
also because when my father and mother had all
that money by drokraben it never used to do them
any good, but always in some old bother to spend
it until it would all be gone. Then we should
have quietness; and Heaven was more pleased with
us when we did drop it. We tried both public and

private life, but the public was all to no much benefit;
and I suppose there has not been a drokraben done
in Wales, not to call it one, these thirty or forty
years.

"I think I have read of one later than that in
England, some twenty-five years ago; and a very
abominable case it was, the only one where I have
any pity for the loser.   Down by Exeter somewhere
a labourer's wife had a daughter ill of consumption ;
and a Romani woman, who called at the cottage, got
twenty-two gold sovereigns off the mother, promising
that the girl should be cured by Friday, when an
angel would appear and return the money."

"A comical angel, sure," said Lementina ; "but
that Romani woman ought to be scandal ashamed ;
burning alive would be too good for she.   Now, I
never told nothing but just by way of pastime, and
everyone must look to pay for that.   *Stealing*,
quotha !" (with an indignant sniff).

"Well, ye-e-s ; I do not myself believe that
dúkeriben, nine times out of ten, is anything graver
than folly—folly enough to be sure.   There was
one of the Toogoods, I remember, górgio brush and
basket dealers, and he was going through Newington,
one of the best parts of Edinburgh, with his caravan.
A lady saw him, and sent her servant out to call
him in, wanted him to tell her fortune, and offered
(I think) ten shillings."

"There ! a man ! and a górgio too !!   Whatever
did he say ?   I'd have worked her."

"He never said one word, but bolted out of the house, for he was perfectly dumbfoundered, frightened by the bare notion of the thing."

"*Too-good* enough; I only wish I'd had his chance. Shouldn't I been a gaby to lose the good money, when I could earn it by two or three nonsense words. But there's some people pretends they wouldn't take it, not if it was put before their nose."

"At any rate, you can't say, Lementina, I ever put the temptation in your way, for I never was dúker'd in my life."

"I wanted to, though, first time I met you at Chester."

"Yes, and I proposed that I should dúker you. No, if I were a magistrate, I certainly would either dismiss all fortune-telling cases, like Mr Harrison, at Ashton-under-Lyne, with the remark, that 'it served silly people right if they lost their money;' or else I would punish the fortune-tellers and their consultors alike; and of the latter, I take it, there would be some three hundred to every one of the former. But did I ever tell you about Georgina Lee? I thought not. Well, she was a Romani woman, twenty years old, with a baby in arms; and she and her husband stopped on Hounslow Heath. One day she called at a gentleman's house near by, and got telling the servant-girls' fortunes, told the cook what she knew to be true, that she was to marry a gentleman. Then the drawing-room bell rang; the lady, it seemed, wanted to hear her fortune too, wished to know if she should be married again within the twelvemonth, and ended by offering Georgina a pound for something that would kill her present husband. So on Friday Georgina returned with a powder in a paper, and the lady then told her that if it did good, she would give her ten shillings ; but Georgina wanted cash down, and, the lady refusing, got hustled out of the house. In the middle of the hustling the happy husband came upon the scene, and gave Mrs Lee in charge for attempting to get money under false pretences. False they undoubtedly were, for the powder turned out to be nothing but chalk ; so Georgina, after a fortnight of remands, was sentenced to three months' hard labour."

"And the lady," Ruth asked, "what did the lady get ? "

" Oh, she got—nothing." [1]

.   .   .   .   .   .

While this chapter was writing, Mr Crofton sent

---

[1] On Fortune-telling generally, see Crabb's *Gipsies' Advocate* (3d ed., 1832), pp. 38-45 ; Liebich's *Zigeuner*, pp. 63-68 ; Borrow's *Zincali*. ch. vi., and his *Lavo-Lil*, pp. 240-44. The special case, above referred to, at Northlew, Devonshire, is given in *Notes and Queries*, 21st Oct. 1854 ; that of Zuba Boswell, at Ashton-under-Lyne, in Smart and Crofton's *Dialect of the English Gipsies*, pp. 206-8. Of a case that resembles Georgina Lee's, a full account may be found in the *Times*, Feb. 17, 21, 24, and March 1, 1862, with which compare the "Trial of Katherene Roiss Lady Fowlis for Witchcraft, Incantation, Sorcery, and Poisoning," 22d July 1590. She was "accusit for sending William M'Oilllevow-dame to the Egyptianis, to haif knowledge of thame, how to poysoun the young Laird of Fowles and the young Lady Balnagoune ;" his errand had failed, since the poison was bought of a merchant in Aberdeen (Pitcairn's *Criminal Trials in Scotland*, Edinb., 1833, vol. i. pt. 2, p. 96).

me two cuttings from American papers, that curiously
illustrate its subject matter. The first, from a New
Orleans journal of 15th April 1880, shows dúkeriben
in its most venial form, as practised to-day on every
English race-course, and "patronised by the royalty,
aristocracy, and gentry of the Kingdom" :—

"The Princess Koket, with twenty Gipsy followers,
passed through Memphis the other day, going to the
usual Spring convocation near Dayton, Ohio, where,
in May, a large number of these peculiar people hold
a festival. The party, over which Princess Koket
holds absolute sway, have been wintering in south-
western Texas and Alabama, but for several weeks
past were on the road to Memphis. They were well
dressed, some in rather gay colours, the Princess
especially so; and their outfit, consisting of six
wagons, eleven horses, and a round lot of camp
equipments, were all in capital order; while the
people looked fat, sleek, and happy. The Princess
Koket was questioned by a number of people during
their stay in Memphis. She proved to be very intelligent, and understood the way of mankind and the
world generally; could tell a fortune in entertaining
style, on short order, and for a single trade-dollar;
and she said she always managed to captivate the
men."

Well, let Her Highness charm the hearts of Mem-
phite wheelbarrows, in Lementinian phraseology (by
the way, how much an Egyptian princess must feel
at home in Memphis!); she may win whole sackfuls

of trade-dollars for anything I care, so long as my neighbour does not encourage organ-grinders. But the second cutting, from the *Daily Picayune* (8th April 1880), what shall I say of it? *De mortuis nil nisi bonum*, and so I say nothing at all, this species of dúkeriben being a lost art in England, where it died lamented twenty-five years ago. Beyond the Atlantic it would still seem to flourish, for on 31st March, " Two aged Gipsies were brought as prisoners into Justice Walsh's court, in Brooklyn, on a charge of grand larceny, preferred by Deputy-Sheriff R. T. Tingle, of Gibson county, Indiana, who accused them of having robbed William Jessop, a wealthy resident of Princeton in that county, of $2150. The prisoners gave the names of Timothy Warton, aged 62, and Mary Warton, aged 61. The deputy said that a band of, Gipsies encamped at Princeton in January last, and the old woman began to tell Jessop's fortune. She pretended to see great things, but said that she could not decipher them unless a large sum of money was put in her hands. To humour her, he took a package of $2150 done up in bundles and bound with paper slips. He placed the money in her hand, and she counted it carefully. Then she spread out the packages, drew a circle, and dropped into a trance. When she recovered, she said that Jessop was to become fabulously rich. She would have to give him two more sittings before she could tell him all, but that the third time it would be all revealed. She tied the money

up in a red handkerchief in his presence, and told
him that it must be put carefully away in his safe,
and that between her visits it must not be touched
or spoken of. The next time she called at his
office, she locked the door and took the package of
money, and again began her incantations. She was
about to repeat some words which, she said, would
bring her nearer to the secret, when she suddenly
started, exclaiming, 'What is that?' as though she
heard a noise. Mr Jessop arose and looked around,
but saw nothing. The Gipsy continued to work with
the package in her hand, and at length said that she
was almost ready to reveal to Mr Jessop a startling
and fortunate event in his near future, but that it
would require one more meeting. He told her he
must have the money by February 10th, as he needed
it in his business. She assured him the spell would
be over by that time; he must not touch the package.
He promised. A fire of doubtful origin, in which
some of Mr Jessop's property was destroyed, put the
Gipsy out of his mind. The Gipsy band disappeared.
Then he went to his safe, untied the red handkerchief
about the package, and, instead of his money, laid bare
a pile of paper cut in the lips the size of bank-notes,
and bound with strips of paper. He put the Deputy-
Sheriff on their track, and he followed them here.
Twelve hundred dollars was found on them." [1]

---

[1] The *New York Herald* (2d April 1880) gave another sketch of
this plot, the one weak point in which is the miscalculation that the
"Hoosier Merchant" would not be fool enough to own his folly.

The final act of the drama I have not seen myself; but I enclosed the above in my last letter to Silvanus, who mentions in his answer that they are thinking of joining his daughter Patience in the States. I question much if they will really go, for the old man vacillates in his purposes, a twelvemonth earlier talking of Glasgow and a bank-directorship, and when we parted of philanthropy.

There it is said that the sum was $2500, and that the Wartons' residence is 99 Hicks Street, Brooklyn. Mary must be Timothy's second wife, since in the Grove Church cemetery, opposite New York, is a marble tombstone, bearing inscription, "Vashti, wife of T. Warton, died Nov. 26, 1851, Æ. 26 yr." Close by it stands another, to the memory of Vashti's sister, "Naomi Davis, who died March 4, 1855, aged 22 years. 'The Lord giveth, and the Lord taketh away; blessed be the name of the Lord,'"—words that are coupled in the Burial Service with First Timothy vi. 7.

Chapter Eleventh and Last.

ON MONDAY the Lovells were to start for Chester, thence to disperse North, East, and South; and I had promised to come and see them start. Approaching the meadow, then, about half-past nine, I was met by a blinding smoke, suggestive of Silvanus's death in the night and a Hindu *suttee* of his widowed queen. But it was only a bonfire of the straw out of all the tents; and yonder was Lementina scraping stray wisps into the flames with a broken tent-rod, and muttering the while, "Nasty Irish breed—never did see such folks for leaving a sleer at every place they goes to—just like a lot of pigs—never thinks of clearing up their rubbish—suppose they'll never want to come again." This, though the state of the meadow might have taught picnickers a useful lesson.

The tents were struck and packed upon the donkeys; the horses stood ready harnessed in the carts; and by the gate Silvanus was talking with

386

the farmer, who was sending a greeting to Sister Cartwright.

Farewells took long, but they were over at last: with Wully the Silent, who all these days had been forgathering with his compatriot gauger; with Plato, who gave me some flies that couldn't help killing; with Loverin, proud owner of the "ondikelous" bear; with one and all of my kindly Romani friends. The last farewell, "Good-bye, old tent-place," was spoken by Lementina; then the procession moved upon its way. Silvanus brought up the rear, and to him Mr Chamberlain :—

"Why, Lovell, you're like the Children of Israel."

EDINBURGH : J. BARTHOLOMEW, CHAMBERS STREET.